Cruising the Library

PERVERSITIES IN THE ORGANIZATION
OF KNOWLEDGE

MELISSA ADLER

FORDHAM UNIVERSITY PRESS

New York 2017

Fordham University Press has no responsibility for the
persistence or accuracy of URLs for external or third-party
Internet websites referred to in this publication and does
not guarantee that any content on such websites is, or will
remain, accurate or appropriate.

Fordham University Press also publishes its books in a
variety of electronic formats. Some content that appears in
print may not be available in electronic books.

Visit us online at www.fordhampress.com.

Library of Congress Cataloging-in-Publication Data
available online at http://catalog.loc.gov.

Printed in the United States of America
19 18 17   5 4 3 2 1
First edition

for V.

CONTENTS

Let's pretend the year is 1990, the season late autumn. Eve Kosofsky Sedg-wick's *Epistemology of the Closet* has just been released. Now envision your-self as a catalog librarian, and the book has landed on your desk. One of the most essential tasks for you as a cataloger is to determine a single location on a library shelf for each book the library acquires. As it is 1990, there is no way you can anticipate the monumental role this book is going to play in the field of sexuality studies. You could have no idea that Sedgwick would come to be regarded as one of the founders of queer theory or that her work would one day be described as having "changed sexuality's his-tory and destiny."[1] Indeed, queer theory had only been called into being a few months earlier as the title of a conference in Santa Cruz, California.[2] *Publisher's Weekly*, a leading source of book reviews that guide librarians' selection choices, suggested that the book was inaccessible and did not recommend it: "Sedgwick does not prove her overstated thesis that homo/ hetero distinction obtains with gender, class and race in determining 'all modern Western identity and social organization.' Obtuse, cumbersome, academic prose limits the appeal of this treatise."[3] You may or may not have seen this review (as a cataloger you probably don't select items for the col-lection, and it is entirely likely that you are not a specialist in the subject), but given this critique it may be a wonder that the book has found its way into your hands. Your decision on how to classify this work will be based upon a perusal of the book description on the cover, the table of contents, and perhaps a skim of the introduction or index. You will want to place the book where its potential readers are likely to look, and you will want to locate it with similar titles in order to bring related works together.

Occupying the position of a librarian in this context, how do you begin to reduce *Epistemology of the Closet* to a single subject within any discipline? If you work in an academic library, you will most likely use the Library of Congress Classification to classify the book. In 1990, available choices within that classification system included sections in the social sciences— HQ76 and HQ71 for homosexuality and sexual deviation, respectively. In the P section nascent subdisciplines were emerging among areas of languages and literature, with homosexuality as a special topic. Depending on the scope and purpose of a particular library, one could have also argued that the book might fit best within philosophy, political science, cultural anthropology, or history.

If you were the cataloger at the Library of Congress, your thinking might have been guided by the awareness that your decision was likely to be replicated across research libraries in the United States and beyond. In fact, Sedgwick actually contacted the Library of Congress directly to appeal their classificatory decision—PS374.H63—one that positioned *Epistemology of the Closet* with books on homosexuality in the history of American literature. An apparently hurried staff note in the catalog record for the book reads, "Author protested mildy [*sic*] at PS class since incl. (she says) 1. Irish, British, German, and French is [*sic*] well; chapters are on Melville, Wilde, James and Proust."[4] In spite of the fact that the class PN56.H57 was an available option, designated for the topic of homosexuality within theory and general literature [Literature (General)—Theory. Philosophy. Esthetics—Relation to and treatment of special elements, problems, and subjects—Other special—Topics, A–Z—Homosexuality], as were a variety of other possible classes in other disciplines, her objection was all but ignored. To this day you will find the book shelved with American literature in libraries around the globe, including Hong Kong, Toronto, Sydney, and across the United States.[5] The Library of Congress produced the original catalog record for the book while it was still in publication, and by virtue of the fact that this classification is printed on the verso of the title page and that standardization and copy cataloging technologies have made replication automatic, this class assignment has been repeated in nearly every research library that owns the book and uses the Library of Congress Classification system to organize its collections.[6]

My hope is that you are beginning to sense the power and responsibility the job of library cataloging inheres. I start with the cataloging of *Epistemology of the Closet* to locate and make sense of the processes by which "perverse" subjects are both constituted in and resist these systems. Critically reading the classification systems and the library catalog reveals the paradoxical nature of classifications: The techniques that bring bodies of literature to life by placing related books together and making them accessible are necessarily constraining and bound by relations of power. Such readings also illustrate the role and purpose of the Library of Congress and its knowledge organization systems in informing the U.S. citizenry and Congress. The consequences and implications of library classifications vary across texts and their classificatory assignments, and throughout this book I show various ways in which library techniques divide and define bodies of literature by putting books into play with others within certain disciplines and segregating them from others. We could venture to guess all kinds of reasons for the Library of Congress's classificatory choice and refusal to change the location of *Epistemology of the Closet*, but the more important message here is that singular cataloging decisions like this one, guided by sets of rules and standards, accumulate to give form and function to bodies of literature in the library.

Indeed, an important distinction needs to be made between the systems and their applications. This book is systemic in focus: I treat the classifications produced by the Library of Congress as primary historical documents that inform American studies, sexuality studies, and the sociology of knowledge. One of my central claims is that these systems must be understood as tools that have contributed to the construction of a national history and identity of the United States, and I suggest that the subjects were not only arranged in relation to one another but in relation to an imagined nation and its interests. As the Library of Congress is the oldest federal cultural institution in the United States, its knowledge organization systems must be analyzed as instruments of statecraft.

I use examples of library classifications in their applications to specific texts to make sense of such tensions and to assess the performativity of these systems. To be clear, the examples that appear throughout this study are not intended to be an indictment of any individual or group of catalogers. Cataloging is hard work, guided by excruciatingly detailed rulebooks on how to describe and categorize bibliographic texts. Like many rules, the Library of Congress's are open to interpretation, and every cataloger arrives at a text from a particular point of view. Given the options set by the Library of Congress standards, any two catalogers are likely to disagree about where to put a book. What is important to register is that the subject cataloging standards produced by the Library of Congress and deployed in libraries of all types designate possibilities for where works can be placed and how they can be described. The Library of Congress and its systems direct conversations and connections by setting the rules for ranking and ordering works, distributing them across the disciplines within the library space, and providing authorized terms for subjects. For this book I've collected and cataloged some of the ways in which library subject cataloging standards inform the history of sexuality and the processes by which norms and authority over reading and research practices have taken hold. The production of "perverse" subjects in library classifications has mapped and indexed normal and abnormal sexualities and bodies.

The conceptualization of the "subject" is a utilitarian one in library science; it is a tool for finding information. Ronald E. Day has suggested that the library subject took on particular significance in the early twentieth century when controlled vocabularies and classifications facilitated the findability of documents through the technique of representing "aboutness."[7] A subject of a work was reduced to what that work was about, and aboutness came to be defined by subject headings. However, the literal strings and notations that facilitate access must also be read as subjectifying mechanisms. The constitution of subjects in the library is the result of certain processes advanced by scientific principles and mediated by technologies, and the techniques of bringing library subjects into being operate by naming, categorization, exclusion, and control. By viewing texts as belonging to bodies of literature, we can theorize library subjects as we do human subjects and subjectivities and consider the ways in which they are constituted in indexing processes.

Cruising the library is not simply a metaphor but a method, inspired by José Esteban Muñoz's *Cruising Utopia*, for understanding the ways in which the library inhibits intersectionality and intertextuality by reducing bodies of literature to disciplined, discrete subjects distributed across the library.[8] The notion of cruising embraces promiscuous and perverse readings. The shelves are the streets, and when browsing or cruising the library, the classification roughly serves as a map to guide our desires. Although we might imagine the library as a kind of Utopia—an island, in a sense, that houses a great bounty of literature and knowledge to which access is granted equally to all members of society, the idea of a library as a perfect place crumbles when we understand how access by subject is organized.

This project claims a kinship with Muñoz's work in other regards—foremost is a shared hopefulness, which for me has derived from nearly a decade of historical, critical analysis of an institution I hold dear—librarianship, and specifically the Library of Congress. This work is entirely personal and political, full of a huge range of emotions from elation to despair. But now, having come to terms with the processes by which library subjects are ordered and named, I feel more than ever that new ontologies based in queer relationality are not only necessary but endlessly possible and hold real potential for expanding opportunities for desiring subjects. The library seems to me an ideal space for unmaking and remaking meaning through the reorganization of knowledge—"for new thought images for queer critique, different paths to queerness."[9]

Libraries have a variety of mechanisms of control at their disposal by which to provide and restrict access via subjects: subject headings, bibliographic classification, and labeling. Each of these terms refers to a specific set of practices in library cataloging.

Subject headings provide a way for seekers of texts to find books in the catalog by searching for a topic with words. Headings belong to controlled vocabularies, which are designed to ensure uniformity and universality within and across library catalogs or other information retrieval systems so that locating information is predictable and precise. Terms like "Paraphilias," "Gay librarians," and "African American lesbians" are strings of words arranged into hierarchical and associative relationships of broader, narrower, and related terms. They are created and maintained by a group of authorities, and in the case of the most widely used controlled vocabulary in the world—the Library of Congress Subject Headings—the authority is the Library of Congress.[10] A librarian's goal is to select and apply the terms from that controlled vocabulary that readers would most likely use if they were searching for books on a given topic. Of course, patrons of libraries of different types and in various communities may have disparate expectations, desires, and needs. Anticipating those desires is key, but the possibilities for meeting them are limited by the options set forth by the set of authorized terms.

In contrast, the call number on the spine of the book is a coded notation, designating a class—PN56.H57 or HQ71, for example. A *bibliographic classification* from which the call number is based is an elaborately designed hierarchy across the disciplines, and it supplies direction for readers in finding their books. Class assignments provide a sense of where librarians think a given book belongs in relation to others in the library. Catalogers try to place similar texts together to provide the best browsing experience for readers and to track inventory of books on any given subject.

Library labeling is a specific type of naming and classification that designates a book as restricted for a particular type of use or reader. For instance, rare or valuable books will sometimes be restricted for their protection, or sexually explicit materials might be in a locked case. In the case of the Delta Collection (the topic of Chapter 2), the Δ (Delta) label relegated books to a restricted hidden collection of obscenity in a specific area of the library—a practice that carried special significance during and after World War II.

In the chapters that follow, I examine the function of each of these mechanisms in producing and disciplining sexualized subjects at the Library of
Congress. Sedgwick's body of work is woven through the book in order
to demonstrate through examples the ways her scholarship is put into play
in the library. Her theoretical positions on the performativity and relations of texts to one another and their readers undergird each chapter to
varying degrees, and the chapter on the restricted Delta Collection demonstrates the frame of the closet. The methodology throughout the book
is to enter into each chapter with an example that illustrates how the texts
are arranged in the library through classificatory techniques and then to
broaden the analysis with a historical account of the processes by which
the systems have organized and designated what bodies of literature can
become and how they inform American studies and sexuality studies.

  The Introduction provides the interdisciplinary context for the project
by putting theories of sexuality and knowledge organization into conversation. Echoing Sedgwick and drawing upon Michel Foucault and Gilles
Deleuze, I call for *becoming perverse readers* in order to challenge the disciplinary boundaries in the library, and I ask what a body of literature can
do within and outside the parameters of the classificatory arrangements
for sexual perversion. I also describe the intertwined histories of sexuality
and librarianship. Bringing these fields' respective taxonomies into direct
dialogue reveals how they reinforce one another, overlap, and perform as
layers of support for normative ideas about sexuality.

  Chapter 1 discusses the authorization of the subject heading "Paraphilias" as the term by which library patrons are meant to find books on sexual
perversion in the catalog. In 2007 "Paraphilias" replaced "Sexual deviation," which had been changed in 1972 from "Sexual perversion." I demonstrate that this heading, although authorized in the interest in being
"neutral," was born out of and continues to reproduce the assumption that
variant sexualities are medical problems. The chapter reveals that this subject heading carries a history of pathologizing and disciplining sexualities,
beginning in 1898, when the first Library of Congress subject headings
were created, and it problematizes the recent adoption of "Paraphilias" for
its assumptions regarding sexual practices outside of particular norms. I argue that the assignment of medicalized terms to works that announce their
disavowal of these terms and the medical model is an act of disciplining—a
means to ensure that deviant works are rounded up under the same name.
Crucially, the absence of nonmedical terminologies for the concept in the
controlled vocabulary means that these materials are not readily appre-

hended by members of the public who are not members of the psychiatric discipline. The chapter brings the heading "Paraphilias" and its earlier versions into conversation with early sexologists and then puts it in dialogue with the ongoing negotiations of definitions of the concepts within and outside the American Psychiatric Association. I trace the first use of the word "paraphilia" back to the Austrian psychoanalyst Wilhelm Stekel in the 1920s and then show how John Money influenced the adoption of the term by the American Psychiatric Association in the 1980s. I explore ways that the Library of Congress (and by extension, local libraries everywhere) has engaged and reproduced certain controversies by enacting this term in the catalog. Using J. Halberstam's methodological frame of "perverse presentism," I also show how the heading unjustly affects meaning and access to literature on sex and sexuality—particularly with regard to literatures across temporalities and disciplines other than psychiatry. The chapter closes with brief case studies on particular books and topics from various periods to reveal the disciplinary effects of "Paraphilias" as well as some of the ways in which the books exceed the application of the heading.

Chapter 2 unveils the history of the Delta Collection, maintained by the Library of Congress's Keeper of the Collections from 1940 through 1963. I lean on Sedgwick to theorize the epistemology of the Delta Collection as a closeted body of perverse and obscene literature. I also work from my guess that librarians named this collection for Daedalus's symbol, signifying a closed room that harbored monstrous knowledge within the labyrinthine library. The collection contained a massive amount of materials, many of which had been seized by the U.S. Customs Bureau and the Postal Service and left to the Library of Congress to store, disseminate, or destroy. This secret Delta Collection served to protect valuable and vulnerable materials from the hands of the public who might damage or steal such items; it also protected the public from perverse ideas and images. It gained political significance as a repository of materials believed to be dangerous during the McCarthy era, when sexual perversion was perceived as a threat to national security and obscenity was considered subversive. The chapter explores a particular labeling policy and how Alfred Kremer, the Keeper of the Collections, struggled with his responsibilities in overseeing this collection. Perhaps more critical is the fact that the Library of Congress did in fact store materials in this collection in part for the purpose of cooperating with other federal agencies in their efforts to crack down on sexual perversion and homosexuality during the postwar era. It also examines a still-unsolved case of theft from the Delta Collection and how the McCarthy-era homosexual panic shaped the FBI's investigation of the case.

Chapter 3 provides a close reading of the library shelves on which the books are placed, with a critical mapping of sexual perversion in the Library of Congress Classification system. A class determines the call number, which indicates the precise location of a book. A class also brings topically related materials together—a process called collocation—ideally placing similar books in the same section, according to where they fit within a given discipline. Drawing upon Foucault's analysis of disciplinary power and governmentality, I analyze the Library of Congress's bibliographic classification as a national history-making instrument. I map the temporal and spatial relationships involved in the Library of Congress Classification system and diagram some of the architectures and arrangements of books on perversion in the library. Focusing on psychiatric and social scientific classifications regarding sexual deviance and disorders, the chapter provides an analysis of the works placed in classes across the library as well as insight into how HQ71, a class within the social sciences, came to be the primary home for books on "Sex practices outside social norms. Paraphilias." It reveals how this classification system separates books off from one another, marking some as deviant and others as strictly medical. And it shows how the classification has mapped and supported dominant American discourses about sexual perversion over the past 115 years.

One thing that became apparent in doing this research is the way in which the universality of these systems results in certain blindnesses. The organization of unified subjects around a heteropatriarchal universality that assumes whiteness inhibits analysis that interweaves sexualities with racial and ethnic dimensions. To dig into questions about the classification of race, Chapter 4 extends the critical geographical analysis into other sections of the library. It opens with Roderick Ferguson's *Aberrations in Black* and provides a queer-of-color analysis of the library's treatment of African American subjects. Here is where cruising the library becomes vital; by cruising library subjects, I unearth the ways that the divisions into discrete categories preclude possibilities for intersectionality. The chapter is framed around the cataloging of Ferguson's book to illustrate how it has been put into relation with other works on homosexuality and race and to witness the Library of Congress Classification as a universal classification that relies upon and reinforces heteropatriarchy. The chapter reveals quite clearly that this classification must be read as a history of U.S. nation building, and it examines how African American subjects have been incorporated into particular spaces within the discipline of U.S. history and in the margins of a huge range of other disciplines. A queer-of-color critique of the classification brings new depths to the analysis by showing how racialized and sexualized subjects are written into and out of American history and how the nation has relied upon unified, discrete subjects.

Chapter 5 reveals the failures of disciplinary classificatory marks in confining bodies of literature and the books of which they are composed. It situates the significance of libraries in the digital era and in the current political economic context of neoliberalism and argues that libraries should be privileged and protected for their role in the public sphere. The chapter concludes on a perverse and optimistic note, suggesting that the areas of study that elude classifications may in fact hold a position of privilege, as by their very nature they defy and deterritorialize the disciplining forces of the academy and the state. Inspired by Haraway's discussion of the cat's cradle game, Deleuze and Guattari's rhizomatic taxonomies, and Sedgwick's intertextual fiber art, I begin to imagine alternative ways to draw connections across texts in the library. Working from Sedgwick's reparative and perverse reading practices, I suggest we find and create reparative taxonomies. Through the lens of perversion and processes of unmaking and making anew the hope is that we invent a variety of creative and critically productive remappings of knowledge about sexuality.

The book closes with a reading of Kafka's "In the Penal Colony," relocating the colony and its executional machine to the Library of Congress and demonstrating the very perversity of the library classificatory apparatuses. I provide my own perverse reading of the Library of Congress and suggest that with bodily investment, the masochistic library user freely engages in knowledge/power games in the library.

CRUISING THE LIBRARY

Introduction: A Book Is Being Cataloged

> Nothing—no form of contact with people of any gender or
> sexuality—makes me feel so, simply, homosexual as the evocation
> of library afternoons of dead-end searches, "wild" guesses that, as
> I got more experienced, turned out to be almost always right.
>
> —EVE KOSOFSKY SEDGWICK, "A Poem Is Being Written"

> Though in the higher forms at school the children were no
> longer beaten, the influence of such occasions was replaced
> and more than replaced by the effects of reading. . . . In my
> patients' milieu it was almost always the same books whose
> contents gave a new stimulus to the beating-phantasies.
>
> —SIGMUND FREUD, "A Child Is Being Beaten"

In her 1987 essay "A Poem Is Being Written," Sedgwick wrote about her
own encounters with the organizing practices in the library, hinting that
cataloging effectively withholds information and stifles interpretation. She
suggested that the erasures of potential homosexual readings in the library
are instructive in doing the history of sexuality: "The wooden subject, author, and title catalogues frustrate and educate the young idea."[1] It seems
that her experiences of libraries informed one of the central arguments
she subsequently developed in *Epistemology of the Closet*—that the "performative aspects of texts" and "reader relations" are "sites of definitional
creation, violence, and rupture in relation to particular readers, particular
institutional circumstances."[2] Sedgwick held that silence is as performative as speech and that it depends upon the privileging of ignorance over
knowledge. Her theorizing of homosexual readings was in no small part inspired by the disciplinary acts that hide queer interpretations from desiring
readers and from her own frustrating visits to the library, where she found
literary works and their relations reduced in ways that prohibited intertextual encounters. Umberto Eco has arrived at similar conclusions, stating
that "eventually there arose in libraries the function of making materials

unavailable, and thus of not encouraging reading," implying a history of techniques that have taken on the appearance of systematically hiding texts.[3] Carrying forward this notion that the library silences particular interpretations and intertextual relations, it follows that libraries are complicit in privileging and circulating ignorance—inhibiting rather than opening up bodies of literature as sources of various knowledges. The classifications in the library unabashedly perform a kind of definitional creation by putting texts into play, organizing them in relation to one another, and authorizing the rules for how terms and classes are created and applied.

In other words, the tools and techniques involved in determining where books are to be placed on library shelves and naming them in authorized terms are classificatory mechanisms that reduce texts and their readings to disciplined subjects. The books on the shelves, organized according to standard systems like the Library of Congress Classification (LCC) and Library of Congress Subject Headings (LCSH), not only reflect and give form to the academic disciplines, but, as I will reveal in the pages that follow, the categories that designate what library books are about actively produce, reproduce, and privilege certain subjects and disciplinary norms. I am interested in the temporal and spatial dimensions and the relations of power at play in the library and in how, regardless of the multiple readings and trajectories of any given book, library classifications designate and delimit relations across texts and readers. Below I present the historical foundations that ground this project and the cross-disciplinary theoretical conversations with which it is in dialogue.

Becoming Perverse

A social and intellectual history of perversion and perversity that reads the library shelves and catalog as primary sources provides a unique lens through which to do the history of sexuality. Given the centrality of the library to the academy, part of the aim of this work is to bring libraries into interdisciplinary conversations about the histories of knowledge production, taxonomies, sexuality, and the state. An intertextual reading of relationships among the subject headings, the medical and social scientific classifications for sexual variance, and the works to which these are meant to afford access problematizes the catalog and classification systems as interfaces where prevailing attitudes and assumptions in scholarship emerge and produce universalized terms and divisions. It shows the shifts over time in scholarship, including changes in what counts as a perverse expression or behavior and what counts as knowledge, by confronting the treatment of perversion by different disciplines and the treatment of the disciplines by libraries. Perhaps unsurprisingly, where we locate "perverse" subjects, we find that that the classifications fail to capture them. The concept of perversion pushes these systems to their limits, dismantling and opening them up to more just ways of organizing and finding knowledge in the library. By problematizing the systems and exposing their failings, the hope is that we find possibilities for creating new ways of facilitating queer and perverse readings. Using Sedgwick's account of her own reading practices as a guide—that for her, "becoming a perverse reader was never a matter of my condescension to texts, rather of the surplus charge of my trust in them to remain powerful, refractory, and exemplary"—we gain a sense of the potential that such a practice holds.[4] In becoming perverse readers it becomes differently possible to forge alternative, creative relations with texts and to gain insights into how we might facilitate rich and productive intertextual relationships and subjectivities across the library.

The failure of the catalog record for *Epistemology of the Closet* in capturing the aboutness of the text confirms that certain books simply do not lend themselves to classificatory acts. Certainly, sexuality does not easily submit to a spatially or temporally fixed position or set of terms. I use the concept of perversion as a lens through which to analyze the limits of the classifications and the potential for literatures to challenge those limits because, while the term has all kinds of sexual connotations, it can be applied to a more general condition of refusal and resistance to normative forces and laws. Perverse subjects of various sorts have negotiated their positions in relation to scientific research over time, in part by confronting norms, by failing or refusing to obey the law, and by enacting desires that resist regulatory categories. And if we recall from history the moments in which sexual perversion has been policed in order to strengthen the U.S. citizenry—and that the most persecuted "perverts" have been homosexuals—we recognize how this term "perversion" has been and is still deployed as a tool to regulate, normalize, and punish.

My aim is not to reclaim or reappropriate "perversion." Nor am I using "pervert" or "perversion" as identity categories, types, or sites. Rather, I echo Patricia MacCormack's conceptualization of perversion, which for her is a tactic rather than a subjective mode of being. I am not advocating or interested in any move toward identifications with becoming a pervert, whatever that means. Instead, we can view perversion as a becoming—an opening, a process that challenges normative categories and ideals. For MacCormack, perversion "is found in *how* the constellation of sexuality, desire and the flesh are thought, not the way this constellation fits into established sexual definitions and meanings."[5] Becoming perverse means that we are not working toward any identity claim but that we are moving toward destabilizing the mechanisms that structure and sustain normative sexualities and identities. It means that we are challenging the systems that assert, catalog, and control thinkable subjects while rendering others unspoken and unthought. Rather than being a question of reappropriating or reterritorializing, perversion is an endless questioning of and resistance within relations of power with the aim of disjoining subjects from the system and its names and notations. It foregrounds the ways in which normalization and normativity require "forgetting that perversity is the grounds of possibility for sexuality itself."[6]

What I am pursuing here is a trajectory that aims at viewing perversion as *action* that carries a positive force, similar to the use of "queer" as a verb. I wish to seek ways in which perverse readings and subjects can be understood as resisting dominant forces. The library is a space where difference has been "used as an instrument of an archival mode of power," reinscribing and reiterating the categories upon which power depends.[7] This project disjoins the category of perversion from the discourse of truth in which it has been enforced and deployed in service to power, in order to push the category and the classificatory systems from which it operates beyond their limits. The perverse pushes back, exceeds, and refuses the mechanisms presented in this book, thereby revealing spaces where the systems break down. Rather than giving themselves over to convention, we might say that perverse readings, composed of "disciplinary excessive" figures and subjects, have no "bibliographic shape" and invite a multiplicity of interpretations and significance.[8]

We might also, as MacCormack suggests, think of perversion as "an ethical tactic towards transformation as much as it is a subversive one, because it refutes the desirability of being accepted within dominant discourse, without refuting its own history or forgetting the accountability of the dominant."[9] As with Julia Kristeva's account of abjection, perversion is that which "disturbs identity, system, order. What does not respect borders, position, rules."[10] Indeed, Kristeva makes this association, as well—"the abject is perverse because it neither gives up nor assumes a prohibition, a rule, or a law; but turns them aside, misleads, corrupts; uses them, takes advantage of them, the better to deny them."[11] To be perverse may be to live well, as it is by way of perversity that we dismantle oppressive systems and the hierarchies upon which they are built. Perversion turns the system on itself. It reveals the absurdity and impossibility of mastering the bibliographic universe.

My use of perversion aims to challenge laws that are deployed to uphold unjust power relations. To be perverse is to be vulnerable because being illegible and outside the law is to be at risk of being coerced into a category with a name and its rules or to suffer the painful consequences of failing or renouncing the law. Arguably, it is within states of domination that we need always to be in the process of becoming perverse. It is where arms of the state reduce and normalize subjects to narrowly or broadly defined names and classes in service to power that we need to disturb. I do not advocate any and all of the sexual or other kinds of perversions, and, surely, care must be taken in choosing how to go about resisting the law. I would not at all suggest that anything goes, nor would I call for any act or position that abuses others. At the same time, I think it's important not to disavow all power relations and their games because, as Foucault tells us, "Where there is desire, the power relation is already present."[12] Rather, we should guard against an abuse of power, which occurs where "one imposes one's fantasies, appetites, and desires on others."[13] If we heed Foucault's call for a concern for the care of the self, we might take comfort in the recognition that we can find ways to resist relations of power without becoming what we protest against. Indeed, the care of the self includes a care for others and aims to manage the space of power relations in a manner that upholds others' freedom. Becoming perverse in this spirit means to honor freedom.

For Foucault freedom becomes possible only with self-knowledge. Linking ethics to a game of truth, he contends that to know oneself one must know the "rules of acceptable conduct or of principles that are both truths and prescriptions."[14] Knowledge and care of the self mitigate the risk of dominating others. This is why we should care about the classification of subjects in the library. It is by way of names and disciplinary norms that we arrive at knowledge in libraries. It is via markers that draw lines between normal and abnormal, often in cruel and punishing ways, that we learn about ourselves and the world. Countless stories describe sexually curious people learning about their bodies and inclinations through library books.

We might also think in terms of object relations, as explained by Deborah Britzman: "Object relations are not just a story of how we use objects but rather how, through relating, we begin to inaugurate and structure our very capacity to position ourselves in reality and phantasy, and so, to the very work of thinking."[15] I suggest that the relations set forth in the library are integral to reading practice, and the structures that organize knowledge affect the circulation and reception of texts. As knowledge about sex and sexuality has been organized according to particular schemes drawn up by the Library of Congress, it is of utmost importance that we interrogate the authoritative mechanisms at play in order to arrive at an understanding of how "subject[s] fit into a certain game of truth" and how, for what purposes, and for whom knowledge is organized and circulated within that game, as well as the ways those mechanisms structure reading practices and self-knowledge.[16]

My sincere hope is that this book will be viewed as a work that conducts and invites creative critique, with the aim toward inventing new ways of thinking about knowledge organization. This project, which investigates the normative, regulatory categories advanced in power-knowledge-sex relations in the library, is one that aims to undo and remake. It is one of perpetually questioning norms and refashioning, reconceptualizing, and repairing where necessary. Indeed, it is invested in presenting the library as perverse, in a sense that we most often regard as dangerous for its abuse of power. And I view the "perverse" as ethical subjects that call the library into question. It is not simply a reversal but a reworking of the assumptions we live by.

What Can a Body of Literature Do?

Action and becoming perverse are at the heart of the theme underlying the tensions expressed in this book. Relying on the notion that all entities take shape in relation to other entities, this project has everything to do with the question "What can a body do?" Applying Deleuze's reading of Spinoza to library books, this question cleanly drives at what is at stake. What can a body of literature become within the disciplinary conventions of the academy and the library? How does a classification map relationships among books and disciplines? How do perverse subjects subvert these dividing lines? What kinds of bodies and connections become possible with the deformation and dissolution of the systems and the opening and release of texts? Is it possible to imagine more fruitful ways of organizing the library and facilitating intertextual readings?

Ian Buchanan has explained that Deleuze's joy in reading Spinoza derived from the way in which Spinoza presents the body as a model: "He does not simply modify our knowledge of the body, he presents the body as knowledge."[17] For Spinoza and Deleuze the body and mind must be thought together, with the awareness that what happens to the body also happens to the mind. Extending this line of thought, I am interested in what bodies of literature do in the minds of readers but also in how works speak and respond to one another and give rise to other texts and ideas. I consider the ways in which organizational structures animate bodies of literature and in fact make it possible to find books—that they may be thought to bring the bodies of literature to life and render them meaningful and usable. As all "bodies are site- and time-specific according to the inscriptions of language and other modes of writing," and as "subjectivity is granted to bodies only through the co-presence of other bodies in space," the spatial and temporal relations on the shelves and in the catalog reveal much about the contours and relations across subjectivities and how they are granted.[18] The structuring mechanisms in the library give a certain kind of presence to relations of power in time and space by displaying the organizational schema on the shelves and in the catalog. Reading the shelves shows how bodies of literature have grown and shifted through the accumulation of texts in different spaces in the library. In the words of Deleuze and Guattari,

> We know nothing about a body until we know what it can do, in other words, what its affects are, how they can or cannot enter into composition with other affects, with the affects of another body, either to destroy that body or to be destroyed by it, either to exchange actions and passions with it or to join with it in composing another more powerful body.[19]

Deleuze measures the health of a body by its capacity to form new relations and what those relations then produce or decompose. A healthy body is one that has a multiplicity of affects and corresponding relations. It follows, then, that a "healthy" body of literature is one that has and engages a multiplicity of readings and that relations among texts give rise to more texts and more readings. To my mind, the ideal library is one that facilitates as many fruitful readings and reader relations as possible.

Similarly, Sedgwick moves beyond the questions of whether a piece of knowledge is true and "how do we know?" to questions of utility and consequences: "What does knowledge do—the pursuit of it, the having and exposing of it, the receiving again of knowledge of what one already knows?" How, asks Sedgwick, "is knowledge performative, and how best does one move among its causes and effects?"[20] A critical subtext across Sedgwick's body of work is, in fact, bound to knowledge organization, or the inquiry into what taxonomies and their categories *do*—what bearing they have on how we come to know and what that means for how bodies of literature and knowledge are activated, circulated, and grow. Of great consequence are the authorities under which taxonomies are produced and the cultural and political contexts that play into the question of what counts as knowledge.

I have conducted this research in part as a response to the specious claim that library classifications simply reflect the literature and are necessarily flawed because the published literature presents certain, limited points of view. In doing this work, it has become apparent to me that this argument fails to hold for a range of subjects. With regard to sexuality, the library has privileged particular (mostly scientific and medical) literatures from which to draw what librarians call "literary warrant"—the principle on which subject authorization is based. In the case of headings, the Library of Congress's policy is to "establish a subject heading for a topic that represents a discrete, identifiable concept when it is first encountered in a work being cataloged, rather than after several works on the topic have been published and cataloged."[21] This language suggests that a new heading should be created when a work is cataloged and there is no existing subject heading that adequately represents the aboutness of that work. When it comes to sexuality, however, this principle is often disregarded. "Queer," as a case in point, has not been added as an authorized heading as of 2016, despite the fact that hundreds of books on queer culture and people feature the term. The proliferation of "queer" across literatures would otherwise have surpassed the minimum requirements of literary warrant, but because it is viewed to be controversial and offensive to some, warrant is considered insufficient for authorization.[22] By ignoring "queer" subjects, the library in effect denies the existence of a field of inquiry and an identity category. "Queer theory" was added as a LC subject heading in 2006, many years after it appeared in the literature, but this heading is limited in application and scope to theoretical works.

The project is also in part a response to a pervasive sentiment revealed in the following exchange between a library patron and the chief of the Subject Cataloging Division at the Library of Congress. Upon browsing her library's shelves at the University of Washington in 1989, the patron noticed that books on child molestation were shelved next to books on gay men and lesbians. She wrote to the director of Bibliographic Control and Access Services at the University Library and asked that the books be recataloged.[23] The librarian forwarded the letter to Mary K. D. Pietris, chief of the Subject Cataloging Division at the LoC, who then responded directly to the patron:

> I can understand your concern that works on sex crimes class next to
> works on gays, but this is an accident of classification, in which some

topics must appear next to other topics although there may be no relation between them except that they are a subtopic of a larger subject.
. . . To even begin to contemplate any intent other than to arrange
works on distinct topics on the shelves boggles the mind.[24]

The book before you provides an account of an attempt to perform this
mind-boggling work. Taking the LoC and its catalog and classifications
as primary historical sources—as documents, archives, and archival instruments—it demonstrates that this problem is not simply "an accident
of classification" but the result of deeply embedded practices with social,
political, and historical roots that have organized and circulated normative discourses about sexuality.[25] Sexual variation has been organized into
medical and scientific categories, and this has a bearing not only on how
books are accessed but also on how bodies of literature and fields of study
are formed.

Let me be clear: This study has been an act of love. I view libraries
to be absolutely essential in a democratic society, but I also believe that
critique opens a field of vision so that we see where we can do better. It is
a credit to the institution of librarianship that these tools are open to the
public and available to criticism. In sharp contrast, the taxonomies that
support proprietary search engines like Google are impossible to view,
and the paths by which we come to knowledge in commercial spaces are
made possible by intrusive surveillance and marketing techniques. Libraries uniquely serve their publics, whether they are scholarly communities or
local residents, and the Library of Congress provides an invaluable public
service by providing bibliographic technologies that facilitate access and
sharing around the globe. At the same time, libraries have a complicated
history that is inextricably tied to the history of the United States, and the
classifications reveal some of the ways in which the making and expansion
of democracy is marked by violence and control.

Power/Knowledge/Classification

Assuming the frame "knowledge is power," Patrick Wilson, in his 1968
essay on bibliographic control, suggested that the organization of knowledge is in fact "power over power."[26] It is true that each individual cataloger holds a degree of power, but more significant is the fact that the
standard-bearing institution in bibliographic control and the organization
of cultural memory in our research and public libraries is, in fact, tied to
the state. As the oldest federal cultural institution in the United States and

the largest library in the world, the Library of Congress serves the U.S. Congress and the U.S. public and also sets the standards by which libraries around the globe are organized. It occupies a critical space where medical, social science, political, literary, and other discourses from around the world are collected, arranged, standardized, and disseminated. The LoC has a direct role in knowledge organization for Congress and the public, and as Samuel Collins argues, "the work of the Library [of Congress] in the 'information age' is not only a matter of arranging and classifying 'information,' but about positioning 'citizen-readers' in relation to it and, by synecdochic extension, to the reins of government and the power of the State."[27] Indeed, the LoC collects and catalogs much more than books. It is home to an expansive archive that contains documents including the Declaration of Independence and collections of papers from people such as Sigmund Freud, Abraham Lincoln, Hannah Arendt, and Frederick Douglas. It has the largest map collection in the world and houses important artifacts, including the Farm Security Administration/Office of War Information photographs, as well as objects and texts from around the world. As the LoC must also be considered a museum and an archive, this book is in direct conversation with the growing body of research on the role of archives in national and colonial narratives. It is also in dialogue with the expansive body of work on taxonomies for sexuality and race—particularly those works that consider the ways in which classifications contribute to the production of national ideals, identities, and ideologies.[28]

Foucault suggested that it was the selection, organization, and centralization of knowledges that brought the possibility of the modern state. The disciplines were used to construct a historical discourse that allowed "the State to talk about itself."[29] In fact, reading the classifications as documents, we see that the arrangement of subjects into disciplines is a narrative about how librarians have viewed sexualized objects of study—not only in relation to one another—but in relation to the project of nation building. I read the Library of Congress Classification and Subject Headings as histories of the United States and as technologies of the state, where categories have been "inscribed in the order of the imaginary."[30] Such an analysis reveals the extent to which the nation relies on unified categories in order to write its history and confirm the universality of the state as well as the ways in which the classifications support national interests. Placing the LoC within a group of federal bureaucracies that developed categories for constructing ideas about the nation and its citizens reveals library classifications to be tools of metaphysics and political economy. Indeed, Barbara

Tillett, the former director of the Cataloging Policy and Standards Office
at the Library of Congress, has acknowledged that choices about subject
headings and classifications tend to reflect the attitudes and beliefs of the
federal government.[31]

This point became publicly evident just before this book went to press.
In March 2016 the Library of Congress announced that it planned to introduce two subject headings, "Unauthorized immigration" and "Noncitizens," to replace the existing "Illegal aliens."[32] Prompted by a petition
circulated by a group of students and librarians at Dartmouth College to
the LoC to change "Illegal aliens" to "Undocumented immigrants," the
two new headings are meant to convey more clearly the concepts in current language.[33] The authorization was quickly met by protest from the
U.S. House of Representatives, members of which are pressuring the LoC
to retain "Aliens" or "Illegal aliens." Conservative members of the House
Appropriations Committee introduced a provision to maintain the heading in its report accompanying a bill for the funding of federal institutions,
including the Library of Congress, in fiscal year 2017. On April 13, 2016,
Representative Diane Black (R-Tenn.) introduced the bill H.R. 4926,
known as the Stopping Partisan Policy at the Library of Congress Act,
directing the LoC to retain "Aliens" and "Illegal Aliens." And on May 16,
2016, four members of Congress, including former presidential candidate
Ted Cruz, issued a letter to the acting Librarian of Congress, requesting a reversal of the change and accusing the LoC of bowing to "political
pressure of the moment."[34] In profoundly conservative fashion, the con-
gressmen indicated that "alien" has such tremendous historical weight that
changing it would impede access to information for immigration scholars,
jurists, and sociologists who are accustomed to the term. Citing William
Blackstone's eighteenth-century *Commentaries on the Laws of England* as
exemplary of the types of texts that use "aliens," they charged that changing the heading is an Orwellian tactic that would have grave consequences.
The letter demonstrates their ignorance with regard to the principles of
literary warrant and currency of language, but much more interesting is
the fact that these members of Congress view subject headings to matter and were compelled to intervene. Indeed, Representative Black argued
that the subject heading change is a "needless policy change," as if the
authorization of taxonomic terminology for access to information should
be regarded as federal policy making.[35] As of this writing, the LoC has
posted an online survey for members of the public to offer comments on
the proposed heading change.

In the case of books on sexual perversion, broadly and strangely defined in the eyes of the library, bodies of literature have occupied positions in service to a medicalized discipline or as agents of the federal government in sexual policing. By looking at the cataloging of texts on a range of sexual expressions, acts, and identifications, we find that more often than not these classificatory mechanisms produce absurd, unjust, or otherwise peculiar bodies of literature. The subject headings, classification marks, and symbols that are all created in this massive government library act as components of an elaborate regulatory machine that renders bodies intelligible, normalized, and unified under academic disciplines, while those subjects that don't obey a norm are rendered invisible or marginal. By reading library classifications against the grain, we find spaces where abstractions of state discourse mask state violence.[36]

Library classifications and the institutions from which they arise—in this case, the Library of Congress—remain underexamined apparatuses in the production of subjects. Although the disciplines of the academy are neatly laid out and displayed on the library shelves, little attention has been paid to the complex processes of disciplinary power that take place at the LoC. These systems are, in fact, apparatuses that create and organize subjects and give rise to bodies of literature with methodologies, languages, audiences, and topics for discussion. The arrangement of books on the shelves displays the participants in dialogue in relation to particular disciplines. It would be shortsighted to suggest that the shelves simply mirror the academic disciplines. As I will continue to point out, the LoC is selective in determining how to reflect and reproduce the disciplines. The academy and its libraries are mutually reinforcing, and their reproductive power extends far beyond library and university walls as they embed and circulate normalizing state discourses about citizenship and belonging. By examining LoC cataloging technologies as apparatuses, we begin to see the role of libraries in situating knowledges about sexuality in privileged domains and naming them accordingly. We also find that the library's arrangements of gendered and racialized subjects are enmeshed in and reinforce particular ways of historicizing subjectivity and citizenship. As these standards are repeated across a globalized network of libraries, the catalog reveals itself to be a colonized space where the classifications of knowledge about humans and the humanities are designed in ways that fortify the state and convey an imagined nation. The Enlightenment era–inspired devices organize library subjects into discrete categories in a vast rational and scientific infrastructure to serve and produce an informed citizenry.

I regard the classifications as apparatuses in Agamben's sense, which includes "anything that has in some way the capacity to capture, orient, determine, intercept, model, control, or secure the gestures, behaviors, opinions, or discourses of living beings."[37] Agamben calls for us to think beyond panoptic prisons, factories, and schools and to consider the pen, computers, and even philosophy and language to be apparatuses that capture and subjectify. He places all objects in the world into two categories: living beings (substances) and apparatuses, and he offers an in-between class—the subject, "which results from the relation and, so to speak, from the relentless fight between living beings and apparatuses."[38] With subjects in the library, I suggest it is the language of the library classifications that brings form to bodies of literature, breathes meaning into them, and facilitates engagement. These classifications give the illusion that a subject can be attained and contained—that a work can fit into a reality present in one place on the shelves. This frame brings into view the tensions derived from the materially organizing taxonomic apparatuses that bring order and make a collection usable even as they simultaneously constrain works within the collection.

The disciplinary lines drawn by such systems are tenuous at best, but surely in their attempts to delineate what books are about, they control and cordon off would-be intertextualities, entanglements, and interdisciplinarity.[39] As Agamben might suggest, however, although the apparatus is what brings the text into being, the text cannot be reduced to the librarian's disciplinary act.[40] Indeed, the text will take on a life of its own—one that escapes the controls of the classifier, the position on the shelf, the author, and even the text itself. How that book is taken up by others, circulated, read, interpreted, and cited is out of anyone's or any system's hands. Literary bodies and their readers are anything but docile.

My hope is that readers will share with me the pleasure in removing the boundaries between human bodies and bodies of literature. That is to say that I seek pleasure in these texts and the intertextuality among the books, the bodies of literature, and the bodies who read and write and take shape by ingesting the texts while giving new life to the texts through their readings. Bodies of literature and fleshly bodies here are all regarded as texts that proliferate meaning and have material effects on one another and in the world. In the library of my dreams I envision a terrific intermingling of bodies of all types, inscribing one another with meaning in flesh and paper and blood and ink, acting out love and desire and fantasy and violence on the shelves and in the rooms of the library. I see something like Foucault's *bibilotheque fantastique*, where the books dream other books.[41] I imagine a time before any classificatory apparatus took hold, before the "universe of language . . . absorbed our sexuality, denatured it, placed it in a void where it establishes its sovereignty," and placed limits by way of laws.[42] It is a space where the abject and sublime come together.

Of course, I don't want just any book. I do depend on my librarians to act as curators of knowledge by selecting and cataloging books that will fuel my desires. It would be impossible to find them if there were no order in the library. And so it is with gratitude that I peruse the HQ section and then wander over to the philosophy books in the Bs and then the library science section in the Zs. I find tremendous pleasure in seeking books and lingering among the ordered stacks. But then my pleasures are interrupted by certain jarring disciplinary associations, like the shelving of *Gayspeak* (Pilgrim Press, 1981), a book on communication styles of gay people, next to books on child sexual abuse. And I wonder how much I'm missing and why these books are placed where they are. I can't help feeling a certain discord and a sense that I've lost my way. I feel the weight of the relations of power in motion in the library—ones that, until recently, I haven't understood well enough to consent to.

The library is an erotically charged space. Some might even regard the pleasurable experience of browsing and losing and finding oneself in the stacks as an exercise in sadomasochism. The classificatory apparatuses in the library, with their disciplinary divisions and regularizing and shaming techniques, often bar opportunities for cross-disciplinary play, prohibit the intermingling of bodies, and cut the perverse from the normal (as if such an act was actually possible). In the library space, submission to and enactment of technologies of control facilitate and inhibit promiscuousness in browsing, perverse readings, and bodily pleasures.

I have resolved to keep this study to printed and bound books. Stemming from my interest in the preservation of the book and my belief that the digital realm can in no way replicate the sensualities and fantasies of the library and its books, I am delaying discussions of digital technologies until the last chapter. For those of us who are frustrated and troubled by the disappearing stacks, who would prefer to hold a book made of paper and cloth and turn its pages, for those of us who browse and love to linger in the library, it seems that explicitly privileging the printed book is a political statement in itself. I would add that issues of naming and taxonomies are not likely to be solved in the digital universe, and in fact, the questions I raise here are applicable to any technology or topic that operates through categories.

I have also decided intentionally to defer deployment of the term "user" until the very end of the book, where it will take a specific meaning. The idea of the user in libraries and information systems has become so prevalent in the field of library and information studies that the term's significance reaches beyond conceptualization as put forth in the ever-increasing body of user studies research. Ron Day foregrounds the extent to which the user is being used and argues that the user has been constructed, as has her needs, in ways that propagate systems and system designers.[43] Around the same time that describing the "aboutness" of works became the rule, the "reader" was transformed into a "user" who employed tools like classifications to meet information "needs."[44] The user has been manipulated into needing what the systems produce. It is for these reasons that, instead of the term "user," I speak of readers, visitors, and patrons. I will self-consciously introduce the user in the epilogue to put a masochistic user into play in a charged, consensual power play with the library and its systems.

Disciplining Bodies of Literature

The history of librarianship parallels that of sexuality studies, and these fields intersect in critical ways in the creation of classifications and definitions of sexual perversion. The late nineteenth and early twentieth centuries witnessed a surge in bureaucratization and standardization in business and science, and librarianship and sexuality were among the fields that became professionalized with the pretense toward being scientific in order to gain legitimacy. Elaborate taxonomies were central to both the scientific study of sexuality and the scientific management of libraries. For sexologists the goal was to organize sexual variance according to deviations from a norm, and for librarians the mission was to organize the entire universe of knowledge, of which sexuality was necessarily a part. Both contributed to wider projects in organizing citizenries.

The Library of Congress Classification and Subject Headings were designed when the LoC moved into its new home, the stately Jefferson Building, in 1897. Eight hundred tons of books, pamphlets, maps, manuscripts, prints, and music lay in heaps in boxes and on floors, to catalog and shelve (see Figure 1).[45] The enormous task of assessing and organizing such a massive quantity of printed and recorded material required an efficient and expert group of librarians, as well as systems to organize this mass of knowledge. Librarian John Russell Young had begun to make plans for organizing the Library of Congress during his brief period of service, from 1897 until 1899. Young unexpectedly died and was replaced by Herbert

Putnam, who served as Librarian of Congress from 1899 to 1939. William
Warner Bishop, in his tribute to Putnam, described the situation in the
new library building as one that must have been terribly daunting:

> What the new Librarian of Congress thought of the situation he found
> we are not permitted to know. . . . Briefly, he found a small staff lack-
> ing systematic organization, a huge mass of books but ill arranged on
> Mr. Jefferson's scheme of classification, an imperfect author catalogue
> on large slips, but no subject catalogue or shelf-list; meager funds for
> purchases and none for publication; material special in form, that is
> prints, maps, music, manuscripts, and the like, in enormous quantities
> but not well catalogued, arranged, and served by specialists; . . . large
> annual accessions, chiefly from copyright and from exchange; a mag-
> nificent and imposing building, itself a pledge and promise of support
> from Congress.[46]

The efficiency and masterfulness with which Putnam and his team of
catalogers, led by J. C. M. Hanson, sorted and cataloged these materials
is nothing short of remarkable. We must observe, though, that it was in
a particular context and period that the Library of Congress devised the
Library Congress Classification system and Library of Congress Subject
Headings to gain control of this unwieldy collection. And although addi-
tions, changes, and deletions of the names and classes are permitted, some
of the underlying hierarchical structures and the disciplinary arrangements
created in that era have become firmly embedded in library networks over
time and would be very difficult to revise in significant ways.

The Enlightenment ideals that fueled the eighteenth-century quest for
knowledge remained a powerful force in Progressive Era America. The
belief that universal knowledge is possible drove Carl Linnaeus, Francis
Bacon, and Denis Diderot to attempt to name and classify everything in
nature, and seventeenth- and eighteenth-century classifications provided
the models upon which nineteenth- and twentieth-century sexologists and
librarians and other scientific professionals based their systems. In fact,
Francis Miksa has drawn a direct lineage from Francis Bacon's classification of knowledge to the current Library of Congress Classification system, locating Thomas Jefferson's system in between.[47] After the former
Library of Congress, housed in the U.S. Capitol, was burned by British
troops during the War of 1812, Jefferson sold his personal collection to
the LoC. His classification system remained the basis for organizing the
LoC's collection for nearly a century. Jefferson adapted Bacon's universal
system of general categories to his personal collection, which was primar-

Figure 1. "Copyright Deposits in the Basement Before Classifying." *Source*: Library of Congress, *American Memory* (Washington, D.C.: Library of Congress, 1898?). Reproduction number: LC-USZ62–38245. http://loc.gov/pictures/resource/cph.3a38598/.

ily composed of materials on world history, the military, and politics, with some books on the sciences. A significant departure from the Jeffersonian system, the present LoC classification was issued in installments, according to discipline, beginning in 1901, as part of the new efforts to assemble and organize the collections in the new building.

Librarians in the late nineteenth century and early twentieth centuries viewed their role as one of helping to improve society through reading. Melvil Dewey called it the "library faith"—the idea that libraries were contributing to the nation's progress and social order by getting the public to read "good" literature. Wayne Wiegand states that, although it appears that the library profession's mission has always been genuinely beneficent, the truth is that the best reading was agreed upon by library leaders who were "WASP, mostly male, middle-class professionals immersed in the disciplinary and literary canons of the dominant culture."[48] Authority arose from dominant cultures in professional groups, and it was under this authority that the best reading was chosen. As public and academic librarians identified the best books, the LoC contributed to the culture of reading practices by effectively setting the standard with regard to production,

distribution, and use of catalog cards, while creating the universal vocabulary and classification scheme, thereby devising the mechanisms by
which reading materials would be organized and accessed. As I will argue
in Chapters 3 and 4, some of the librarians of Congress were also statesmen
and census takers, and much of the work of the Library of Congress must
be understood in the context of state building.

Herbert Putnam was an outspoken advocate for the Library of Congress and obtained the essential resources needed to manage the collection and advance cataloging standards. Putnam believed that the Library
of Congress should surpass other national libraries' roles as storehouses
of material by organizing services for Congress and other departments of
the federal government and sharing those services and techniques with
other libraries and scholars. Significantly, his success in expanding the LoC
resulted in part from his close friendship with Theodore Roosevelt, a historian who supported the LoC's mission and allocated funds to improve it.
In fact, Roosevelt consulted Putnam for advice on reading materials and
proposed selection ideas. They exchanged letters that included sentiments
such as the following:

> As I lead, to put it mildly, a sedentary life for the moment I would
> greatly like some books that would appeal to my queer taste. I do not
> suppose there are any histories or any articles upon the early Mediter-
> ranean races. That man Lindsay who wrote about prehistoric Greece
> has not put out a second volume, has he? Has a second volume of
> Oman's Art of War appeared? If so, send me either or both; if not, then
> a good translation of Niebuhr and Momsen [*sic*], or the best modem
> history of Mesopotamia. Is there a good history of Poland?[49]

The librarian satisfied such requests from the president by regularly sending him lists of new acquisitions, from which Roosevelt chose books to be
delivered to the White House. According to Paul Heffron, "The whole
correspondence with Herbert Putnam reveals a unique combination of
personal and official ties binding the 26th President to the Library of
Congress."[50] The LoC, by order of President Roosevelt, received the papers of George Washington, James Madison, Alexander Hamilton, Thomas
Jefferson, James Monroe, and Benjamin Franklin, and Putnam noted that
Roosevelt was the only president to discuss LoC matters in executive addresses to Congress.[51]

Putnam envisioned the LoC as a universal library, and in one of his pleas
to Roosevelt for an increase in funds, he expressed its mission in terms
of the potential to influence and standardize library practices across the

United States, providing for us a glimpse of how the Library of Congress was gaining power and authority:

> Libraries of the United States are organizing their work with reference to uniformity in methods, to cooperation in processes, to interchange of service, to the promotion of efficiency in service. They look to the National Library for standards, for example, for leadership in all these enterprises. It is now in a position to "standardize" library methods, to promote cooperation, to aid in the elimination of wasteful duplication, to promote the interchange of bibliographic service.[52]

The Library of Congress began printing catalog cards with subjects in 1898, and libraries across the United States became the beneficiaries of this practice when the LoC shared, exchanged, and sold printed cards starting in 1902, after Roosevelt approved an act of Congress authorizing the LoC to sell copies of cards and other publications to institutions and individuals.[53] This was the origin of copy cataloging, as purchasing printed cards meant that local libraries could save time and resources, and it meant that libraries were adding the same content and form to their catalogs. Putnam declared in that year's annual report, "The undertaking has in various ways so affected the work of the Division that it can justly be said to constitute the most important event in [LoC] history."[54] Putnam boasted at the American Library Association convention in 1904 that the LoC was already printing sixty thousand cards annually and invited librarians to subscribe to the service.[55] Through this sharing and selling of catalog copy, the subject headings and other standards were gradually installed and made common practice in libraries that received or purchased the cards.

The LoC's authority with the wider library community was not immediate, however. Initially, its sharing was more an act of service in the interest of efficiency rather than an attempt to get local libraries to conform to a standard. Indeed, the LoC was primarily concerned with its own collection when creating subject headings and assigning call numbers. With an increase in publishing and demands on libraries in the 1930s, though, there was a call for the LoC to communicate its subject cataloging policies and procedures to the wider American library community.[56] David Judson Haykin became the Subject Cataloging Division's first chief in 1940 and immediately found it necessary to codify and normalize subject cataloging for the entire subject cataloging community in and outside the LoC before it got too unwieldy. His vision was for the LoC to serve as a central bureau for subject cataloging. As Haykin recognized the limitations of the cataloging staff and their inability to be aware of all the changes in every discipline, he began hiring subject specialists, insisting on more and better terminologies. Every year witnessed an increase in the number of new headings added. Haykin produced a manual for creating and applying headings, and this became the textbook on subject headings for libraries across the United States, further establishing the LoC as authority.[57] Miksa credits Haykin with fully propelling the LoC to the status of authority and standard bearer by making LoC products more valuable, more readily available, and more indispensable. The production of the manual gave librarians the perception that the headings were based on authoritative rationales and gave good reason to have confidence in the LoC's products. This confidence, combined with the increasing demand for efficiency, led to the widespread adoption of LoC standards and terms.[58] In the following decades, the advent of machine-readable records for authority headings made the inclusion of LoC headings in thousands of library catalogs even easier and, in fact, automatic. Copy cataloging practices became computerized, and catalogs at the local level were able to house their own databases of authority records imported from large shared systems. Over the course of the twentieth century copy cataloging techniques and technologies became increasingly efficient and also served to embed standards deeply in libraries around the globe.

Efficiency and standardization require simplicity and uniformity, which, according to James C. Scott, were also conditions of statecraft. Scott soundly argues that incredibly complex practices were rendered controllable and legible through categories constructed along a standard grid.[59] During the Progressive Era in the United States a high-modernist ideology—perhaps best conceived as an unwavering faith in scientific and technical progress—fueled classificatory projects in the library and sexological professions, both of which should be recognized as integral to social engineering. Indeed, we find on library shelves a confirmation of Foucault's proposition that, contrary to the notion that sex and sexuality were not talked about in the nineteenth century, the topic of sexuality proliferated in networks and texts as a *dispositif* of disciplinary power. Within the sexological books of the late nineteenth and early twentieth centuries, normal and abnormal were delimited and described, and perversions were ordered and narrated in detail. These classificatory distinctions are repeated in simplified categories on the shelves, as those early sexology texts provided the literary warrant for designing the sections of the classification that continue to organize sexuality today.

The argument frequently expounded by sexuality scholars today—that sex can be considered the organizing principle for everything—is instructive for the history of library classifications. Indeed, this notion was also propelled by Richard von Krafft-Ebing in his *Psychopathia Sexualis*, albeit in the context of a very different worldview. Here are Krafft-Ebing's opening words to his study:

> If man were deprived of sexual distinction and the nobler enjoyments arising therefrom, all poetry and probably all moral tendency would be eliminated from his life. Sexual life no doubt is the one mighty factor in the individual and social relations of man which disclose his powers of activity, of acquiring property, of establishing a home, of awakening altruistic sentiments towards a person of the opposite sex, and towards his own issue as well as towards the whole human race. Sexual feeling is really the root of all ethics, and no doubt of aestheticism and religion.[60]

It was from the *Psychopathia Sexualis*, which is widely considered a foundational sexological taxonomic work, that the LoC seems to have drawn warrant for establishing its hierarchies and naming practices regarding sexuality at the end of the nineteenth century. Translated into English in the same decade that the LoC moved to its current building and developed its subject headings and classification system, it provided the basis for establishing a scaffold in support of the scientific study of sexuality. And it is those same hierarchies that provide the essential structures by which we organize many of our libraries today. John K. Noyes provides us with a particularly astute observation, noting that Krafft-Ebing's rationalization and classification of the perversions required a particular, contradictory conception of doing history—one that dehistoricizes the perversions in order to explain a universal struggle between civilization and nature and the ethical imperatives for taming biological impulses.[61] The nineteenth-century invention of certain perversions as pathological disorders and the organization of those perversions into a system of categories was an attempt—emblematic of modernity—to totalize human sexuality and establish the primacy of sex in a grand narrative about the progress and perils of human civilization.

Foucault notes that it was during the last two decades of the nineteenth century—when Krafft-Ebing wrote his seminal text—that sexual abnormality emerged "as the root, foundation, and general etiological principle of most other forms of abnormality."[62] Sedgwick identifies this decade as the point at which knowledge and sex became inextricably linked, that Enlightenment-era practices had by then become so reified in Western culture as to result in a condition in which "knowledge meant sexual knowledge," and she says that this decade is where we should turn to analyze the intersecting discourses across medicine, law, language, and the "career of imperialism," which collectively inaugurated the homo/hetero binary and taxonomies of perversions and homophobic oppression.[63] One of Sedgwick's central premises is that "the master terms of a particular historical moment will be those that are so situated as to entangle most inextricably and at the same time most differentially the filaments of other important definitional nexuses."[64] Arguably, the primary mechanism by which oppression of homosexuals and other "perverse" people was enacted was through the production of taxonomies, with categories for gender and sexuality and race designed according to binaries of normal and abnormal, or normal and perverse, sexualities. The Library of Congress was the place where knowledge was centralized and organized into disciplines at this time, and where intersecting knowledges were divided up.

It should be clear now that the structures underlying the classifications and naming systems in libraries were born out of and reiterate societal norms of a particular era. Inspired by other Enlightenment-era systems, they were created to organize the library's "universal" collection, and over the course of the twentieth century the library's power and authority over knowledge expanded its reach. The ways that the LoC inscribes difference in this universal system brings to light what Sedgwick observed about universalizing and minoritizing discourses that uncomfortably and uncertainly overlap and come into conflict. There are benefits to naming and categorizing sexual difference, as they bring books about particular minorities together on the shelves. The utilitarian goals of the classifications are impossible to realize fully, however, in part because of the limitations of singular categories. Those limits are the result of the universalization of heteropatriarchy, which has been constructed through and depends upon the exclusion and marginalization of subjects. Indeed, where there are claims to universality—and knowledge organization systems built upon the belief that such a thing is possible—we must interrogate the ethical dimensions associated with the universalisms upon which those systems are constructed and the ways in which minority difference is written.[65] With regard to sexuality, library classifications seem to ignore altogether any notion that, as Freud argued, we are all innately perverse.[66] Rather, derived from Krafft-Ebing's conceptualization of perversion as nonprocreative sex, the classification assumes a "normal" sexuality and marks everything "abnormal" or "perverse" as a marginalized minority. I am inclined to side with Freud and those who claim that we are all perverse, and I suggest that such a notion turns the classification, along with the universalisms it assumes, on itself. A complete inversion or reworking of the classification might be a productive thought experiment, setting perversion as an assumed norm and arranging a proliferation of sexual and bodily variance around a different set of ideals.

Situating Knowledges in the Library

One of the primary purposes here is to unmask knowledge-sex-power mechanisms and to locate the speech of subjugated knowledges erased by or spoken for in the language of more dominant voices: "It is a way of playing local, discontinuous, disqualified, or nonlegitimized knowledges off against the unitary theoretical instance that claims to be able to filter them, organize them into a hierarchy, organize them in the name of a true body of knowledge, in the name of the rights of a science that is in the hands of a few."[67] In order to understand discipline formation, we need to examine discursive practices, which, according to Foucault, "take shape in technical ensembles, in institutions, in behavioral schemes, in types of transmission and dissemination, in pedagogical forms that both impose and maintain them."[68] The Library of Congress is precisely the kind of institution to which Foucault refers. It has acquired and organized and situated various knowledges into disciplines of literature, sociology, medicine, popular culture, legal studies, and so on, serving to normalize discourses within disciplines and privilege certain disciplines over others.[69] The LoC further disciplines sex and sexuality by privileging scientific domains and texts, granting such disciplines authority while obfuscating the humanities, popular literature, and emerging interdisciplinary and local knowledges.

The Library of Congress is not alone in privileging the sciences, and it is best understood as part of a network of institutions that advance such aims. Foucault tells us that inherent in the claim to be a science is an aspiration to power, and his genealogical method demands that we ask a series of questions: "What types of knowledge are you trying to disqualify when you say that you are a science? What speaking subject, what discursive subject, what subject of experience and knowledge are you trying to minoritize when you begin to say: 'I speak this discourse, I am speaking a scientific discourse, and I am a scientist'?"[70] To be clear, I do not propose any kind of annihilation of the sciences; rather, I am interested in how they have come to disciplinary power and privilege in the academy and our libraries.

Such a position carries implications for and informs Donna Haraway's notion of situated knowledges, which privileges partial knowledges derived from various localized positions that together produce a more holistic understanding of the world. Haraway calls for a pooling of local knowledges from various perspectives rather than a single explanation of the world from a "God's-eye" view. The only way to find a larger vision is to be somewhere in particular, rather than seeing from above and determining order. This is in direct contradiction with the aims of library classifications, which were first designed by a group of experts to organize the universe of knowledge. As Haraway tells us, feminist, antiracist technoscience projects like hers "do not respect the boundaries of disciplines, institutions, nations, or genres," nor do knowledges about sexuality.[71] And it through the critical interdisciplines like disability/queer/feminist/ethnic/critical race studies that we see the extent to which a universal system fails to account for partial knowledges. By situating knowledge across the library according to disciplines, various voices are hidden away, and important conversations are likely missed.

Given this awareness of how classification disciplines scholarship and literary works through science, we might think of texts in the humanities as subjugated knowledges, particularly given that the scientific disciplines do, in the case of sexual perversion and other subjects, restrict these texts from speaking on their own behalf, organizing and distributing them in attempts to provide a rational order. Given the nature of classification—a scientific enterprise, to be sure—the humanities and critical interdisciplines may simply be uncatalogable by definition. Under the disciplining apparatuses of classifications and subject headings, the humanities are dominated by the scientific disciplines of psychiatry, medicine, and the social sciences. Where scientists like Haraway have turned to the humanities, pursuing interdisciplinary methods for critical inquiry into scientific norms and technologies, we find it is impossible for the classification to accommodate.

To take Haraway's corpus as a case in point, Figure 2 illustrates the disciplines to which her work has been assigned as well as each of the subject headings assigned to her books. Her body of work is dispersed across the library in disciplines as diverse as agriculture, biology, anthropology, and feminist theory within the social sciences. For example, take her interdisciplinary text *Simians, Cyborgs, and Women: The Reinvention of Nature*, for which the book description at the publisher's website reads: "Although on the surface, simians, cyborgs and women may seem an odd threesome, Haraway describes their profound link as 'creatures' which have had a great destabilizing place in Western evolutionary technology and biology."[72] The book is shelved with books on biological determinism and sociobiology within the discipline of anthropology. If one were browsing a library's

**HQ1190—Women, Feminism—
Feminist theory**

> *Modest_Witness@Second_Millennium.*
> *FemaleMan_Meets_OncoMouse:*
> *Feminism and Technoscience* (1997)
>> Feminist theory
>> Feminist criticism
>> Technology—Social aspects
>> Science—Social aspects
>> Computers and civilization
>
> *How Like a Leaf* (1999)
>> Feminist theory
>> Feminist criticism
>> Sociology
>> Primates—Behavior
>> Human behavior
>
> *Haraway Reader* (2003)
>> Feminist theory
>> Feminist criticism
>> Technology—Social aspects
>> Science—Social aspects

**QL85—Zoology—Human-animal
relationships**

> *When Species Meet* (2008)
>> Human-animal relationships

GN365.9—Anthropology—Sociobiology

> *Simians, Cyborgs, and Women: The*
> *Reinvention of Nature* (1991)
>> Sociobiology
>> Feminist criticism
>> Primates—Behavior
>> Human behavior

**SF422.86—Agriculture—Dog
breeders—Psychology**

> *Companion Species Manifesto: Dogs,*
> *People, and Significant Otherness*
> (2003)
>> Dog owners—Psychology
>> Dogs—Psychological aspects
>> Human behavior
>> Human-animal relationships

**QH331—Biology—Philosophy of
biology**

> *Crystals, Fabrics, and Fields:*
> *Metaphors of Organicism in Twentieth-*
> *century Developmental biology* (1976)
>> Biology—Philosophy
>
> *Crystals, Fabrics, and Fields:*
> *Metaphors That Shape Embryos* (2004)
>> Biology—Philosophy

**QL737—Zoology—Mammals–
Systematic divisions**

> *Primate Visions: Gender, Race, and*
> *Nature in the World of Modern Science*
> (1989)
>> Primates—Research—History
>> Feminist criticism
>> Sociobiology
>> Human biology—Social
>> aspects

Figure 2. Donna Haraway's corpus, as organized by the Library of Congress.

shelves, how likely would one be to stumble upon this text? Should it be with other Haraway texts? Ought it to be in the HQs with other books on feminism and women and queer subjects? Or might we place it with other sociotechnical topics? Where do/could all the cyborgs in the library reside? In what ways does situating it with books on human nature reduce the text and prevent it from comingling with others and would-be readers?

I am certainly not the first to ask these kinds of questions. Roland Barthes recognizes this classificatory conundrum in his writing about the Text:

> The Text does not come to a stop with (good) literature; it cannot be apprehended as part of a hierarchy or even a simple division of genres. What constitutes the Text is, on the contrary (or precisely), its subversive force with regard to old classifications. How can one classify Georges Bataille? Is this writer a novelist, a poet, an essayist, an economist, a philosopher, a mystic? The answer is so uncertain that manuals of literature generally chose to forget about Bataille; yet Bataille wrote texts—even, perhaps, always one and the same text.

Similarly, Derrida asks how we should classify Freud's archive, stating that the deconstruction of the archive concerns the "institution of limits declared to be insurmountable," with one set of questions having to do with classification:

> What comes under theory or under private correspondence, for example? What comes under system? Under biography or autobiography? Under personal or intellectual anamnesis? In works said to be theoretical, what is worthy of this name and what is not? Should one rely on what Freud says about this to classify his works? Should one for example take him at his word when he presents his Moses as a "historical novel"? In each of these cases, the limits, the borders, and the distinctions have been shaken by an earthquake from which no classificational concept and no implementation of the archive can be sheltered. Order is no longer assured.[73]

The librarian's job is anything but straightforward. Both Barthes and Derrida recognized the exasperatingly impossible, practical necessity of classification. The more pressing question, however, confronts the classificatory mechanism itself and the life of the disciplines in the library—or rather—the library in the disciplines. Whereas we all recognize the tensions inherent in classifying works, what this project sets out to do is to understand how the classificatory mechanisms have taken hold through relations of power and how they function. It locates the library as the "ground of both our freedoms and our unfreedoms" in reading practice.[74] It aims to discover ways in which perverse subjects trouble and destabilize the grid of intelligibility upon which fixed and normative subject positions are built. The wager is that undoing the systems in the library will open up possibilities for new ways of conceptualizing and locating bodies of literature through, on, and in perversion.

CHAPTER I

Naming Subjects: "Paraphilias"

You who read me—are you certain you
understand my language?

—JORGE LUIS BORGES, "The Library of Babel"

The first and most important rule is not to
believe the statement that the patient was
attracted to the same sex since childhood.

—WILHELM STEKEL, "Is Homosexuality Curable?"

The catalog record for *Epistemology of the Closet* demonstrates the performativity of subject headings—the authorized terms by which we search for books. I ask you to reassume the position of a cataloger in 1990, and think now of a handful of key words and phrases that represent what *Epistemology of the Closet* is about. Bear in mind that, as a cataloger, you consider what your library patrons would be most likely to seek in the catalog if they were looking for books on the subjects you assign. Subject searches are performed as a gathering technique when readers do not know the titles and authors of the texts but have an idea of the topic they are looking for. If you were properly cataloging this book according to the rules, you would look to the Library of Congress Subject Headings to find the authorized forms of the terms. In 1990 the lists of headings would have been sitting on your desk in a massive five-volume set clothed in red covers. A significant amount of training is required, as is a solid grasp of the subject matter, to be able to apply the headings, add subdivisions, and encode it all adequately. For this text, catalogers chose to provide the major authors addressed by Sedgwick as subjects, as well as four topical subject headings. Recall again that the term "queer theory" had been coined just months before the publication of the book, and it was not officially authorized as a subject heading by the Library of Congress until 2006. I leave this exercise off here and leave it to you to compare your own assessment of what *Epistemology of the Closet* is about (an impossibly absurd task, I realize) with what the Library of Congress chose for the 1990 edition. Next we move to the subject of "Paraphilias," formerly called "Sexual perversion."

> Melville, Herman, 1819–1891. Billy Budd.
> James, Henry, 1843–1916—Criticism and interpretation.
> Wilde, Oscar, 1854–1900—Criticism and interpretation.
> Proust, Marcel, 1871–1922. A la recherché du temps perdu.
> Nietzsche, Friedrich Wilhelm, 1844–1900.
> American fiction—Men authors—History and criticism.
> Homosexuality and literature.
> Gays' writings—History and criticism—Theory, etc.
> Gay men in literature.[1]

The inspiration for this book arose out of my own struggles as a seeker of historical materials on homosexuality and bisexuality via the University of Wisconsin library catalog in 2009—as a disciplined subject, so to speak. I performed a keyword search to locate catalog records that included the term "homosexual" anywhere. Upon finding some entries of interest, I clicked on links to various author names and subject headings, and eventually my wanderings conveyed me to the record for the 1934 edition of Wilhelm Stekel's *Bi-Sexual Love: The Homosexual Neurosis*, which brought my browsing to a halt. I noticed that the record contained no headings for bisexuality or homosexuality. Rather, the only two subject headings assigned to this book were "Neuroses" and "Paraphilias." As the latter term was unfamiliar to me at the time, my first inclination was to think that it must have been a mistake—perhaps a medical heading, or a relic that somehow never got updated. I then clicked on the heading to see if it was applied to other works in the catalog and discovered that it was included in over three hundred bibliographic records.

Perplexed, I searched the Library of Congress's catalog and WorldCat (a shared catalog across 72,000 libraries) and found that it was clearly a currently authorized subject heading.[2] I consulted the authority record for the heading in the Library of Congress authorities database, which indicated that "Paraphilias" was authorized in 2007 to replace "Sexual deviation" (see Figure 3). The record also revealed that the reasons for preferring this term were supplied by psychiatric literature. The 1934 Stekel book was assigned this heading because of the technological application called "global" or "batch updating," which allows a librarian to update automatically all catalog records that contain a given heading to the current form. Stekel's book, then, which had originally been assigned the headings "Sexual perversion" and "Neuroses," is now cataloged with "Paraphilias" and "Neuroses," providing no heading for homosexuality, bisexuality, or any reference to this as a historical text.[3] With the global update technology, "Paraphilias" replaced "Sexual deviation" in most catalogs, including that of the Library of Congress, without any human review of the catalog records. This means that, by virtue of automation, texts that were cataloged in the early part of the twentieth century retain formerly held attitudes that associated homosexuality and bisexuality with perversion, but now in anachronistic terms.[4]

While the story of my search is only one personal anecdote, I hope that it resonates with readers and illustrates a sense of being disciplined, which manifested in the jarring experience of struggling to understand my own identifications in unintelligible terms. It demonstrates how the disciplinary apparatus affects both the text and the reader. The classificatory mechanism inscribes a book's subject in the catalog in a language that may be foreign to both the text and the person seeking the text, resulting in a range of effects and affects. I can also draw from other encounters: For example, when I deliver talks on this topic, I often begin by asking my audience if they've ever heard this term. Hands very rarely go up, and while this may have something to do with a risk of exposure, shyness, or disinterest, the regularity with which I face blank stares upon asking this question is notable. In conversation people generally require an explanation if I mention my research on paraphilias. And in my own personal interactions with popular culture, the only time I recall hearing the term is in an episode of *Law and Order: Special Victims Unit.* These encounters lead me to surmise that this is a term that simply doesn't carry meaning for the vast majority of people and is used only in certain circles, like law and medicine. Furthermore, and more important for the purpose of this study, what these

1898–1972	"Sexual perversion"
1972–2007	"Sexual deviation"
2007–	"Paraphilias"

Figure 3. Library of Congress subject headings, by period of authorization.

experiences demonstrate is the contrast between the language of people on the street, of humanities and social science scholars, and of psychiatric professionals and scholars. The consequences of the authorization and use of "paraphilias" are many, including the erasure of a whole range of materials, the misrepresentation of historical conceptions of perversion, and the silencing of voices outside of the medical sciences. Placing the term "paraphilias" at the heart of this chapter illustrates how a single Library of Congress Subject Heading serves to discipline sex and sexualities through the act of naming.

This chapter sets out to perform a history of the present practice of categorizing books on perversion with the heading "Paraphilias" and to seek an understanding of how this medicalized term has taken hold in the library catalog. The Library of Congress is in dialogue with and reinforces psychiatric norms in a conversation that silences would-be interlocutors, particularly from the humanities and the street. But perhaps more significantly, the history of these terms in knowledge organization practice provides a glimpse of how the Library of Congress participated in the development and refinement of categories alongside other federal bureaucracies that were trying to gain a conceptual mastery over perversion in order to define both desirable characteristics for citizenship and the deviations by which to exclude people from membership.

Subject Heading Practices and Procedures

The Library of Congress Subject Heading (LCSH) authorities database contains a half-million subject authority records, which designate the terms that can be used to catalog works by subject and how these terms are structured in library catalogs. LCSH is a syndetic system, meaning that it connects related terms, synonyms, or variants by using cross-references in a database within the catalog. Online library catalogs often provide links to "Use" or "See" references, so that patrons are directed to the authorized terms for their searches, charting the correct course that will lead readers to their books. For those who search a catalog by subject using a nonpreferred term—"Sexual perversion in literature," for instance—the authority mechanism will redirect the seeker to the correct term—in this case it will say "See: Paraphilias in literature." Not only is LCSH a controlled vocabulary, but the terms are authorized by a governing body that determines which terms are valid and the processes by which they become authority headings; in this case it is a committee composed of cataloging staff at the Library of Congress. The potential for reach of the vocabulary has been expanded with the recent creation of the Library of Congress Linked Data Service, which "enables both humans and machines to programmatically access authority data at the Library of Congress."[5] LCSH and other vocabularies are part of the public domain and terms are accessible through uniform resource indicators (URIs).

> Sexual perversion in literature
> **Titles:** 0
> **Type:** Library of Congress subject headings
> See: **Paraphilias in literature**

The database also helps people find terms that are related to the topic of interest. They may be broader or narrower terms in a hierarchy, as with "Baby bonnets," which is a member of "Hats," or they might be topically associated, as "Baby bonnets" is related to "Infants' clothing." Figure 4 provides a map of the social network of terms most closely related to "Paraphilias." Most are narrower terms: "Sadism," "Masochism," "Voyeurism," "Lust murder," "Bestiality," "Fetishism," "Exhibitionism," and "Pedophilia." One term is provided in the authority record as a "See also" term (meaning that related items might be found with another heading): "Psychosexual disorders."[6] The illustration also shows all of the narrower and related terms for that level, connecting terms that are considered related. One could easily carry this exercise on, extending related terms nearly endlessly, playing a game of "six degrees of paraphilias."

One is likely to be struck by the presences, absences, and relationships produced by the network of authority records. Why, connected to "Fetish," are there only the types "Foot," "Boot," "Sock," and "Shoe"? Have books only been written on these fetishes, and why does it get so specific with regard to the extensions of the foot? The category "Psychosexual disorders" is a bizarrely exclusive collection of terms—that "Transvestism" is in this grouping is troubling, especially when displayed in relation to the other terms in this family of "disorders." "Paraphilias" is two degrees from both "Sex crimes" and "Murder" via "Lust murder." If we extend a map of "Sex crimes," we see that the "Paraphilias" are not far removed from all sorts of criminal acts, and we see some disturbing notions of what counts as a sex crime (Figure 5).[7]

Aside from the medical and criminal associations, there is the concern about the terminology chosen for the concept. One of the Library of Congress's principles states that it will create a new heading when it appears

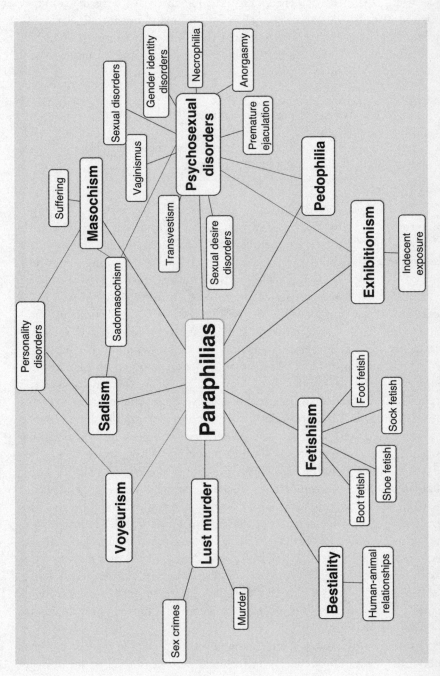

Figure 4. Terms related to "Paraphilias."

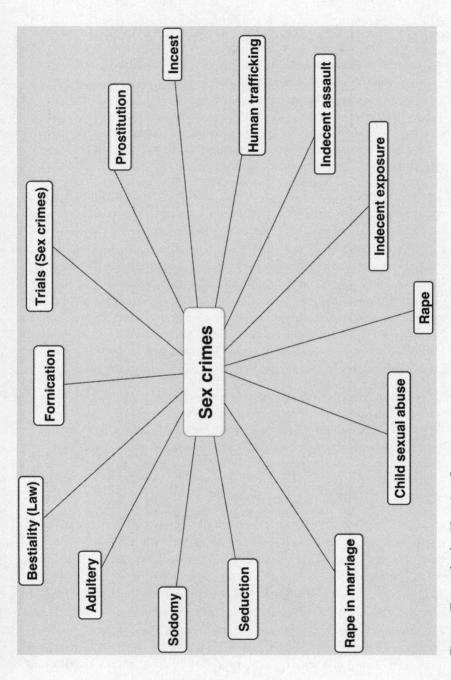

Figure 5. Terms related to "Sex crimes."

in the literature, but it also has a policy to authorize terms in general use, rather than jargon.[8] The American Library Association and the Library of Congress endorsed a statement issued in 1975 stating:

> The authentic name of ethnic, national, religious, social, or sexual groups should be established if such a name is determinable. If a group does not have an authentic name, the name preferred by the group should be established. The determination of the authentic or preferred name should be based upon the literature of the people themselves (not upon outside sources or experts), upon organizational self-identification, and/or upon group member experts.[9]

Although "paraphilias" does not name a group or an identity category, it could be argued that the term refers to people and their sexual practices; it is a diagnostic category, and it would seem that such a diagnosis may carry the assumption that a person has a disorder or is disordered. The medicalization of a set of behaviors should not so readily be taken as given, however, and I would suggest that those who engage in, carry an identification with, or are curious about any of the practices that fall within this category should be considered in decisions regarding what they are called. In using medical jargon, the Library of Congress effectively marginalizes not only a set of practices but also those who engage in any of the acts or seek information about them. As Sedgwick so elegantly states:

> To alienate conclusively, *definitionally*, from anyone on any theoretical ground the authority to describe and name their own sexual desire is a terribly consequential seizure. In [the twentieth] century, in which sexuality has been made expressive of the essence of both identity and knowledge, it may represent the most intimate violence possible. It is also an act replete with the most disempowering mundane institutional effects and potentials.[10]

In 2016, over 650 books in the Library of Congress collection are cataloged with the subject heading "Paraphilias" or with a heading that contains this word, such as "Paraphilias in literature." Approximately 560 are unique titles, and 360 of those are originally written in or translated into English.[11] Searching WorldCat for the 360 unique titles written in English revealed that the total number of U.S. library holdings for these books approaches 50,000, with the majority of libraries being general academic libraries, followed by public libraries. Medical and law libraries comprise a relatively small minority of holding libraries.[12] It is likely that those libraries have cataloged the books in the same terms both because Library of Congress Subject Headings are the primary mode of subject access for nearly all library catalogs in the United States and across the globe and because copy cataloging ensures a degree of uniformity across catalogs.

Researchers, practitioners, and the public have long disagreed on what counts as sexual perversion or a paraphilia, and the definitions of perversion have changed over time. Even the psychiatric community has not been able to agree on the definition and diagnosis of paraphilias. Charles Moser states that the "creation of the diagnostic category of paraphilia, the medicalization of nonstandard sexual behaviors, is a pseudoscientific attempt to regulate sexuality."[13] Further, he argues, "The equating of unusual sexual interests with psychiatric diagnoses has been used to justify the oppression of sexual minorities and to serve political agendas. A review of this area is not only a scientific issue, but also a human rights issue."[14] Laws and O'Donohue have described the controversy surrounding sexual deviance, suggesting that the *Diagnostic and Statistical Manual of Mental Disorders* (*DSM*) presents an "institutional rather than a scientific resolution to the definitional problem," which is value laden, created and negotiated by committees, and subject to personal and political influences.[15]

Similarly, Élisabeth Roudinesco argues that the adoption of "paraphilias" is of critical significance for the psychiatric and psychoanalytic community and a symptom of a wider shift in the field. In her view, "psychiatry claims to be abolishing the very idea that perversion might exist by refusing to pronounce its name," a move that she believes will have deadly consequences.[16] According to Roudinesco, the erasure of perversion occurred when the *DSM* abandoned the psychoanalytic approach to psychology and replaced it with behavioral criteria that made little to no reference to subjectivity. The *DSM* did away with human difference and rendered subjects as objects to be classified and diagnosed on the basis of disciplinary ideology. The designation of "paraphilia" means that anyone can be under suspicion, and even fantasies become subject to diagnostics. By denuding perversion of any substance, the psychiatric evaluation becomes one of screening and classifying for disease and disorder rather than one of treating the psychic, desiring life of subjects. It must be pointed out that the subject headings "Paraphilias" and "Paraphilias in literature" have both been assigned to Roudinesco's book *Our Dark Side: A History of Perversion* (2009), in spite of her clear preference for the term "perversion" and her argument against the use of "paraphilias."

Despite such controversies, the Library of Congress has chosen psychiatric literature for the sources upon which to base its subject heading. The LC authority record cites several titles that provide literary warrant for the new heading, "Paraphilias," including *Medical Subject Headings* (*MeSH*), the *Thesaurus of Psychological Index Terms*, athealth.com, and *Human Sexuality: An Encyclopedia* (1994), which is quoted in the authority record for justification of the term:

> Paraphilia is defined as an erotosexual and psychological condition characterized by recurrent responsiveness to an obsessive dependence on an unusual or socially unacceptable stimulus. The term has become a legal synonym for perversion or deviant sexual behavior, and it is preferred by many over the other terms because it seems more *neutral and descriptive* rather than judgemental.[17]

The term "Paraphilias" is arguably even more troubling (or at least differently troubling) than the headings that preceded it—"Sexual deviation" and "Sexual perversion." Although the earlier headings were clearly drawn from the medical literature, the words themselves had further reach and would have been intelligible to a broad population, even if offensive or harmful to some. The texts written by "laypeople" during the early twentieth century engaged with the public and researchers by using the term "perversion" to disavow it, to advance cases against the inclusion of inverts, homosexuals, and transvestites in the category of "sexual perverts." In sharp contrast, "Paraphilias" is not only problematic because of its medical origins but because it obscures meaning, rendering the nonnormative sexualities invisible, carrying disciplinary force, and potentially prohibiting access to materials cataloged with this heading.

The very existence of "paraphilias" as the sole term for access to this concept in the library catalog relies on the assumption that nonnormative sexualities, in their various manifestations, are medical problems. It presupposes the notion that sexual variance is a medical condition to be explained, classified, and, when necessary, treated. Furthermore, what is considered a perversion or a paraphilia is subjective and differs from person to person, culture to culture, and over time. The assignment of the term to materials from the humanities, social sciences, and popular literature—to works that do not use the term and for audiences for whom this term does not resonate—is a blatant disregard of the language used by a range of authors and readers through the imposition of medical jargon, the use of which the Library of Congress has expressly indicated it avoids.

Moreover, if we consider the Library of Congress classifications to be tools for writing a national history, the terms authorized from 1898 through the present—"sexual perversion," "sexual deviation," and "paraphilias"— have all helped construct and preserve ideals about a national citizenry by marking and pathologizing abnormal sexuality and opposing it to assumed norms. While the earlier headings created a binary distinction, "Paraphilias" nearly writes perversion out of public history and knowledge production by making it virtually invisible to all but psychiatric professionals.

Perversion—Deviation—Paraphilias

An account of "paraphilias" in the catalog would be incomplete without tracing the dialectical exchanges that contributed to the word and its meaning within the psychiatric community that uses it. Indeed, arguments dating back to the late nineteenth century continue to be at the root of some of the central questions regarding the identification, diagnosis, and treatment of paraphilias, even in the 2013 edition of the *Diagnostic and Statistical Manual of Mental Disorders*. We begin this investigation by looking to the ways in which "sexual perversion" was used by the sexological community and imported into the catalog. We find that the taxonomies in sexuality studies and libraries are, in fact, coextensive even as they shift over time, and they serve to reinforce dominant norms and ideas about sexuality.

Richard von Krafft-Ebing is widely regarded as the sexologist who in the late nineteenth century set the course for modern sexuality studies in Europe and the United States. As Henry Oosterhuis has observed, Krafft-Ebing was one of the first to synthesize medical knowledge about sexual perversion "by naming and classifying virtually all nonprocreative forms of sexuality."[18] His *Psychopathia Sexualis*, which was solely intended to be a reference text for lawyers and doctors, underwent twelve revisions between 1886 and 1903, with the first translation into English published in 1892. Krafft-Ebing was an assistant physician at an asylum and became one of the first expert witnesses for the Austrian and German courts. He collected case histories from his practice and court cases, which then went into his books. The first edition of *Psychopathia Sexualis* was a detailed, graphic account of forty-five case studies based on the lives and confessions of his patients. The preface to the first edition reads, "A scientific title has been chosen, and technical terms are used throughout the book in order to exclude the lay reader. For the same reason certain portions are written in Latin."[19] Despite efforts to keep the text out of the hands of laypeople, the publication was widely circulated beyond his intended audience and generated a huge response and correspondence. Krafft-Ebing used this material for subsequent editions, with the 1903 edition including 203 cases.

In providing physicians with a textbook and bringing rationalism to the legal treatment of sexual perversions, Krafft-Ebing gave impetus to the degeneration theory of sexual perversion, broadly defining it as any nonprocreative sex, or otherwise put "pleasure without utility."[20] He considered sex acts without procreative goals to be the result of a psychological and moral disorder and that they indicated overall degeneracy, and he believed that such defects were embedded in the body. Such ideas relied on a master discourse of evolution and classed populations, which ranked individuals from primitive to civilized. People could progress, become arrested and fail to reach maturity, or degenerate and slide to more primitive conditions. Heredity was a key to development, and class, race, nation, ethnicity, and religion were evaluated using measures of mental abilities, bodily configurations, and cultural productions.[21]

A key mechanism for assessing sexual deviance was the identification, classification, and cataloging of all deviant sex behaviors and physical characteristics that might indicate inversion or degeneration.[22] Krafft-Ebing's classification shifted and expanded over the editions but maintained the evolutionary framework, reiterating hierarchies of racial progress. For instance, in "primitive races," perverse behavior might be characteristic of the arrested development of the entire group, but among "advanced races" it was considered to be pathological degeneration or individual arrested development. By discovering inversion and homosexuality in "primitive" societies, doctors and anthropologists argued that these were signs of evolutionary regression in "civilized" societies. As Lisa Duggan has noted, "The result was a hazy, unstable distinction in the text's analytical framework between vice or immoral perversity, most characteristic of those lowest on the vector of development, and the condition of perversion, which might be found without hint of vice at the higher end of the vector."[23] Women were also separately placed on the evolutionary hierarchy; even the most "civilized" women were less evolved than the men of their nation, race, and class. Sexologists struggled to figure out how to explain inversion in women and often contradicted themselves. Were they advanced because they were mannish; were they freaks; were they degenerate? According to Duggan, they eventually created expansive taxonomies that were flexible enough to deal with such contradictions.

Critically, for Foucault, the notion of perversity was entirely a game of medical and judicial qualification and came to "authorize the appearance of a range of manifestly obsolete, laughable, and puerile terms or elements in the discourse of experts who are justified as scientists."[24] Foucault likens the textbooks of the late nineteenth century to children's books, with their overly simplistic, disciplining terminologies that act as terms of translation across the medical and judicial fields, and he suggests that perversion provided the ideal "switch point" upon which to regulate deviance. Foucault understood the criminalizing response to the pervert as a response to danger and asserts that "danger and perversion constitute . . . the essential theoretical core of expert medico-legal opinion."[25]

For most sexologists in the late nineteenth century, a small number of homosexuals were considered congenital inverts, and the rest became inverts or engaged in inverted behaviors as a result of a compound of nature and nurture. Krafft-Ebing described this and other perversions in terms of a difference between *perversion* and *perversity*:

> *Perversion* of the sexual instinct, as will be seen farther on, is not to be confounded with *perversity* in the sexual act; since the latter may be induced by conditions other than psycho-pathological. The concrete perverse act, monstrous as it may be, is clinically not decisive.

Perversion, for Krafft-Ebing, was a disease that could only be understood through an examination of the whole person, whereas a whole range of external factors might lead a normal person to perform a perverse act. The distinction between perversity and perversion continues to play out in present-day discussions and debates about the identification and diagnosis of paraphilias and, more broadly, about whether paraphilias are, in fact, disorders.

For the moment it is important to situate the creation of "Sexual perversion" as a subject heading at the Library of Congress in this late nineteenth-century sexological context. The Library of Congress Classification, which is the topic of the third chapter, actually cites the *Psychopathia Sexualis* in its HQ71 class as an example of books about "Abnormal sex relations." There is no question that it was scientific sexological books that served as literary warrant for creating the heading "Sexual perversion" and determining how it would be applied in the catalog. This is especially significant when we acknowledge the fact that texts written by John Addington Symonds, Edward Carpenter, and others presented accounts of variant sexualities (primarily homosexuality and inversion) from the perspective of experience, repudiated pathologizing explanations, and actively rejected the label "perversion." Books that disavowed the term were assigned the heading "Sexual perversion" from 1898 onward, and I would argue that this must be read as a disciplinary action with silencing effects.

Perhaps surprisingly, none of Freud's works have been categorized as being about perversion in the Library of Congress catalog. Even his seminal *Three Essays on the Theory of Sexuality*, in which he elaborates an entire theory of perversion—one that has held as a prevailing frame for analysis—was not assigned the heading "Sexual perversion." His theories would become corrupted and adapted to various purposes, but their influence on sexological thought remains, particularly in psychoanalytic approaches to sexuality. Still, each edition held by the Library of Congress, including the German version published in 1910, is assigned only one barely descriptive subject heading: "Sex."[26]

Freud's contributions are essential to understanding the development of the current situation with paraphilias. Foremost among these is his theory on the universality of perversion among humankind, writing that "there is indeed something innate lying behind the perversions but that it is something innate in everyone, though as a disposition it may vary in its intensity and may be increased by the influence of actual life."[27] He believed all humans are *polymorphously perverse* in childhood, meaning that a child's sexuality consists of partial sexual instincts that originate in various erogenous zones of the body. Relatedly, Freud also asserted that all human beings are innately bisexual. As Juliet Mitchell explains, the term "bisexual" is used today to indicate the sexual attraction to both sexes, but for Freud in the late nineteenth century, bisexuality had to do with the fact that "whatever one's object choice, whether hetero, homo or ambi-sexual, somewhere one is, psychically, both sexes."[28] Any of these inclinations can give rise to perverse or healthy behaviors in adulthood, and in his early theories, the distinction between normal and pathological depended upon whether the perverse desires were pursued to the exclusion of procreative sexual intercourse.

Although Freud's work was not about sexual perversion in the eyes of Library of Congress catalogers, some of his followers' publications were assigned the heading "Sexual perversion." Among those authors was the inventor of "paraphilias," Wilhelm Stekel, who coined the term in *Störungen des Trieb- und Affektlebens*, the second volume of which was translated into English in 1922 and entitled *Bi-Sexual Love: The Homosexual Neurosis*—the very text that set me off on this investigation![29] The German *paraphilie* also appears in Stekel's *Die Geschlechtskälte der Frau: Eine Psychopathologie des Weiblichen Liebeslebens* and *Die Impotenz des Mannes: Die Psychischen Störungen der Männlichen Sexualfunktion*, both published in 1920. The Library of Congress assigns "Paraphilias" to Stekel's later volume, *Sexual Aberrations: The Phenomena of Fetishism in Relation to Sex*, first published in German in 1923 and translated into English in 1930. That book sets out to explain the psychopathology of fetishism by focusing on sadism and masochism. In it Stekel defines the following terms: "parapathia stands for neurosis; paralogia for psychosis; and paraphilia for perversion."[30] Like other texts of this era on sexual perversion, the sale and distribution of this book was restricted to medical professionals, psychoanalysts, and scholars.

The definitions of fetishism and paraphilias as provided by Stekel demonstrate the centrality of maleness and heterosexuality to definitions of normal sexuality. He wrote of the perverse human as if he can only be male (with a few rare exceptions), and he described homosexual fetishism as "a condition that can be totally explained as a retreat from the female, flight from woman."[31] As with Freud, who believed that perverse inclinations are universal, Stekel asserted that paraphilias are universal, and he distinguished pathological ones as those that take the place of heterosexual, genital intercourse: "We cannot sufficiently emphasize the fact that all these forms of paraphilia are a part of the make-up of all normal humans."[32] For Stekel, a "true fetish lover dispenses with a sexual partner and gratifies himself with a symbol," whereas "normal fetishism aids the man in the conquest of the woman and even promotes his libido."[33] He regretted the lack of studies on perversion and attributed this to "Freud's opinion that paraphilia is something complete; that it is not reducible or analyzable to any further component elements."[34] He believed that Freud's theory on perversion was too simplistic, and contra Freud, he asserted that the paraphilia (perversion) can often be viewed as a positive of the parapathia (neurosis). Importantly, in a personal letter, Freud expressed regret about having initiated Stekel to psychoanalysis, and their relationship deteriorated over time.[35]

Stekel further broke from Freud and the more progressive sexologists, including Magnus Hirschfeld and Havelock Ellis, in his radical assertion that homosexuals were diseased, incapable of real love, and required treatment. He believed that homosexuality in men resulted from pathological families with strong mothers and weak fathers and that homosexual men's dread of women is rooted in a form of sadism. Stekel accused Hirschfeld, who firmly believed homosexuals ought not to be treated as criminals or psychiatric patients in need of curing, of creating homosexual propaganda, and he claimed he could cure the willing patient of homosexuality with two to three months of treatment.[36] Jennifer Terry has suggested that this kind of rhetoric supported the U.S. "War on the Sex Criminal" launched in 1937. J. Edgar Hoover later stated in 1947 that the most rapidly increasing type of criminals was the degenerate sex offender.[37] Increasingly, as postwar homophobia spread, the fear of conspiracies and infiltration and uncontrolled sex perversion led to the passage of laws to police "perverse" acts and bodies at the federal and local levels.

Indeed, the Library of Congress Subject Headings reflect a change in discourses during and after World War II, with the addition of

"Homosexuality" to the lexicon of subject headings in 1946. Until then, homosexuality had been subsumed under the heading "Sexual perversion," along with a variety of uncataloged sexual practices. "Homosexuality" was first applied as a heading to an Italian book entitled *Homosexualismo em Medicina Legal*, by Antonio Bello da Motta, and was added to the printed list of headings in 1948.[38] When it first appeared in LCSH, it was cross-listed with "Sexual perversion" (a reference that would remain until 1972) and given a "see also" note to "Sodomy." The call numbers assigned to it were defined as "Social pathology" and "Medical jurisprudence." Further direction was supplied to patrons regarding the heading: "Works on the criminal manifestation of homosexuality are entered under the heading Sodomy."[39] It was around this time that the Library of Congress began to more formally codify subject cataloging, while its authority with the wider library community was beginning to grow.[40]

A few speculations regarding the motives and consequences of this addition seem conceivable. It may be the case that the increase in subject specialists at the Library of Congress around this time contributed to the added heading. It may also be that J. Edgar Hoover's "War on the Sex Criminal" had brought heightened attention to homosexuality, calling for more precision within the broad category of perversion. Or it may be viewed as part of the larger federal sexual policing project that wrote new knowledge about sexual perversion into policy, in effect "helping to produce the category of homosexuality through regulation."[41] Perhaps the heading served to bring visibility to the form of perversion perceived to be most dangerous at the time. It also seems reasonable to think that this categorization helped propel homosexuality into mainstream discourses about sex, granting it a status of recognition and providing access to literature while maintaining the dominant attitude toward homosexuality as one of disdain and the perception of homosexuality as pathological and deviant. In the final analysis, it seems likely that all of these conditions brought the heading into being and significance. We will see in the next chapter that the addition of "Homosexuality" as a subject heading coincides with addition of sex crimes in the HQ71 and HQ72 sections of the bibliographic classification—the classes designated for abnormal sex relations (and subsequently sexual deviation).

Six years after the publication of the printed list of LC subject headings that included "Homosexuality," the first edition of the *Diagnostic and Statistical Manual of Mental Disorders* of the American Psychiatric Association was published, with a brief section on "sexual deviations," categorized as a "sociopathic personality disturbance." The 1952 *DSM* advises: "Individuals to be placed in this category are ill primarily in terms of society and of conformity with the prevailing cultural milieu, and not only in terms of personal discomfort and relations with other individuals."[42] In this early edition, psychiatrists seem to have recognized deviations as having more to do with social norms than with biological conditions. This was a progressive stance, but according to De Block and Adriaens, the writers of the *DSM* would grow increasingly interested in pursuing a theory-neutral or an atheoretical nomenclature with subsequent editions.[43] Indeed, John Noyes demonstrates that the 1980 *DSM-III* indicated that cases concerning disturbances between individuals and society must be understood as social problems and should not be grounds for diagnosis. Rather, the *DSM-III* was to focus on "behavioral, psychological, or biological dysfunction."[44] Noyes is quick to point out that such distinctions break down once we recognize the political and cultural underpinnings of the *DSM*, including its reliance on and universalization of heteronormative ideals. The *DSM-IV* goes even farther in its distinction by drawing a line between "real" and "simulated" sadist and masochistic acts, failing to recognize the view established in psychoanalytic circles that understands masochism as aiming to unsettle precisely these boundaries. It would seem that the diagnosis is also an annihilation of the masochistic subject.

Although the term "sexual deviation" had long been the predominant and preferred term with the American Psychiatric Association (since 1952), the Library of Congress did not authorize it to replace "Sexual perversion" until 1972, by which point a growing body of literature supported the notion that sexual deviations are socially constructed. Although the Library of Congress trailed the American Psychiatric Association in its adoption of "deviation," it was ahead of the APA in its removal of "Homosexuality" from that category. When the authorized heading changed from "Sexual perversion" to "Sexual deviation" in 1972, the Library of Congress also cancelled the inclusion of "Homosexuality," placing it with the more general (or normal) sexual relations (see Figure 6). This preceded the removal of homosexuality as a sexual disorder in the *DSM* and in the *Medical Subject Headings* (*MeSH*) and resulted in part from the activism of gay and lesbian librarians. The Task Force on Gay Liberation of the American Library Association—the first gay and lesbian professional organization in the United States—was instrumental in changing the terms by which we access LGBTQ materials in libraries.[45]

Barbara Gittings, the coordinator of the Task Force on Gay Liberation from 1972 until 1988, was a prominent lesbian activist whose testimony before the American Psychiatric Association with Frank Kameny contributed

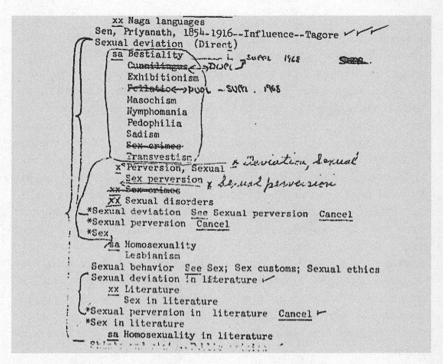

Figure 6. LCSH Weekly List, with handwritten changes to Sexual deviation and its cross-references, 1972. *Source*: American Library Association Papers, University of Illinois, Urbana/Champaign, 31/48/5.

to the removal of homosexuality from the *DSM*. Although not a practicing librarian herself, Gittings believed that access to information and reading materials was vitally important for gays and lesbians and the movement. The Task Force on Gay Liberation successfully organized a number of campaigns, including one to improve subject headings and classifications, an annual Gay Book award (now called the Stonewall Book Awards), and annual releases of bibliographies of gay-positive titles to assist in library selection. Sanford Berman and the Task Force on Gay Liberation were extremely effective in eliciting changes in Library of Congress subject headings and classifications for materials on homosexuality in the 1970s and 1980s. Petitions signed by librarians and scholars were submitted to the Library of Congress to demand new headings in place of or in addition to existing headings. Not only were pathologizing links to sexual perversion eliminated, but new terms were also added to the vocabulary to provide access to materials that had formerly been rendered invisible or perverted by inadequate cataloging. Indeed, that activist work toward making gay

and lesbian literatures available and visible in American libraries is arguably one of the more significant and effective long-term projects in pulling
LGBTQ materials out of the categories of perversion and deviation and
into the hands of readers.[46]

This movement among librarians was deeply tied into the larger push
to remove homosexuality as a disorder from the *DSM*. Robert Spitzer, the
APA psychiatrist who led the *DSM* revision project, was emphatic in his
belief that a diagnosis depended on the definition of "disorder," and he
determined that, in order to be considered a mental disorder, a condition
must cause "subjective distress or regularly be associated with some generalized impairment in social effectiveness or functioning."[47] According
to De Block and Adriaens, it was this definition of "social effectiveness or
functioning" that would distinguish homosexuality from the other sexual
deviations. They suggest that the retention of deviations other than homosexuality in the 1973 *DSM* was largely political, pointing out that even
Spitzer was not convinced that all sexual deviations were mental disorders
according to the distress and disability model.[48] However, the removal of
homosexuality fit within the gay liberation agenda, which may have been
compromised if other behaviors were accepted as normal. It was the political action of activists that motivated the removal of homosexuality, and
with a lack of an equivalent movement lobbying for the removal of other
deviations, the APA went to lengths to maintain the placement of the more
general category "sexual deviations" in subsequent editions of the *DSM*.

While psychiatrists debated the meanings and diagnoses of disorder
and deviation, library collections grew to reflect the expansion of sexuality studies to fields outside the medical and psychiatric disciplines, where
normative ideas of sexuality were becoming highly contested. Looking to
the broad spectrum of literatures assigned "Sexual perversion" and then
"Sexual deviation" in the 1970s, we witness a decline in the pathologization of sexual deviations as well as a decrease in the number of books on
homosexuality assigned to the category. But we also find that it is increasingly difficult to find common threads among the books, as those written
by psychiatrists were primarily concerned with sex offenders, a number of
books offer historical and literary accounts of sexual deviations, and others provided social analyses of sexuality. Corresponding to the diminished
pathologization of homosexuality was the advancement of other perspectives, particularly that of sociologists, who promoted Howard Becker's and
Erving Goffman's theories of deviance and increasingly distanced themselves from making ethical judgments. This served to legitimize a wider
range of perspectives on sexual variance by bringing more voices from

and to different areas of the academy and the public. Vern Bullough stated that historians had been silent until the 1970s, and he argued, "A major obstacle to understanding our own sexuality is realizing we are prisoners of past societal attitudes toward sex. . . . I have accepted the notion that no form of sexuality is against nature, and although I find some expressions of sexuality more distasteful than others, I have tried to avoid condemnation."[49] Some of the texts written at the beginning of this shift, like those by Bullough, published in the mid-1970s, discuss homosexuality at length as part of an argument to remove it from the stigmatized position of sexual deviation.

By this time, library activists had also gained visibility. Sanford Berman had built an extensive network of librarians who petitioned the Library of Congress to revise its biased headings, including those for gay and lesbian topics. Having already persuaded the Library of Congress to change "Sexual perversion" to "Sexual deviation," it was around this time, in 1975, that the American Library Association and the Library of Congress issued the statement that advocated creating headings in terms that groups or communities prefer for themselves. At least in part as a result of Berman's massive petitioning efforts, which included headings for a huge range of marginalized and excluded subjects, the Library of Congress formed the Subject Authority Cooperative Organization (SACO) in the 1990s, allowing librarians to propose new headings if they can demonstrate that the terms do appear as main topics in published literature. Participating librarians submit formal proposals for new headings and classes, which then go to a Library of Congress committee for approval. SACO currently includes over eight hundred institutional members and has contributed thousands of new headings and classifications since its inception. As of 2015, over 63,000 new headings, 14,800 heading changes, and 26,600 new class numbers have been authorized through the SACO program.[50] Today the vocabulary includes hundreds of terms for subjects that (had they been written about) would have formerly been subsumed under the broad heading "Sexual perversion." For instance:

Lesbian nuns
Lesbian mothers
Lesbian motorcyclists
Lesbian rabbis
Lesbian students
Lesbian libraries
Lesbians, Italian American

Lesbians on postage stamps
Lesbian photographers
Lesbian physical education teachers
Lesbian police officers . . .

. . . You get the idea. Since around 1990 we have witnessed a huge increase of headings for gay, lesbian, bisexual, and transgender subjects. "Paraphilias" seems not to have been affected by these developments, however, nor have the relations among categories like sadism and masochism to paraphilias been challenged. Even as libraries have become havens for some LGBTQ subjects and patrons, certain topics remain to this day under the broad pathologizing (and potentially obliterating) category of "paraphilias."

Authorizing "Paraphilias"

The American Psychiatric Association, in keeping with its scientific, theory-neutral approach, introduced the term "paraphilias" in the 1980 *DSM-III* to replace "sexual deviations," arguing that "it correctly emphasizes that the deviation (para) is in that to which the individual is attracted (philia)." Such a description focuses on the sexual object rather than the sexual aim, indicating the position of the APA, which also defines "paraphilias" on the basis "that unusual or bizarre imagery or acts are necessary for sexual excitement," with "sexual objects or situations that are not part of normative arousal-activity patterns and that in varying degrees may interfere with the capacity for reciprocal affectionate sexual activity."[51]

John Money was a key figure in the revival of the term "paraphilias," bringing it into common practice among psychiatrists.[52] Money promoted the use of the word on the basis that it best represents the biomedical nature of sexual abnormality. Comparing it to other terms and their uses, he wrote, "Kinky and bizarre are the popular words for paraphilic sexual fantasies and practices. Legally, they are called perverted and deviant."[53] Motivated by his belief that paraphilias—particularly those sexual activities that cause harm to others—can be understood and treated through science, as well as by his interest in the "sexual rights" of humans, Money wrote a popular text to support the identification and treatment of paraphilias. Following the course of previous influential sexologists, Money created an elaborate classification, assigning forty paraphilias to one of six categories: "sacrificial/expiatory; marauding/predatory; mercantile/venal; fetishistic/talismanic; stigmatic/eligibilic; and solicitational/allurative."[54] Particularly in the 1980s, Money published widely on the topic of paraphilias in professional journals, popular literature, and reference texts. The term took hold among psychiatrists but has yet to become part of the vernacular of the general public.

Again, as Freud had similarly asserted, the APA recognized that paraphilias could play a part in a healthy relationship, and so what distinguished a disordered behavior from an acceptable one "was its exclusivity and/or repetitivity in arousing sexual excitement." Indeed, the "DSM-III seemed to follow Freud's characterization of the paraphilias here, thereby ignoring its very own definition of mental disorder, which it *did* use to legitimize the removal of homosexuality."[55] The diagnosis had to do with the belief that the paraphilias impair people's ability to have normal, loving, reciprocal relationships with others, whether or not the individuals regard themselves as ill or distressed. This almost disarmingly recalls Stekel's view that homosexuals and other perverse individuals were incapable of love. What's more, John Noyes observes that the *DSM-III*'s definition of sexual masochism is inherently heteronormative, as it describes dysfunction in biological terms or in a refusal to seek pleasure in the reproductive act itself.[56] The APA repeatedly revisited certain distinctions, puzzling over questions concerning the boundaries between criminality and illness, with some of these determinations falling along lines of perversion and perversity, fantasy and acting on fantasy, and cultural situations.[57]

Although the Library of Congress did not directly cite the *DSM* as a source for literary warrant when it authorized "Paraphilias" in 2007, it did use other encyclopedic texts in psychiatry. It would have been from the fourth edition of the *DSM* that these other sources (and by extension, the Library of Congress) would have drawn their definitions. It is worth quoting the *DSM* here for its definition of the term:

> The Paraphilias are characterized by recurrent, intense sexual urges, fantasies, or behaviors that involve unusual objects, activities, or situations and cause clinically significant distress or impairment in social, occupational, or other important areas of functioning. The Paraphilias include Exhibitionism, Fetishism, Frotteurism, Pedophilia, Sexual Masochism, Sexual Sadism, Transvestic Fetishism, Voyeurism, and Paraphilia Not Otherwise Specified.[58]

According to a lead cataloger at the Library of Congress, the 2007 heading change was intended to "reflect contemporary medical and psychological thinking and usage."[59] In light of the psychiatric community's ongoing disagreement on the meanings of "deviation" and "paraphilias," however, the LoC's simultaneous deference to the psychiatric literature and claim to authority over knowledge is particularly fraught.

A reading of all of the works held by the Library of Congress and assigned this heading from 2007 to the present reveals that, although it may reflect current *psychiatric* usage, it does not at all represent usage in the majority of texts whose catalog records bear this name.[60] By deferring to the psychiatric literature as the authority and by medicalizing nonnormative sexualities, it seems that the Library of Congress has effectively made it much harder to find information on this topic, committing the act of "bibliocide"—a term Sanford Berman assigned to practices that annihilate material through poor cataloging. While librarians and the authority record state that this term is preferred because it is neutral, the truth is that the term is anything but, as it is a term authorized by the *DSM*, which pathologizes certain sexual behaviors. Indeed, Dean Spade calls for an examination of "systems that administer life chances through purportedly 'neutral' criteria, understanding that those systems are often locations where racist, sexist, homophobic, ableist, xenophobic, and transphobic outcomes are produced."[61] One might speculate that the neutrality here derives from the fact that people aren't familiar with this term and therefore it is rendered meaningless. If this is true, then it is a clear case of censorship by cataloging, which, according to Berman, is pervasive in libraries. He suggests that sex is one of the most highly censored subjects, "particularly if it's in the form or photos or film or deals with beyond-the-pale topics like anal intercourse or S&M."[62] Among these techniques is the "inadequate, if not outright erroneous cataloging, as well as restrictive shelving practices, rendering much material inaccessible even though it is in the collection."[63] Relatedly, the National Coalition for Sexual Freedom stated in a white paper, "we must conclude that the interpretation of the Paraphilias criteria has been politically—not scientifically—based."[64] The striking lack of materials on these subjects on mainstream library shelves observed by Berman may be both reflective and productive of this silence.[65] It is true that relatively few contemporary library books touch on these subjects with a nonclinical or popular approach, despite suggestions that such materials should be collected and made accessible in public libraries for those who are curious or need to know safe practices, without confronting shaming techniques.[66]

The fifth and most recent edition of the *DSM* (2013) again revised its stance, this time by distinguishing between "paraphilias" and "paraphilic disorders." Now a person can act on or fantasize about nonnormative objects without being disordered. Additionally, the paraphilias have been moved out of the section on "Sexual and Gender Identity Disorders" to their own section. To be considered a disorder, the paraphilia must be one "that causes distress or impairment to the individual or harm to others."[67] The current method of diagnosis is complicated: There is, first, the identification of a paraphilic activity or object choice, and, second, there is the determination of whether there is harm to the individual or others. These two criteria vary in language depending upon the paraphilia in question, but the example of sexual sadism disorder illustrates the logic and course of diagnosis:

A. Over a period of at least 6 months, recurrent and intense sexual arousal from the physical or psychological suffering of another person, as manifested by fantasies, urges, or behaviors.
B. The individual has acted on these sexual urges with a nonconsenting person, or the sexual urges or fantasies cause clinically significant distress or impairment in social, occupational, or other important areas of functioning.

For a diagnosis to be administered, both criteria must be met. Therefore, the person can be a sexual sadist without being disordered if the activities and fantasies are not causing distress and are carried out with consenting adults.[68] Although the distinction between disordered and nondisordered (normal?) paraphilias is widely regarded as progress, many view the existence of the diagnosis at all to be a problem, particularly for its reliance on repronormative and heteronormative frames. In agreement with Noyes's assessment of previous editions of the *DSM*, Lisa Downing maintains that the fifth edition continues to privilege heterosexuality and reproductive sex: "The logic subtending the pathologization of 'paraphilic disorders' remains consistent with that underlying the 'paraphilias' in earlier editions of the Manual."[69] Indeed, the current model still sorts normal and abnormal subjects, and arguably, a person's diagnosis may be based in institutional logics that produce and measure "disorder" and "harm."

Certainly, all of this should carry new meaning into library catalogs, which presently do not distinguish between nonpathological and pathological paraphilias. Over the ten years since the Library of Congress adopted the term, it has already taken on new meaning, rendering the heading differently inaccurate, even according to the psychiatric community. As we will see in the next chapter, the arrangement of paraphilias on the shelves is one that places texts on sex crimes and consensual kinky sex in the same space.

The normalizing effects of the medical professions are at work in the Library of Congress collection and catalog, as they seem to have great influence on subject authorization and knowledge organization. Although "paraphilias" is intelligible to psychiatrists and may be useful for them in finding materials, the term is rarely used by other disciplines. However, the works assigned this heading tend to be aimed at a multidisciplinary audience, and these books are held by a wide variety of libraries—not just medical libraries. It is particularly curious that the Library of Congress would choose a highly medicalized term for a subject that serves a general audience, including literary scholars, social scientists, and the general public, given that the United States has a National Library of Medicine that serves the psychiatric community and has its own controlled vocabulary.

The Perversely Presentist Catalog

Taxonomic discourses for sexual practices and identities are constantly changing, expanding, reappropriating, offending, and refusing to be pinned down, presenting a challenge for the Library of Congress, which strives to describe its literature in contemporary terms. The goal of fitting phenomena neatly into categories for information retrieval is in direct conflict with the elusive, expansive, and shifting nature of perversion—and, for that matter, all of sexuality. While granting that it would be impossible for a library catalog to get at the complexities and nuances of texts on sex and sexuality, I would argue that the reduction of literatures on nonnormative sexual expressions to "Paraphilias" is loaded with problems derived from disciplinary norms and assumptions. Moreover, the effects of assigning this name are to render some texts invisible to their potential readers and to render other texts perverse—even as they themselves reject such a label—not to mention that a majority of works are caught by the trappings of time. What we have is a motley mix of texts from different eras and perspectives all brought together under this heading.

Presentism is a persistent historiographical dilemma for anyone trying to explain the past by using current terminologies that did not exist or have significantly changed in meaning since the period under investigation. Historians of sexuality are keenly aware of the changing nature of taxonomies and the inherent struggles in understanding past sexual practices, identities, and concepts in the context of the present and conveying them in intelligible terms. The work of sexuality scholars depends on and contributes to the study of how categories have emerged, expanded, disappeared, and changed over time as well as how these categories have been explained and defined in terms of identities, behaviors, conditions, and difference.

"Perverse presentism," as proposed by J. Halberstam, is a methodology that attempts to account for and overcome the problems of presentism by denaturalizing the present as a point toward which all of history is moving and improving and applying "what we do not know in the present to what we cannot know about the past."[70] Using present-day terms and definitions to describe the past greatly oversimplifies and distorts the historical record. When speaking of subjects in sexuality studies, it may inaccurately or un- fairly render certain acts and identities as essentially perverse, carrying pathological connotations derived from psychiatry. However, an awareness of the limitations of language and the capacity to know the present and the past, as well as efforts to learn about the past in its own terms, expands the opportunities to interpret the historical record. Halberstam uses this methodology to study nineteenth- and early twentieth-century same-sex desire among women, taking care not to use "lesbian" as a blanket term to describe women who desired women during an era when "lesbian" did not exist. Halberstam argues that considering women who desired women as lesbians or protolesbians erases their histories and the specificities of such identities and activities as tribades, female husbands, and a whole range of expressions.

At stake in the case of "Paraphilias" is not only whether the term is useful or intelligible today but also the kind of descriptive power it car- ries with regard to older works. In both senses, the perversion of mean- ing carries implications for access to texts across space and time as well as the broader disciplinary effects on knowledge about sexuality. One could certainly argue that the catalog should retain certain associations of the era in which a text was produced. Situating older texts on homosexuality with texts on perversion would maintain a degree of historical integrity. But things get very interesting and mixed up when we see a variety of time periods intermingled in the catalog under a single term. The use of the term "paraphilias," which carries historically and culturally specific de- notations and connotations, erases the prevailing attitudes and beliefs of previous eras by imposing new definitions and terms on past meanings. We know that homosexuality was considered a perversion or deviation for most of the twentieth century, so it is unsurprising to find such terms used to describe works that promoted such points of view. But something is seriously altered and confused when an automatic replacement occurs in bibliographic records, applying the new term "paraphilias" for such varied works as *Sexual Feeling in Woman* (1930), *Venus Castina: Famous Female Im-*

personators, Celestial and Human (1928), *The Invert and His Social Adjustment* (1929), *Sex Variant Women in Literature* (1956), *The Case Against Pornography* (1972), and *The Erotic Minorities*.

Exceeding "Paraphilias"

The remainder of the chapter is devoted to highlighting a handful of cases for which the assignment of "Paraphilias" fails to apply. It might be thought of as a very abridged catalog of works that are underserved by this heading. Much is left unaccounted for, but the cases presented below stand out as some of the most remarkable.

ANOMALY

While most late nineteenth- and early twentieth-century sexologists were intent on diagnosing, classifying, and treating various behaviors and desires, there were some scientists, as well as humanists and "laypeople," who objected to the idea that inversion, homosexuality, and transvestism should be considered perversions.[71] These voices have been persistently ignored by library catalogers, and to this day, catalog records for their works carry a stigmatizing notion of perversion, but now in a vocabulary that would have been completely foreign to these authors. The voices that opposed the pathologizing explanations tended to identify as inverts or transvestites themselves and often wrote as advocates, as in the case of *The Invert, and His Social Adjustment*, written under the pseudonym Anomaly in 1929. Such texts tried to advance an understanding of their experience as human beings rather than as patients or case studies, and they served as a means of resistance to dominant authorized discourses. Anomaly was well aware of his position and justified his own merits in his second chapter, entitled "By What Authority":

> It is my wish to outline briefly some of the social factors of inversion which, naturally enough, are not dealt with by those whose interest lies in the symptoms of neurosis. My views will suffer discount because of the "the phenomenon known to psychologists as 'rationalization,' especially the so-called 'defence reaction'" . . . Critical readers will ask by what authority I presume to offer advice on a subject which has been dealt with, in many of its aspects at least, by men of eminence whose names carry the weight of scholastic approval. . . . I make no apology for concentrating on the personal note, for what value this book may

have will lie in the fact that its based on personal experience and first-hand knowledge.[72]

Texts like Anomaly's provide critical evidence of the human suffering that came at the hands of medical professionals, and they offered practical advice for others who might share similar experiences or may want to learn about those who do. That books written from the personal experiences of homosexuals and inverts rank among those most widely held in American libraries, as this one does, suggests that a significant number of libraries held books that represented the voices of those who would be diagnosed alongside the medical texts doing the diagnosing.[73] It does seem that the Library of Congress disregarded their language from the start by choosing sexological/medical terminologies for subject headings, even when inverts, homosexuals, and transvestites clearly didn't accept the label "sexual perversion." This means that, from the earliest headings, the Library of Congress engaged in the disciplining of nonnormative sexualities. What's more, the term "Paraphilias" was not in use when this text was written, so the application of the recently adopted, highly medicalized term grossly distorts the meaning and accessibility of the work.

LESBIANS

"Lesbians" was added as a Library of Congress Subject Heading in a 1974–1976 supplement, indicating that the LoC finally recognized lesbians as people. Prior to that the LoC only named a condition with the heading "Lesbianism," which was authorized in 1956. Before 1956, anything about lesbians would have been found by looking for the heading "Sexual perversion," or if it was published between 1946 and 1956, it might have been assigned "Homosexuality."

In contrast to the medical texts of her day, Katharine Bement Davis wrote about marital hygiene from a less clinical standpoint, arguing for rational sex education, women's sexual rights, and access to safe contraception. Davis belonged to a minority of scientists who "saw single women, including lesbians, as key sources of information for determining what made women happy."[74] Davis's study began in 1920 (the same year as ratification of the Nineteenth Amendment) in the wake of key historical developments and shifts, including women entering the paid workforce and obtaining college educations, lower birth rates, increasing divorce rates, and the promotion of women's rights.

Studies like Davis's initiated the sociological analysis of sexuality, considering individual traits and behaviors through empirical methods and statistical analysis to find variance. Such methods contrasted with clinical models that studied "abnormal" individuals based on assumptions about what constitutes "normal." Davis studied the "normal" woman because she felt that sex, other than in its pathologized forms, was an unexplored science, but she defined "normal" as a woman who was "capable of adjusting satisfactorily to her social group"; same-sex desire among these women was not uncommon.[75] Davis conceptualized lesbianism as a continuum of variations and believed it was much more common than previous sexologists thought. For example, among her findings were the following: Half of the unmarried women experienced intense emotional relations with other women, and over one-quarter said that a relationship was "carried to the point of overt homosexual expression."[76] Davis concluded that sexual satisfaction depended on knowledge and was an important factor in the well-being of normal women.

Given that the study intentionally sought out "normal" subjects to gain an understanding of healthy marriage, it is curious that the 1929 edition of the published account, *Factors in the Sex Life of Twenty-Two Hundred Women*, was assigned the heading "Sexual perversion" and today retains the updated form "Paraphilias" in the Library of Congress catalog. The other headings, "Women—Health and hygiene" and "Marriage," in their overgeneralizations are only marginally descriptive of the contents of this text.[77] Interestingly, the more general "Sex" was not applied. The author herself did not consider these women's actions to be generally perverse, but clearly a cataloger did, and this attitude continues to be reproduced and modernized by cataloging technologies.

Thirty years later, Jeanette Howard Foster published *Sex Variant Women in Literature*, the catalog record for which is displayed in Figure 7. The pathbreaking guide to lesbian references in literature (written by a Kinsey Institute librarian) was originally assigned "Sexual perversion in literature" because it was published ahead of the authorization of the headings "Lesbians" or "Lesbianism" or "Lesbians in literature."[78] Those terms would also have been subsumed under the broad "Sexual perversion" at that time.

In fact, there are no words for lesbians or homosexuals anywhere in this record.[79] Later editions of the book are cataloged with more "appropriate" headings, including "Lesbians in literature." Even this might be a case of perverse presentism, though, according to Halberstam, as the Foster book discusses same-sex desire among women from its earliest appearance in literature to Foster's present. Additionally, Foster's use of "sex-variant" is ignored. In a similar vein, *Diana: A Strange Autobiography*, a memoir published under a pseudonym in 1939, is also currently assigned

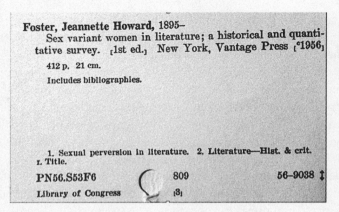

Figure 7. Catalog card for *Sex Variant Women in Literature*, obtained from University of Wisconsin–Madison Libraries.

"Paraphilias," as is Marion Zimmer Bradley's 1960 *Checklist: A Complete, Cumulative Checklist of Lesbian, Variant, and Homosexual Fiction, in English, or Available in English Translation, with Supplements of Related Material, for the Use of Collectors, Students, and Librarians*.[80]

SEXUAL DEVIATION / DEVIANCE

Leading up to the change from "Sexual perversion" to "Sexual deviation," attitudes about sexual deviations had shifted quite dramatically, particularly in the years after World War II, and the literature reflects this change. For instance, one of the more widely held books cataloged with "Paraphilias" in U.S. libraries, Frank S. Caprio and Louis S. London's *Sexual Deviations*, is almost entirely about homosexuality and intended for a general audience. Published in 1950, the authors followed the contemporary approach to studying sexual perversion (again, primarily homosexuality) as illness. As the book was written with the belief that marital troubles stem from misinformation and a need for laypeople to know the "sexual deviate" to prevent sexual perversion, the frontmatter reads, "The prevalent lack of understanding toward sexual problems—coupled with the growing public concern over sex crimes—make this book an invaluable guide to the layman." Although the Library of Congress acquired and cataloged the book after "Homosexuality" was approved as a subject heading, catalogers did not see fit to assign the term to this book. In fact, the bibliographic record does not include any reference to homosexuality, even as a keyword. It was simply given the heading "Sexual perversion," and the full suite of disciplinary apparatuses discussed in the present study was enacted on this text: It was shelved with books on perversion in HQ71, and at some point it was locked away in the postwar Delta Collection.

Alternatively, deriving from symbolic interactionism theory in sociology, the edited volume *Sexual Deviance*, published in 1967, states that deviance is determined by social practices. Gayle Rubin regards the book as a landmark in shifting the way we study sexuality.[81] Its editors, John Gagnon and William Simon, trained at the University of Chicago and hired by the Kinsey Institute, "virtually reinvented sex research as social science," reframing homosexuality as normal and ordinary and challenging heteronormative assumptions that led to the pathologization of homosexuality.[82] According to the editors, interactions of institutionalized norms that produce definitions of "normal" and "deviance" should be understood in terms of social structure, social situation, and the character of the actors:

> A form of behavior becomes deviant when it is defined as violating the norms of some collectivity. Usually, the collectivities that are relevant are those formally empowered to sanction deviant behavior in general, though for certain forms of sexual behavior only informal and covert sanctions are applied by selected collectivities. . . . Deviance exists in social systems as a necessary complement to conformity . . . to speak of one is to imply the other.[83]

Still, as with the 1950 example, what is key to our understanding of cataloging practices is the complete absence of terms in the catalog record referring to the actual topics covered in this text: homosexuality and prostitution. In this later case the authors interrogate the inclusion of these two categories within the broader category of sexual deviance by studying the role of norms within "deviant" communities. Nevertheless, the original bibliographic record was assigned only "Sexual perversion" as a heading, and there are no terms referring to homosexuality or prostitution that might turn the record up in a keyword search. Such an absence is striking, given that both concepts were well established in LCSH at the time this book was cataloged. It may be because of a lack of effort, or it could have been an instance of active bibliographic censorship. Perhaps the oversight could be explained as a case of inadequate expertise of the cataloger, who may have simply read the title, *Sexual Deviance*, and applied "Sexual perversion" as a heading (publication of the book preceded the subject heading's change to "Sexual deviation" by a few years). If the cataloger had turned to the introduction and table of contents, however, she would have seen that the book gives an overview of theories of sexual deviance and then applies these specifically to homosexuality and prostitution. She might have surmised that the authors were in fact distancing the work from the psychiatric profession and its terms.

One observes a related problem in the record for the Swedish psychiatrist Lars Ullerstam's *The Erotic Minorities*. When published in English in 1966, the book was assigned "Sexual perversion." In *The Erotic Minorities*, however, far from pathologizing behaviors, the author of the book advocates a greater appreciation for sexual deviance, condoning and at times celebrating acts that fall under the category of perversions: "Should we not rejoice," he writes, "that we have been provided with various potentialities for the experience of joy, and help each other to achieve it in our various ways, even if these should happen to be of a sexual nature?"[84] In fact, the author explicitly states that "perversion" is a "poison label," and he advocates for social policy that allows a wide range of sexually deviant behaviors. Writing in Sweden, the author found homosexuals to be in an enviable position, with clubs and leniency in law and society. He wanted to see similar accommodations for people with deviant desires and inclinations, such as bestiality, fetishisms of various sorts, paying for sex, and pornography.

Overwhelmingly, authors writing in the 1960s and 1970s used the term "perversion" only in a historical or critical sense. Extremely few works include the word "paraphilias," and that term occurred nowhere in the social sciences and humanities literatures. A number of the texts avoid using terms "deviation" or "perversion" altogether, or like James Henslin, they may redefine or clarify "deviance." He writes in his *Deviant Lifestyles*, "my use of the word deviant to modify lifestyle does not mean bad, sick, perverse, or even undesirable. . . . These terms simply mean nonnormative or departing from generalized expectations, often in such a way that negative sanctions are the typical result."[85] These texts ushered in studies of the social construction of gender and sexuality and preceded Foucault's *History of Sexuality*, which, incidentally, is given the single subject heading "Sex customs—History."

"Paraphilias in Literature"

One of the more blatantly spoken-over fields is literature and literary studies, with the heading "Paraphilias in literature." This is perhaps the most absurd of all the cases, as the heading medicalizes the literary study of sexual perversion and annuls the literary voice as well as temporal and spatial dimensions. Literary scholars simply don't include the term "Paraphilias" in their texts. Book titles include *The Sadomasochistic Homotext: Readings in Sade, Balzac, and Proust, Ovidian Myth and Sexual Deviance in Early Modern English Literature*, and Jonathan Dollimore's core text, *Sexual Dissidence: Augustine to Wilde, Freud to Foucault*. The very idea of condensing a work of literature into its "aboutness" or its critique into a few terms chosen from a vocabulary authorized by a national authority is laughable.

DRAG

The heading "Sexual perversion" had been associated with the narrower and related terms "Exhibitionism," "Homosexuality," "Lesbianism," "Masochism," "Nymphomania," "Sadism," "Sex crimes," and "Transvestism."[86] When "Sexual perversion" changed to "Sexual deviation" in LCSH in 1972, all cross-references, except for one to the related "Sexual disorders," were eliminated, but apart from "Homosexuality" and "Lesbians," most of these and other headings would slowly reappear as cross-references in subsequent editions. "Transvestism" was the first of the sexual behaviors or phenomena to reenter the hierarchy under "Sexual deviation" in 1980, along with "Sexual disorders." "Transvestism" was also associated with "Impersonators, Female," a heading whose 1988 scope note indicated: "Here are entered works on men impersonating women. Works on women impersonating men are entered under the heading Impersonators, Male. Works on impersonation of the opposite sex as a manifestation of sexual perversion are entered under the heading Transvestism."[87] "Transvestism" first appeared as a subject heading in 1948 (decades after the Library of Congress acquired Magnus Hirschfeld's 1910 *Die Transvestism*), and "Transvestites" was added in 1989.[88] Because the terms "transvestism" and "transvestite" have become identified with the language of psychopathology, many people who cross-dress have come to prefer terms other than "transvestism." Indeed, the Library of Congress still links "Transvestism" (but not "Transvestites") as a narrower term under "Psychosexual disorders."

Even in recent years the Library of Congress has continued to resist honoring requested changes to "Transvestites" and related headings.[89] Sanford Berman proposed the heading "Drag queens" on August 24, 2005, and other librarians followed suit, including staff at the Tretter Collection in GLBT Studies at the University of Minnesota. In a 2006 letter to Berman, Barbara Tillett expressed that "Drag queens" was among the headings the Library of Congress was evaluating for approval.[90] Berman was pleasantly surprised that this was under consideration, noting that previously Tillett "unequivocally stated that 'The term "drag queens" is an upward see reference to "Transvestites," which we continue to feel is appropriate.'"[91] Berman seemed to find it curious that Tillett so quickly had a change of heart. Whether she truly did have a change of heart remains unknown; "Drag queens" was not authorized in 2006 and has not been adopted as of this writing.[92]

In the years since the Berman/Tillett correspondence, very little has changed. "Transvestites" is still the preferred term for cross-dressers, "Female impersonators" remains the preferred term for "Drag queens," and "Male impersonators" is used in place of "Drag kings." The Library of Congress now distinguishes between female/male impersonators and transvestism based on whether the act of dressing in the manner of the opposite sex is for entertainment or for psychological gratification. The scope note for "Female impersonators" reads: "Here are entered works on men who impersonate women, generally for purposes of entertainment or comic effect." "Transvestism" and "Transvestites" have identical scope notes: "Here are entered works on the practice, especially of males, of assuming the dress and manner of the opposite sex for psychological gratification."

Although "Transvestites" is no longer a narrower term under "Paraphilias," and "Female impersonators" never was, the 1934 edition of *Venus Castina* is currently assigned "Paraphilias" as the sole heading in the Library of Congress catalog. The inclusion of "Paraphilias" in that record reveals that the prevailing attitude toward the type of female impersonation written about in *Venus Castina* was that it was a perversion, but again, it comes through in anachronistic language. Perhaps ironically, the record for the earlier 1928 edition includes only the heading "Female impersonators." And so, while the refusal of the Library of Congress to adopt "drag" is troubling, in the case of *Venus Castina*, the term "Female impersonators" is arguably more suitable, as it is more appropriate for the time period. The term appeared in the book and in other literature of the period.

THE TWENTY-FIRST CENTURY—REINVENTING "PERVERSION"

Applications of "Paraphilias" after the heading was authorized in 2007 reveal another set of problems. The book description for the 2011 *Part-Time Perverts: Sex, Pop Culture, and Kink Management* explicitly states what the author sets out to do, which is to distance herself from the psychiatric community and talk about kink and alternative sexualities in nonpathologizing language.[93] The author even proposes a new way of classifying "perversion management":

An interdisciplinary exploration of sexual perversion in everyday life, *Part-Time Perverts: Sex, Pop Culture, and Kink Management* starts from the premise that, for better or worse, everyone is exposed to a continual barrage of representations of sexual perversion, both subliminal and overt. Our involvement, Dr. Lauren Rosewarne contends, is universal, but our management strategies cover a spectrum of behavioral possibilities from total repression to total immersion. It is those strategies that she examines here. Drawing on her own experience, as well as on pop culture and a multidisciplinary mix of theory, Rosewarne shifts the discussion of perversion away from the traditional psychological and psychiatric focus and instead explores it through a feminist lens as a social issue that affects everyone. Her book examines representations of perversion—from suppression to dabbling to full-body immersion— and proposes a classification for perversion management, and charts the diverse strategies we use to manage, and perhaps enjoy, exposure.[94]

Rosewarne's book is woefully undercataloged, with only the headings "Paraphilias" and "Sex customs." There is nothing about feminist critique or popular culture. Fortunately, the title provides key terms that are likely to be found by a patron conducting a keyword search.

Similarly, the subject headings for the book *The Other Side of Desire*, written by Daniel Bergner, are "Paraphilias—Case studies" and "Compulsive behavior—Case studies." Nothing in this record indicates what the book is truly about: It is a collection of case studies about foot fetishism, acrotomophilia (sexual interest in amputees), sadism, and a man's desire for his stepdaughter. Its pairing of "Compulsive behavior" with "Paraphilias" resembles the association of "Sexual perversion" and "Neuroses" in the record for the much earlier Stekel text.

Interestingly, this title is held by more public libraries than academic libraries, with the total number of holdings in the United States exceeding four hundred. Perhaps this signals a shift in public librarians' collection development policies and attitudes as well as a broader societal curiosity about perversion. In her review of the book, Lori Gottlieb tells readers that it altered her frame of mind, causing her to question her own beliefs about perversion.

After reading Daniel Bergner's unsettling but riveting new book, *The Other Side of Desire*, I'm no longer sure where normal ends and abnormal begins. Take the people Bergner, a contributing writer for *The New York Times Magazine*, introduces us to: a devoted husband with a foot fetish, a fashion maven who's a sadist, a man who becomes sexually attracted to his young stepdaughter (Woody Allen, anyone?) and an advertising executive who lusts after amputees.

Are all of them deviant? None of them? Or is deviance a matter of time and place, the way that a century ago, fellatio and cunnilingus were regarded as perversions in some psychoanalytic circles? I'll ruin the ending for you right now: these questions are unanswerable, but that's precisely what makes the asking so engrossing.[95]

This reviewer recognizes precisely the issues brought forth by my study, but unfortunately, libraries are not supplying this type of information to their patrons. Rather, the book is effectively hidden by undercataloging and by the use of a term by which few public library patrons are likely to search. If they do locate it by way of the catalog, they receive the patholo-gizing message carried by the headings. Other recently published titles that might be said to defend or explain "perversion" are Jesse Bering's *Perv: The Sexual Deviant in All of Us* (2013) and James Penney's *World of Perver-sion: Psychoanalysis and the Impossible Absolute of Desire* (2006). I have already mentioned Roudinesco's critique of "paraphilias" and the application of the term to her book *Our Dark Side: A History of Perversion*. Perhaps the question is, then, whether the Library of Congress should readopt "per-version" to describe and reflect these perversion-positive texts as well as all of the others—particularly in the humanities—that use this term. Or as I will suggest in Chapter 5, perhaps there is something to be said for the inscrutability of perversion within the normalizing hierarchies of the Library of Congress's classificatory systems.

CHAPTER 2

Labeling Obscenity: The Delta Collection

"Closetedness" itself is a performance initiated as such by the
speech act of a silence—not a particular silence, but a silence that
accrues particularity by fits and starts, in relation to the discourse
that surrounds and differentially constitutes it. The speech acts that
coming out, in turn, can comprise are as strangely specific. And they
may have nothing to do with the acquisition of new information.

—EVE KOSOFSKY SEDGWICK, *Epistemology of the Closet*

To tell of courage to face the unknown with
intelligence, tell of Theseus.

—PAUL KUNTZ, "What Daedalus Told Ariadne, or, How
to Escape the Labyrinth: The Minotaur"

In the history of libraries there have always been spaces and texts to which
access has been barred and certain patrons and patron types for whom access has been denied. Libraries will often have a restricted collection—a
locked case, a unit of shelving behind the circulation desk, or a special
room—that requires readers to obtain permission from a librarian to view
the books within. Very often the restricted materials contain explicit adult
content or valuable illustrations. During and after World War II the Library of Congress held one of the largest collections in the world of this
kind, composed mostly of erotica and items considered to be pornographic
or obscene. The Library's Delta Collection, which included books, motion
pictures, photographs, playing cards, and other materials, was separated
from the general collection, and access was highly restricted. Many of the
materials in the Delta Collection had been seized by the Customs Bureau
and the U.S. Postal Service, and the Library of Congress made the final decision regarding destruction, storage, and circulation of such items.
Others were obtained through the Copyright Office and were considered
vulnerable to theft and damage. The Delta Collection served to protect
materials from mutilation, preserve the cultural record, protect citizens

from harmful obscenity, and serve as a repository of sample materials for consultation by federal agencies up through 1964.

This collection undoubtedly carried a certain epistemology, and underlying this chapter is Sedgwick's theory of the closet, which serves as a guide in considering the ways in which the materials in the collection acquired a special status and how their silences tell a key story about the production and regulation of knowledge about sexuality. The Delta Collection was quite literally a closeted-off set of materials deemed to be perverse, and except for certain books that were considered to have intrinsic value as part of a cultural record and in need of protection, the Delta Collection served as a mechanism by which to classify works out of U.S. memory and identity. For Sedgwick, "the closet is the defining structure" for oppression based on sexuality, and she argues that it operates by way of a series of juridical formulations that were constructed to support and sustain a heteronormative culture.[1] In contrast to the subject headings featured in the previous chapter, and the bibliographic classification in the next, what the Delta Collection did for the writing of U.S. history was not only disciplinary, but it enacted a more extreme series of erasures and silences. Materials that contained ideas, images, and information about "aberrant" sexual practices, whether they were about homosexuality or contained otherwise "obscene" content, were not to be housed within the library's general collection. Many of these texts did not match the ideals of the project of constructing a national citizenry, and their sequestration was arguably aimed at the prohibition of citizens becoming perverse readers. The Delta Collection served the nation by functioning as a juridical device, as the materials held within were to be used as evidence for federal agencies and Congress. And reminiscent of the scarlet letter "A" affixed to Hester Prynne's breast, the sequestered materials in the Delta Collection were stamped with the delta symbol: Δ.[2]

The panic surrounding World War II and postwar sexual perversion held certain knowledges to be a central threat, and keeping obscene materials out of the hands of citizens was a frenzied and impossible effort at preventing the spread of perversion by censoring it and circulating silence and ignorance. At this point, definitions and understanding of what constituted obscenity had not been officially determined in law and policy, so methods for policing it were inconsistent and heavy handed.[3] In the 1940s and 1950s U.S. librarians found themselves at the center of heated discussions about censorship and the freedom to read. As a federal agency, the Library of Congress occupied a very particular position in that debate. The Delta Collection is far from cohesive, and it reflects the confusion surrounding definitions of obscenity and what to do with it. The unifying principles were that the materials were assumed either to pose or be subject to a threat of harm. It contained books on perversion and homosexuality but also works on heterosexual relations and birth control; literary works that were contested in the courts, such as *Ulysses* and *Lolita*; rare books; and some of the more ribald pornography of the time. What was contained in the collection was knowledge that was viewed to require a measure of special protection. As we will see later in this chapter, however, the Delta Collection was not as secure as was intended.

Finding the Delta Collection

The Library of Congress's participation in the postwar regulation of obscenity is an untold portion of the story of government policing of sexual deviance in the United States. Scholars have explored the roles of the Customs Bureau, the Postal Service, and the Federal Bureau of Investigation in intercepting, seizing, and storing materials deemed to be obscene.[4] They have not, however, examined the Library of Congress's role in this process. Paul and Schwartz's 1961 account of federal censorship does give the LoC's involvement a brief mention, praising it for saving materials from the agencies that would destroy them:

> Material that is seized is either destroyed or sent to the Library of Congress. The Library does not collect obscene or pornographic materials as such; it receives such materials because it is a repository for publications produced the world over. . . . Selection criteria are broad, for the Library is not worried about protecting the public; it is worried about retaining all materials—anything which may reflect some facet of the world's culture or may be useful for research.[5]

While this position is perhaps limited and uncritical, it would be equally shortsighted to argue that the LoC's actions described below simply constitute a sweeping act of censorship.

Indeed, it's quite complicated. As Alison Moore suggests in her analysis of similar collections at the Bibliothéque Nationale de France and the British Library, one might view such hidden collections of obscenity and erotica as ones "that sought to contain desire, to designate it and to command its parameters while sanctioning sexuality as an inherently validated system of meaning."[6] The next sections demonstrate some of the central tensions that obscenity brought to the Library of Congress and how the Delta Collection provides a window into the function of labeling as a mechanism in what seem to be ideologically opposed efforts to contain and preserve, censor, and serve the federal government. The LoC was one of many institutions that struggled to come to terms with the charge to protect resources, protect rights of individuals, and protect the public from the harm of an ever-increasing amount of sexually explicit materials. In addition, the LoC's employees were interested in protecting the library itself—as well as their own positions within it.

My own encounter with the Delta Collection began with the catalog—as it did with my study of "paraphilias." In fact, it was in searching for materials cataloged with that heading at the Library of Congress that I discovered a number of bibliographic records that contained, instead of call numbers, a note that read, "Problem location." Most of the titles designated by this location turned out to be in the Rare Books Reading Room, but a few searches ended up in dead ends, with librarians looking everywhere they could think of, only to return empty handed. For example, *Night in a Moorish Harem* was one that was missing. A few librarians had mentioned the Delta Collection in passing during my visit to the LoC, simply stating that such a thing once existed and that I may want to look into it. Attempts at finding published information on the collection proved to be fruitless, even with the assistance of LoC historians and reference librarians. Encyclopedias, indexes of subject collections, and historical accounts of the LoC do not provide any information about the Delta Collection.[7] Cheryl Fox, head archivist in the Manuscript Reading Room, suggested consulting a collection of papers from the Office of the Keeper of the Collections. This archive turned out to hold a wealth of information that revealed a virtually unknown history of sexuality at the Library of Congress.

Although the Delta Collection is described in unpublished annual reports, these accounts were never entered into the published reports submitted to Congress. Among the keeper's papers, however, are records of transfers of materials to the LoC, excerpts of the keeper's diary detailing his thought processes regarding the Delta Collection, correspondence with other internal and external offices, policies, meeting minutes, and reports of items designated for destruction. Although the archival record is quite rich in certain regards, it seems that nearly every staff member tried to maintain distance from the Delta Collection, and no one wanted to claim authority on the topics of pornography and perversion. This means that the historical record is, in fact, quite sparse: Only certain official positions were written down. Many of the documents are difficult to decipher, as discussions of what to do with the Delta materials was an apparently uncomfortable and deeply fraught topic.

Postwar Federal Sexual Policing and Censorship

On August 8, 1963, seven uncataloged and unprocessed publications were loaned from the Delta Collection to Congressman John Dowdy (D-Tex.), during a hearing on a bill to ban homosexual groups from soliciting funds.[8] The impetus for the bill proposal was an application for a license to solicit charitable contributions for the Mattachine Society, an early activist organization that worked toward improving the rights of homosexuals. As there was no municipal or state law prohibiting homosexual social and activist groups from receiving donations, Dowdy proposed a federal law to prevent such actions. In his statement to Congress, Dowdy proclaimed:

> If the laws of the District of Columbia indeed do not authorize the refusal of a solicitation license or any other official recognition to a society such as this, whose illegal activities are revolting to normal society, then I feel that it is our duty to provide such authority without delay. The Mattachine Society is admittedly a group of homosexuals. The acts of these people are banned under the laws of God, the laws of nature, and are in violation of the laws of man.[9]

The bill died in the Senate, so the Mattachine Society remained relatively unharmed, but what this case begins to reveal is the LoC's role in the policing of sex and sexuality after World War II. The librarian's correspondence does not indicate which publications Dowdy viewed, but the record clearly states that the materials were obtained from the library's restricted Delta Collection on the day before Dowdy brought the bill to the floor. On another occasion, the Library of Congress made an exception to the rule that prohibited browsing of the Delta Collection for the Honorable Judge Leonard P. Moore, nearly three months after he upheld the decision of lower courts that had determined that *Lady Chatterley's Lover* was not obscene. Librarians provided the judge with small table and chair and a space "to exam[ine] volumes of particular interest at leisure."[10]

While the historical record on how the Delta Collection was used is meager, these examples remind us that the Library of Congress is not simply a storehouse of information but that its primary role has been to serve the U.S. Congress and government officials. As such, the LoC was a participant in the postwar regulation of sexuality through the restriction and provision of evidence in an antihomosexual campaign as well as in wider projects to regulate proper sexual citizens. "Sex perverts" were classified as reliability risks, prone to pressure from foreign agents, and the Library of Congress was part of the nation's apparatus for finding perverts and censoring obscenity.[11]

It is important to note that some of the texts housed in the Delta Collection also served as evidence of crimes. Those that were acquired via the Postal Service and Customs Bureau were seized through an arresting act, may have served as the basis for prosecution, and then were made available for federal officials and Congress as sources in other investigations. The archival records reveal details of transfers from customs offices across the nation, complete with names and addresses of those from whom materials were impounded. One gathers the significance of the connection between the LoC and the wider antiobscenity campaign when one recognizes that books confiscated in headline-making arrests may have been among those that still bear the Delta marks today. For instance, the *Evening Star* reported in 1958 that five thousand items impounded over eighteen months by New York customs and postal authorities were to be delivered to the Library of Congress. Many of the items were confiscated from seamen and students returning from Europe.[12] The same year, Lawrence Gichner, who authored three works housed in the Delta Collection and whose collection was admired by Alfred Kinsey, was arrested by eleven Morals Division detectives, who seized from his home fifty crates full of "erotic literature from every corner of the world."[13] Such observations call into question the wholesomeness of the Library of Congress in its mission to protect and preserve materials for the cultural record, as these resources arrived via punitive mechanisms and were then designated for use by federal agencies and Congress.

In a 1953 speech President Dwight D. Eisenhower proclaimed, "Don't join the book burners. Don't think you are going to conceal faults by concealing evidence that they never existed. Don't be afraid to go into your library and read every book." Eisenhower seems to have been assuming that the public can trust their librarians to select the materials worthy of being read and that they should, in fact, read subversive literature, if only to know the enemy. Dissenting voices must be brought into view, and the citizenry ought "to have them at places where they are accessible to others." Censorship, Eisenhower suggested, should be reserved for documents that "offend our own ideas of decency."[14] "Offensive" materials, it was presumed, would not likely be found in a library, and materials containing ideas opposed to normative notions of common decency were to be best left to the censors.

The U.S. Congress has historically acted as censor by enacting laws prohibiting the importation, mailing, and distribution of "obscene" materials. The most influential act was the first sweeping antiobscenity law, now commonly called the Comstock Act, passed in 1873. The act outlawed importation of obscenity from foreign countries and made it a felony to send or receive obscene materials through the mail. Later, the Foreign Agents Registration Act of 1938 required the registration of all foreign agents and foreign political propaganda disseminated in the United States, essentially bringing war propaganda and obscenity under the same umbrella of outlawed subversive materials.

Hysteria over censorship during and after World War II resulted in part from an increasing struggle to strike a balance between the desire to allow adults to decide for themselves what to read and the mass exploitation of commercial forms of speech that were viewed as potentially harmful to the public. Whitney Strub suggests that beginning in the 1940s the American public tried to reclaim moral authority from Comstock's disciples, insisting on their right to make decisions about their own media consumption. At the same time, though, Cold War efforts "consisted of programs to normalize and reproduce atomized nuclear families—predicated on heterosexual marriages in which wives avoided the workplace—in an effort to sustain the consumer culture that had begun to replace industry as the heart of the American economy."[15] Opening obscene books with their suggestions of nonprocreative sex, vice, homosexuality, and other perverse acts to the public might render the entire citizenry vulnerable to outside forces. As scholars have pointed out, "whereas communism embodied the greatest political perversion," homosexuality and other sexual perversions posed the greatest domestic threat.[16]

World War II and the postwar era also brought heightened passion from the American Library Association. The ALA adopted the Library Bill of Rights in 1938 to outline its position on intellectual freedom in response to the 1938 House Committee on Un-American Activities to investigate subversives. In 1948, with the expansion of World War II and McCarthyism, the ALA strengthened the Library Bill of Rights by taking a firmer stance on censorship and intellectual freedom, stating that libraries have a responsibility to challenge coercive measures that limit access to resources that inform moral and political opinion.[17] The LoC, however, opposed or disregarded many of the ALA's resolutions, and in 1948 Chief Assistant Librarian of Congress Verner Clapp led the opposition to the ALA's Resolution Protesting Loyalty Investigations in Libraries.[18]

In 1951 the ALA issued a "Statement on Labeling," derived from the Library Bill of Rights. The statement resulted from a series of events beginning in 1950, when Rutherford D. Rogers, chair of the Intellectual Freedom

Committee (IFC) of the ALA, reported that a number of groups, including the Sons of the American Revolution, had petitioned libraries to implement labeling systems for restricting access to communist and subversive materials.[19] Such labels would not only have marked materials as subversive but would have placed them in a segregated collection, to be given out only upon application. In response the IFC drafted a six-point statement on labeling that echoed Eisenhower's sentiments, asserting that labeling is a censor's tool that deterred the democratic ideals libraries hold:

> Although totalitarian states find it easy and even proper, according to their ethics, to establish criteria for judging publications as "subversive," injustice and ignorance rather than justice and enlightenment result from such practices, and the American Library Association has a responsibility to take a stand against the establishment of such criteria in a democratic state.

The ALA firmly indicated its position as anticommunist but stated their opposition to labeling and "any group which aims at closing any path to knowledge."[20] The statement on labeling was approved as policy by the ALA Council on July 13, 1951. The Delta Collection stood in opposition to that statement, as the collection served to hide items from view and placed a Delta symbol on the spine labels of the books. It should be pointed out, however, that, as Eisenhower's speech on book burning suggests, obscenity (a concept that was still not well defined) was generally agreed to be outside of the scope of materials that should be protected from censors. But what must be emphasized here is that, as with many locked cases, this act of labeling was not simply a censoring act; it was a part of a mechanism designed to protect materials from destruction or theft. Also, as the nation's library, the Library of Congress holds a position unlike any other library in the United States, and so the guidelines on intellectual freedom and labeling set forth by the ALA can be disregarded if in conflict with the demands of the U.S. government.

In 1952, in what Eli Oboler considers one of the most extraordinary bills ever to come before Congress, former FBI agent Representative Harold Velde (R-Ill.) introduced "a bill to provide that the Librarian of Congress shall mark all subversive matter in the Library of Congress and compile a list thereof for the guidance of other libraries in the United States."[21] The bill died, but presumably the Delta materials would have been conscripted into this proposed effort to assist librarians in nationwide censorship efforts. In 1956 Congress passed a law that permitted the Post Office to impound mail suspected of promoting fraud, obscenity, and gambling, except for publications with second-class mail privileges.[22]

By 1957, according to Louise Robbins, "the 'obscene' had begun to overtake the 'subversive' as the target of censorship."[23] Increasingly, accusations of homosexual and communist tendencies became interchangeable. For example, Alfred Kinsey was accused of aiding communism and was censored based on the perception that his work would undermine the status and power of the United States in the world.[24] Around the same time the Supreme Court's *Roth* decision tested the constitutionality of the conviction of a New York man for mailing obscene materials. It ruled that obscenity was not protected by the First Amendment and upheld the conviction of Samuel Roth for sending obscene materials through the mail. The ruling also stated that the "federal obscenity statute, 18 U.S.C. 1461, punishing the use of the mails for obscene material, is a proper exercise of the postal power delegated to Congress."[25] Additionally, as Robbins has revealed, the LoC participated in the 1947 Federal Loyalty Program, which included the purging of homosexuals from its workforce in the early 1950s because homosexuals and other "perverts" were viewed to be weak and susceptible to blackmail. Although the LoC was not required to participate in the federal loyalty program because it was not an executive branch agency, it did engage in the federal investigations and firing of employees. Robbins found that "according to the congressional investigation, between April and November 1950 fifteen LoC employees were charged with 'perversion.' Nine resigned under pressure, one was fired, and five cases were pending."[26] More people lost their jobs during this phase of the purges at LoC than during any other.

It was amid this tense climate of sexual policing that the Library of Congress was faced with the responsibility of assessing and storing sexually explicit materials that arrived through the Copyright Office, the U.S. Customs Bureau, and the Postal Service.

Keepers of the Collection

A local Washington, D.C., publication, undated but published when the Delta Collection still existed, claimed that the origins of the Delta Collection date back to the 1880s, with the bequest of a valuable rare book collection from a California tycoon. Included in that collection, according to the author, were such titles as the *Khamasutra*, the eighteenth-century spanking novel *Fanny Hill*, and a version of the fifteenth-century *The Perfumed Garden*. The author states: "The greater part of the erotic treasure was saved by an anonymous administrator with foresight. He realized, regardless of its contents, or because of them, the collection was rare."[27]

Although the article is quite sensational—and as of yet its assertions about the early formation of the collection remain unsubstantiated by LoC employees or archival evidence—it is worth entertaining the idea that Ainsworth Spofford was the librarian who inaugurated this secret collection.[28] Spofford is now recognized as a visionary who, emblematic of his era, promoted the "best" reading, but he also recognized the cultural value of books of that might be considered to be of lower quality.[29] He distinguished the mission of smaller public libraries from that of a national library and said that, while books of questionable morality may not belong in a small public library, "national libraries . . . would be derelict in their duty to posterity if they did not acquire and preserve the whole literature of the country."[30] He also observed, "what is pronounced trash today may have an unexpected value hereafter, and the unconsidered trifles of the press of the nineteenth century may prove highly curious and interesting to the twentieth, as examples of what the[ir] ancestors . . . wrote and thought about."[31] This position paralleled those of librarians who maintained closeted collections at the British Library and the Bibliothéque Nationale de France around the same time.[32]

The Delta Collection had always contained a sampling of books that would generally not be held by the LoC, and part of the rationale for retaining these items was preservation of the cultural record. Although LoC policy was to not maintain a collection of obscenity for its general collection, a 1954 acquisitions document outlined a policy for adding items of value for the history of manners and customs, art and literature, or those having a bearing on psychological or legal studies, even if they had some pornographic aspects. Pornographic or obscene materials that did not fit such categories were to be acquired in order to serve as samples.[33] It certainly wasn't only homosexuality, or even pornography, for that matter, that the Delta Collection contained. As with the Bibliothéque Nationale and the British Library collections, the Library of Congress's Delta Collection held a mix of scientific/sexological texts along with what was considered erotica and pornography, as well as the literary texts that were challenged in the courts. There was a remarkable number of books on sexual relations within a marriage and on birth control. And many of the works in the collection contained illustrations, which would have been easy prey for vandals if available in the general collection.

The documented history of the Delta Collection seems to begin in 1920, when a librarian wrote to a member of Congress requesting he return the book *Madeleine*, which had recently been identified as immoral and out-lawed. The letter stated that the book was either to be withdrawn or kept in a special collection in the Copyright Office as part of the legal record there.[34] This may have been the precursor to the Delta Collection, or it may have actually been the Delta Collection. The earliest correspondence that actually names the Delta Collection dates from 1936, when U.S. Congressman Millard Caldwell (D-Fla.) wrote to the Librarian of Congress, concerned about obscene items that might be in the LoC's collection. Librarian Herbert Putnam informed Caldwell that the books were indeed held by the Library of Congress in a restricted collection. An attached letter from the superintendent of the Reading Room to Putnam specifies that the four books in question were copyright deposits and "Items 1 and 2 are now in the 'Delta' Colletcion [*sic*] (a collection whose use is restricted to adults and only consulted under supervision in the Rare Book Room). Items 2 and 3 are in process of being catalogued and classified and will soon also be part of the 'Delta Collection.'"[35]

Arguably, the collection was initially formed in an effort to preserve the historical record, and while the Library of Congress maintained this as its mission (even as it was burning materials), the political significance that the Delta Collection assumed during the McCarthy era distinguishes it as much more than a preservation mechanism. Not unlike the Collection de l'Enfer at the Bibliotheque Nationale, which has a much longer history, these preservation efforts were entangled in state regulatory projects. In the final years of the ancien régime, for instance, the state seized and stored pornographic works during arrests. According to Moore, it was during the Second Empire of Louis Napoleon that these materials were secured in the restricted collection, marking the point at which the ambivalence of the collection became apparent—that the preservation and integrity of materials, which were in fact acquired in efforts to rescue banned books, derived from state censorship activities.

The Delta Collection officially became the purview of the first and only Keeper of the Collections, Alfred Kremer, when he was appointed by Librarian of Congress Archibald MacLeish in 1940. The keeper's primary duties were to protect collections from war damage.[36] MacLeish also appointed Luther Harris Evans director of the Legislative Reference Service (currently the Congressional Research Service) in 1939 and chief assistant librarian in 1940. On May 30, 1942, Evans delivered the address "The Library of Congress and the War" before the Librarian's Council, during which he told council members that the library, in support of the war, had increased its circulation of books and opened its facilities and

services to researchers. Evans also described the struggle to find a balance
in the LoC's role as a national library in serving the federal government
and the general public. He reported that over four hundred employees of
other federal agencies were conducting research at the Library of Congress and that 150 other people were designated by the Coordinator of
Information at the LoC to do research on foreign countries.[37] Wishing to
play a more personal role in the war, MacLeish resigned as Librarian of
Congress on December 19, 1944, and Luther Evans was appointed acting
librarian by President Truman in 1945. It was with a patriotic spirit that
LoC leaders made decisions regarding the selection and maintenance of
war-related and subversive and obscene materials. This climate no doubt
altered the very nature of the Delta Collection from being a repository
of the cultural record to being a political actor in the postwar era, one
with increasing significance as McCarthy's policies and rhetoric came to
dominate.

In 1952 (the year before he became director general of UNESCO),
Evans wrote to the commissioner of the Customs Bureau to express concern that subversive materials were being destroyed in customs and postal
seizures. The Library of Congress had been receiving materials that the
Customs Bureau and the Postal Service had confiscated for years, but there
was no official policy requiring these deposits. He petitioned to amend
the *Customs Manual* to require the delivery of seized items to the LoC.
The amendment stated:

> Printed matter of all kinds . . . for which an assent to forfeiture has been
> obtained, will be forwarded by the Bureau to the Library of Congress.
> . . . If libel action is necessary in connection with items of the above
> specified kinds, the United States attorney shall be requested to have
> the condemnation decree provide . . . for the delivery of such items to
> the Library of Congress for official use in lieu of destruction.[38]

These materials, which would have included propaganda, obscenity, and
other items considered subversive, were then placed in a Federal Agents
Collection, with selected obscene materials going to the Delta Collection.
When the *Customs Manual* was first amended to deliver items to the LoC,
the library requested that up to fifty copies of each text should be kept for
distribution to other government agencies. By 1953 the range of shelving
was overflowing, as they received an average of two to three mailbags of
subversive materials per day.[39] The understanding was that items used for
official use would either be destroyed or returned to the Customs Bureau
once they had been withdrawn from the Library of Congress.[40]

The 1956 unpublished annual report of the Exchange and Gift Division stated that the Post Office Department transferred 224,113 pieces of war propaganda, which were excluded from the mails in accordance with the *Postal Manual*. Two copies of each were segregated for the LoC's collection, and those not selected by other federal agencies were pulped monthly. Approximately four thousand pieces (mostly press releases and tourist information) were received under the Foreign Agents Registration Act. Of these most were sent by the British Information Service, the Australian News Information Service, and the Turkish Information Office.[41] That year the Bureau of Customs also transferred "several thousand pieces of obscene literature and motion picture films" as required by the *Customs Manual*. Representative selections were kept for the collections of the LoC, and the remaining items were forwarded to the Keeper of the Collections for disposal.[42] The amount of obscenity relative to the quantities of other types of materials is not readily knowable.

The massive quantities arriving at the LoC proved to be virtually unmanageable, hindering efforts to preserve and protect. It seems that, for the most part, the erotic and pornographic materials were disposable, at least in the eyes of the Keeper of the Collections. He lamented in his notes that the volume of the seized obscenity held and the labor required to evaluate and select from the materials just didn't seem to be worth the trouble. He resented the fact that earlier policies resulted in a chaotic and overwhelming amount of obscene materials, with which he was left the responsibility of overseeing in addition to his other duties as preservationist. It should be noted that the keeper used terms like "pornography," "obscenity," and "erotica" interchangeably and used words like "dirt," "filth," and "perverted" to describe such materials. On July 17 and 30, 1956, his diary entries read:

> I visited the Delta Collection to survey the status of "inventoried" intercepts and large quantities of unprocessed filth. . . . A sizable quantity of seized dirt was obviously sent to the former custodians of the Delta Collection with little or no formality involved in the transactions. . . . I still hold the view that the value of the materials selected from this source is hardly equal to the expense in time required by the messes thus far.[43]

Still, the keeper did not have jurisdiction over selection of materials. That was left to the subject divisions and selection officers, and in his diary Kremer expressed frustration about waiting for selectors to wade through the accumulated materials that he would have preferred to destroy.

I have to be very careful in not giving the impression that I am med-
dling into the affairs of the Processing Department and possibly, into
the affairs of the Reference Department in connection with this very
touchy business. Believe me, any residue of this seized material which
will be fed to us in the future will be destroyed just as quickly as we can
get it off the premises.[44]

Kremer was also frequently perplexed by protocols concerning the Delta
materials and about where his responsibilities began and ended. There was
clearly disagreement among the staff about what to do with the materials received from the Customs Bureau and the Postal Service. Without
the authority to burn materials, Kremer was careful not to overstep his
bounds. He finally made a formal request to be granted such authority on
February 19, 1957, when he found himself burdened by innumerable cartons of unselected films, books, and other printed material.[45] As he wrote
in his unpublished annual report for 1957, he "assumed an active role as the
Library's Security Officer in sponsoring action leading to the appropriate
disposition of large masses of such material, and finally established and ef-
fected the security measures resulting in satisfactory disposal measures."[46]
Once these policies and procedures were enacted, Kremer set out to reduce the amount of obscenity coming into the library and destroying the
bulk of the LoC's existing holdings of "filth."

Around that time, the *Customs Manual* was again amended to state that
only one or two copies of intercepts should be sent to the LoC, and in 1958
it was decided that five hundred duplicate copies of Delta items needed
to find a new home, preferably in another library.[47] These particular duplicates had mostly come through copyright and were not viewed to be
grossly obscene but, rather, were sealed away to prevent mutilation by the
public. The materials received from the Postal Service and Customs Bureau were not to be exchanged or transferred.[48] Great precautions were
taken before exposing this collection to other libraries because, although
the vast majority of the surplus designated for this removal was not obscene
or pornographic and had come through normal copyright or gift channels,
the librarians expressed concern about revealing the other contents of the
Delta Collection.

Reports of quantities retained or discarded do not seem to have been
kept with regularity, but in 1960 it was reported that 1,233 total pieces in
the Delta Collection were selected from intercepts through 1960's fiscal
year, including 917 photos, 158 printed matter, twenty-six prints, eight
decks of playing cards, three handkerchiefs, and a variety of other types

of materials.[49] At the close of fiscal year 1961 there were 1,343 items in the collection.[50] In 1962, the last year that the number of Delta materials was reported, 227 pieces were added, totaling 1,570 items. The keeper reported that certain Delta items were to remain unprocessed and contained in a secure area of the Rare Books Division.[51]

A May 23, 1963, report indicated that 123 burn bags were filled with Delta materials and that six hundred books and five hundred magazines still awaited review.[52] On November 5, 1963, 487 monographs sent from the Customs Bureau were rejected and designated for destruction. Nine monographs were sent to the Descriptive Cataloging Division to be forwarded to the Delta Collection through regular processing channels, and seventeen sample monographs were sent to the Delta Collection without cataloging. Fifty-six serials were discarded, and thirteen were selected for the sample file and forwarded to the Delta Collection.[53]

Toward the end of his tenure at the Library of Congress in 1963, Alvin Kremer indicated that he was firmly opposed to the idea of placing the Delta books in the general collection.[54] However, Coordinator for the Development and Organization of the Collections Robert D. Stevens wrote:

> I can make no claim to a knowledge of the workings of the perverted mind. Consequently, I asked the Keeper of the Collections, who has had some experience in this area, to assist me to the extent of pointing out publications he felt to be particularly vulnerable to mutilation or theft. He did not care to prepare this advice. The recommendations that follow then are solely my own based on my best rational judgment.[55]

It appears that Kremer and Stevens had serious differences of opinion regarding the preservation and access to the Delta books. Stevens recommended transferring the entire collection (with the negligible exception of a few discards) to the open shelves. In fact, all items except for those determined to be rare were moved to the general collection beginning in 1964. Librarians ceased adding to the collection in 1964 and then interfiled most of the materials within the general collection, after the office of the Keeper of the Collections was eliminated upon Kremer's 1963 retirement.[56]

The Book, the Thief, the Librarian, and His Lover?

On August 6, 1953, it was reported that plates and other illustrations had been removed from valuable books in the Delta Collection. As the Delta

Collection was kept under lock and key, it was assumed that an employee had committed the offense. Director of Personnel Robert M. Holmes said that the books contained photographs of nude women and that the theft was "probably the work of a sexual pervert."[57] The book that precipitated an extensive FBI investigation was *Erotic Color Prints of the Ming*, a book valued at $200 at the time and which had never been officially charged to a reader. Forty-two pages of prints had been removed from the book. Ironically, the book had been sent to the Delta Collection only a month earlier in error, and it was during its transfer to the Orientalia section that the damage was discovered. Upon further investigation of the collection, it was estimated that 151 volumes and thirty-five periodicals had been "mutilated," meaning that pages had been cut or torn out. Kremer determined that between 550 and one thousand illustrations and photographs had been stolen.[58]

While the Keeper of the Collections was in charge of decisions regarding preservation and conservation concerning the Delta Collection and other areas of the library, there were people that worked more directly with the collection on a regular basis. Frederick Goff was chief of rare books, which contained the Microfilm Reading Room, the Delta Collection, and other sections, from July 1940 until July 30, 1953. Phillip Melvin began working at the library in 1947 and was transferred to the Microfilm Reading Room, under the supervision of Faustine Dennis in 1948, and on June 1, 1953, he was promoted to librarian in charge of the Microfilm Reading Room and the Delta Collection. This happened just at the beginning of a larger restructuring in which the Microfilm Reading Room, the Delta Collection, and the bookstacks were transferred from Goff in Rare Books to Colonel Millett Webb. At that time there were approximately four thousand items in the Delta Collection, but no official inventory had been conducted at the time of the transfer from Goff to Webb.[59]

Melvin was the primary suspect in the case of the mutilated books, in part because staff members perceived him to be "highly emotional, having effeminate characteristics, and [he] has shown an above normal interest in pornographic literature."[60] In his interviews with FBI agents, Melvin stated that he had no interest in the Delta Collection and had requested several times that it be transferred from his care. Staff members, however, reported that he took too much interest in the Delta Collection, at the expense of his microfilm duties, and that he sometimes showed his friends Delta books to satisfy their curiosity.[61] The record reveals that Melvin had also been subjected to an FBI federal loyalty investigation in 1948 but was cleared by the Library of Congress Loyalty Review Board.[62] He had been a member of the U.S. Navy in 1945 and was honorably discharged for medical reasons.[63] Much of the record has been redacted on the grounds that disclosure would be an unreasonable invasion of personal privacy, but if he was investigated under the loyalty program, it is likely he was a suspected communist or homosexual. Holmes stated that Melvin had been the victim of a case of blackmail a few years earlier, in association with Father Herbert Clancy of Georgetown University, but again, so much of the record has been redacted that one cannot ascertain the details of the relationship or the blackmail.[64] What is apparent is that there was a great deal of speculation as to Melvin's character and sexual proclivities and that those assumptions surrounding his interests influenced the investigation of the mutilated books.

Melvin and Assistant Curator Emily M. Jahn were the two people who possessed keys at the time the mutilation was discovered, and a third key was held in the guard office and available only to the lieutenant of the guard. Holmes ruled Jahn out as a suspect because she was a "married woman of fifty-eight years of age, having several children, and has been a very trust-worthy employee of the Library of Congress for the past twenty-three years."[65] Jahn seemed to be convinced that Melvin was responsible for the crime. She and others suggested a number of possible suspects or informants, including Melvin's personal friends, acquaintances, and male roommate. The FBI tried on at least two occasions to press Melvin to agree to a search of his apartment. It seems that the offender left a trail of evidence, including mounting papers and scraps of cuttings that were left out, shoved between ring-binder pages, or on the floor. These and the mutilated books, filling four and a half cartons, were delivered by hand to the FBI by Carl Voelker and Alvin Kremer for fingerprint analysis on August 21, 1953.[66] Fingerprints were compared with those of Library of Congress employees, including guards and librarians who had contact with the collection, but no matches were found. After that, Jahn suggested more possible contacts of Melvin's. These people were interviewed and fingerprinted. In the end, the case was closed on April 22, 1954, and remains unsolved.[67]

What I find remarkable about this case is the extent to which the aims of the library collection collided and cohered with the methods the FBI undertook. By all appearances it seems that it was immediately determined that this crime could only have been perpetrated by a sexual pervert, and the selection of witnesses and suspects for questioning followed this logic, indeed to the point of farce. The library had long dealt with vandalism like this—theft of entire volumes or specific pages from its collections was not uncommon. Without question, the fact that the stolen materials were taken from a locked collection makes this particularly curious, and it is highly likely that it was an inside job. Still, it seems that alternative motives and suspects that might have been worth pursuing were lost given the singular focus on catching the sex pervert. In fact, another high-profile case had occurred fourteen years earlier, when fingerprint analyses connected a razor blade left in the Rare Books Reading Room to Mary Frances Anderson, a "shy and retiring" freelance historian and former federal employee. She was investigated in 1939 by J. Edgar Hoover, with Alvin Kremer's assistance, for the removal of 1,300 images from volumes on natural history—primarily birds and flora.[68] Over the course of three to five years these images were cut and sold to dealers, and there might have been a significant "vandalism syndicate."[69] While that earlier case remains a mystery in many respects, it is clear that the extensive theft from restricted collections was motivated by a desire for personal proprietary gain. Certainly, similar aims might have motivated the theft of sexually explicit images in and before 1953. It is also plausible that an employee destroyed the volumes in acts of censorship, one of the primary reasons for which collections like the Delta Collection are locked away. Although protection of the public from obscenity is one of the considerations for restricting materials, the protection of valuable resources is arguably the primary reason.

Strangely, Frederick Goff was hardly questioned, although the collection had been under his supervision until just days before the thefts occurred. In fact, Goff's remarks contradict those of Melvin's in important respects. For example, whereas Melvin claimed that Goff had instructed him to hide particularly sensitive titles—*Fanny Hill* and *Night in a Moorish Harem*—Goff denied that he ever suggested such a thing. (Perhaps it's not a coincidence that *Night in a Moorish Harem* is one of the titles that was lost in 2010!) Goff did admit that Melvin reported to him earlier in 1953 that the Delta Collection had somehow been "disarranged" but that Goff was not concerned and did not look into it.[70] While Goff admitted that theft had long been a problem, he was not aware of any recent concerns. He named a reader who might have stolen materials, but that person was not located or called in for questioning. It seems quite likely that, since an inventory was not taken at the time of the transfer of the collection and that readers had been allowed to view materials, in the same way that Mary Frances Anderson had years before, someone might easily have removed images before or while Melvin was charged with the task of overseeing the collection. Also, the accusation that he took too much interest in the Delta Collection seems unfair, given the fact that he had just been assigned to oversee the collection; one would assume that he should have concerned himself with the collection in order to manage it. Additionally, there were over thirty guards who might have had access to the key. While it was only supposed to be accessible to a lieutenant of the guard, one guard admitted that sick leave or other circumstances could have resulted in other guards temporarily assuming responsibility over the Delta Collection.

Given the range of possible motives and people who might have come in contact with the materials, the necessity of the perpetrator being a sex pervert withers away. More troubling, however, is how readily Library of Congress staff accused and pursued Phillip Melvin based on his appearance and their perceptions of his predilections. For them he most closely fit the profile of a sex pervert. That he was first submitted to a 1948 federal loyalty investigation and then accused of theft are perhaps indicators of the political obligations of the Library of Congress more than they are of Melvin's guilt. Holmes, as director of personnel, was an active participant in the Federal loyalty investigations held at the Library of Congress. On June 28, 1962, for instance, he interrogated library employee Nevin R. Feather, who was asked to deliver a notarized written statement responding to certain allegations:

> It has been reported that during 1961 you disclosed to representatives of another government agency that, on a couple of occasions, you had permitted a man to perform a homosexual act (fellatio) on you. Also, that you related that you find members of the male sex attractive; that you have been in bed with men; and that you have enjoyed embracing them.
>
> 1. Is this report true? If it is, please state whether or not your conduct in this respect has been confined to the foregoing, and if it has not, please explain.
>
> 2. If the above report is true, then please explain your negative answer to that part of item 20 on the Standard Form 89, "Report of Medical History," which reads "Have you ever had or have you now homosexual tendencies?"[71]

It is probable that Melvin faced a similar set of questions from Holmes, either in his 1948 federal loyalty investigation or later, along with the interrogation regarding the theft. That he was so singularly pursued as a suspect, even when lead after lead went cold, is quite telling of the time and place during which these events occurred. In hindsight it appears that the Library of Congress and the FBI were more interested in ferreting out sex perverts from within their ranks than in finding answers to the question of who mutilated the books. While I can only speculate, it does seem that the case was dropped when they realized they could not find their pervert.

"The Beast in the Closet"

Librarians of Congress must have had an idea of what was at stake when they locked a secret collection of erotica away from the public, and I imagine they named it the Delta Collection after Daedalus's symbol.[72] In myth, Daedalus told King Minos's daughter Ariadne the secrets of the labyrinth, and she, in turn, instructed her lover Theseus in how to navigate its lines and passageways, in order to find the Minotaur and slay it. The monstrous being—the most unnatural kind of offspring, produced by the union of the king's wife and a bull—waited within the depths of the maze to devour its next victim, but Theseus, armed with the key to the Minotaur's lair, conquered the beast, thereby rescuing any Athenians who would otherwise be sacrificed to and devoured by the beast.

The Delta Collection contained knowledge about "natural" and "unnatural" sex acts—the kinds that some may have feared might result in something as bestial as the Minotaur. Those texts threatened to devour the entire nation's citizenry, leaving America's first line of defense—the family—weak and impotent against the communist enemy. Only certain librarians held the key to the knowledge held within—as Ariadne to Theseus, so to speak. No card catalog was available for the public to consult. The classification system that serves as a guide for the general collection did not deliver one to the Delta Collection. One had first to know of the existence of the collection, and then one had to know precisely which volume was sought and request it in person. Browsing was not an option, and viewing of films and photographs was off limits to anyone other than federal officers.

Indeed, the Library of Congress is a library Jorge Luis Borges or Umberto Eco might have written about—labyrinthine and mysterious, with infinite passageways.[73] In fact, readers might easily mistake Herbert Small's description of the library's architecture in the *Handbook on the New Library of Congress* for Borges's "Library of Babel." First, Borges:

> From any hexagon one can see the floors above and below—one after another, endlessly. The arrangement of the galleries is always the same: Twenty bookshelves, five to each side, line four of the hexagon's six sides; the height of a normal librarian. One of the hexagon's free sides opens onto a narrow sort of vestibule, which in turn opens onto another gallery, identical to the first—identical in fact to all . . . Through

this space, too, there passes a spiral staircase, which winds upward and downward into the remotest distance. In the vestibule there is a mirror, which faithfully duplicates appearances.[74]

Now, Small:

Alcoves occupy the space between the inner and outer octagons. Between the two domes—the inner shell and the outer—is vacancy . . . the alcoves behind the screens are in two stories, like the arcading, and are intended to contain a collection of the most necessary standard books on all important topics. . . . One may pass through doors in the partitions from one alcove to another, on either floor; and by means of a winding staircase inside each of the piers one may go up or down, not only from story to story but, on the one hand, into the basement below and, on the other, to the space between the inner and the outer dome above. . . . The stacks are divided into nine tiers, each tier being seven feet high, and into an equal number of stories the same distance apart. This distance was adopted in order that the books on the highest shelf of a tier might not be beyond the convenient reach of a man of average height.[75]

There is order to this labyrinth, though, of which only the librarians can truly make any sense (or obtain access), just as in Borges's tale of the Library of Babel. The principles underlying library classifications depend on a belief in the veracity of the notion that if one understands the logic of the classification, one can bring order to the collection, and that patrons can utilize the system like they would Ariadne's thread.

One starts to grasp the truth of Borges's idea of an infinite library when one considers the fact that in one hundred years the units of shelving have expanded from forty miles in 1897 to over eight hundred miles, with 12,000 items added daily, forcing the collections out to offsite storage facilities. And we begin to apprehend the reality upon which the library's mythical status has been based, particularly in the works of Borges and Eco, and its self-conscious associations with Greek and Roman gods and goddesses of knowledge and wisdom.[76] Overlooking the Main Reading Room is a towering, fifteen-foot-tall marble mosaic of the goddess Minerva. And Theseus makes an appearance on the walls of the library, as well. As painted by Walter McEwen, we meet him after he has slain the Minotaur, when Minerva commands him to leave his lover Ariadne behind on the island of Naxos, so that she can be betrothed to Bacchus. The painting is part of a series in a corridor that opens onto a richly ornamented reading room for members of the House of Representatives.

In almost every account of a labyrinth there is an accompanying story of mirrors. Borges was obsessed, as was the narrator of "The Library of Babel": "Men often infer from this mirror that the Library is not infinite—if it were, what need would there be for that illusory replication? I prefer to dream that burnished surfaces are a figuration and promise of the infinite." In fact, one of the bronze doors at the main entrance of the Library of Congress features two women—Research, who holds the torch of knowledge, and Truth, who holds a mirror and a serpent, signifying wisdom and the "accurate reflection of external objects . . . joined in order to produce a consistent and truthful impression upon the reader."[77] At the Library of Congress, knowledge was selected and organized to reflect certain images and knowledges to an informed citizenry, and it locked away the knowledge that threatened to undermine the imagined nation.

Indeed, the mirror can also be frightening in its capacity to reveal the truth. In Nabokov's *Lolita*, which once resided among the Delta books, the first conjugal event between Humbert Humbert and Lolita at the Enchanted Hunters hotel involves a hall of mirrors and a closet, presaging a metamorphosis that would occur upon the revelation of certain knowledges: "There was a double bed, a mirror, a double bed in the mirror, a closet door with a mirror, a bathroom door ditto, a blue-dark window, a reflected bed there, the same in the closet mirror, two chairs, a glass-topped table, two bed-tables, a double bed."[78] The Delta collection was not unlike Humbert's hotel room, the effects of which were both to hide and mirror. At this particular point in the labyrinth one's animalist nature is reflected back in all of its horrifying perversities, and the danger within was that encounters with the texts would cause readers to become perverse. Frederick Whiting asserts that the frenzy around *Lolita* derived from an "anxiety about monstrous births, namely, their relation to the illicit desires that conceived them."[79] As with Kafka's Gregor Samsa, who arose out of sleep with his body transformed into an insect, his first vision being that of a picture from a magazine resembling a *Venus in Furs* (suggesting that perhaps this was also the last thing he saw before he went to sleep, inducing his transformation), the encounter with the knowledge of one's own perversity may render one monstrous. This metamorphosis brings to mind the very story of *Venus in Furs*, also held in the Delta Collection and authored by Sacher-Masoch, the name from which Krafft-Ebing derived the term "masochism." And in the first pages of the *Psychopathia Sexualis*, Krafft-Ebing writes: "Man puts himself at once on a level with the beast if he seeks to gratify lust alone, but he elevates his superior position when by curbing the animal desire he combines with the sexual functions ideas of morality, of the sublime, and the beautiful."[80] Encountering the knowledge held within and diving into it, one is transformed—a differently desiring subject, entranced in perverse literatures that one can never erase from memory. The perverse monster is particularly threatening because part of its fearsomeness is its capacity to elicit desire and arousal on the part of the subject. The monster is what, as put by MacCormack, "abjectly pushes us outside symbolic integrity."[81] One must place a distance between oneself and the monstrous, so as not to align oneself with the monster. If one desires the monstrous, then the desiring subject is also monstrous. Best to keep everyone safe by locking the monster away. What remains, though, is the knowledge that there is, in fact, a beast in the closet. And opening the door may unleash its powers. Foucault, too, writes about the kinds of transformations that might occur in the labyrinth:

> The labyrinth is linked to the metamorphosis, but according to an equivocal plan: it leads, like Daedalus' palace, to the Minotaur, the monstrous fruition which is marvel and also a trap. But the Minotaur, by his very being, opens a second labyrinth: the entrapment of man, beast, and the gods, a knot of appetites and mute thoughts. The winding of corridors is repeated, unless it is perhaps the same one; and the mixed being refers to the inextricable geometry which leads to him. The labyrinth is at the same time the truth and the nature of the Minotaur, that which encloses him externally and explains him from within.[82]

Among the books in the Delta Collection were some of the more pornographic productions created during and after World War II. Perhaps the greatest danger of the knowledge contained within this collection is the inevitable self-knowledge to be revealed with the encounter. Moreover, opening the books to the public might result in the confirmation of Freud's and Kinsey's theories on the universality of perversion, and allowing everyone to see their own selves in such a light might in fact render the entire perverse citizenry vulnerable to outside forces. After all, homosexuals were purged from the ranks of federal agencies, including the Library of Congress, precisely because they were viewed to be weak and susceptible to blackmail, in addition to being ineffectual and unable to participate in the national project to increase and multiply.

The threat of perversion was considered particularly dangerous because of the unknowable aspect of the pervert and the paranoid belief that the perpetrator lurked around every corner. As Margot Canaday has pointed out, the federal government produced mechanisms by which they could apprehend the pervert, including a variety of metrics and classifications.[83] With the war on perversion, though, the enemy was the U.S. citizen—a sort of traitor, and all the more dangerous because he (as was usually believed to be the case) was employed in federal agencies, taught in schools, and resided in American neighborhoods, where he could undermine U.S. policy and the American family. What's more, the enemy could quite easily be oneself, and this may in part be why such rigorous policing efforts took hold, particularly during the McCarthy era. Whether it is erotica, hardcore porn, or a titillating sexological text that introduces oneself to previously uncharted desires, the result is to come face to face with one's simultaneous horror, fascination, and arousal. The books that were seized by the Customs Bureau and in the mail were dangerous because they would expose and circulate perverse desires, and anyone could be vulnerable. They brought one face to face with desires that, according to the dominant discourses, were abnormal, unhealthy, and even monstrous. The case of the persecutory investigation of Phillip Melvin reveals the depths to which this kind of paranoia extended, as the case brought librarians and federal agents into contact with the terrifying idea that one of their own might be a pervert.

Foucault marks a shift in our understanding of the monster in the late nineteenth century, around the same time that he marks the invention of the homosexual as a species.[84] It is the same configuration of medical and juridical disciplinary mechanisms that produced sexual deviance that also divided the monstrous body into a multitude of perversions and bad behaviors within the disciplines. By way of the law and psychiatric medicine and the classificatory apparatuses that organized these disciplines, the monstrous—who was formerly outside the law—was rendered intelligible and controllable.[85] Monstrosity—that which defied laws of nature—became the explanatory principle for criminality, danger, and their regulation. I would argue that the Library of Congress's division of normal sexuality and abnormal sexuality, and the further divisions within those respective categories, mirrored this wider societal shift. But the rise of obscenity after World War II, combined with the Red Scare, reinvigorated the fear of monsters. American Cold War politics incorporated a discourse of monsters in order to demonize and dehumanize the enemy and to bring notice to a sexualized threat to the home. Pornography was believed to cause sex violence and childhood delinquency and arrest normal sexual development. Furthermore, one needs the monstrous to see oneself as normal.

In alignment with Foucault's assessment of the problem with monsters, Whiting suggests that in *Lolita*, "Humbert's monstrousness consists not in his criminal acts but in violating that order," with "order" referring to nature. The unintelligibility of the accumulating erotica and porn, in addition to the sexological and rare books initially set aside in the late nineteenth century, could only be made intelligible by treating it collectively as a monstrous body. This body of knowledge, whose reproducibility was even more impossible to measure or predict, could only be managed by containment, erasure, and elimination. The texts were determined to be unlawful by other federal agencies, but at the same time they were incapable of being disciplined by library technologies, and so they were sequestered and hidden away.

Sedgwick would say that this closeted collection informs speech about sexual relations more generally.[86] Whereas the previous and following chapters show how classificatory apparatuses discipline subjects, the Delta Collection illustrates what happens when perversion cannot be made sense of within a given grid of intelligibility. The books within this collection stood outside any rules of library classifications, and so with a single mark—Δ—not a name or a notation but a symbol they were banished to a closed location. The fear and loathing surrounding this collection provides a glimpse into the centrality of sexuality as an organizing principle upon which all else is based. The regulation of sexually suggestive texts and the withholding of such texts from the American people brings to light the extent to which everything, including the safety and security of the nation, comes down to sex. Again, Foucault, on how the monster's lair exists as an alternative, underground space, which perverts and threatens the laws and knowledge upon which society is built:

> The space symbolized by the Minotaur is, on the contrary, a space
> of transmutation; as cage, it makes man into an animal of desire—
> desiring like a wild beast, desired like a prey; as underground chamber,
> it contrives, underneath the states, a counter city-state that vows to
> destroy the oldest laws and pacts; as machine, its meticulous movement,
> supported by nature and reason, gives rise to Antiphysis and all the
> volcanos of madness. It is no longer a matter of the deceptive surfaces
> of disguise but, rather, of a nature metamorphosed into a depth by the
> powers of the supernatural.[87]

Foucault tells us that it is here that "modern perversity" finds its proper space: "The truly transgressive forms of eroticism are now found in . . . the direction of the counternatural, there where Theseus is headed when he approaches the center of the labyrinth, toward that core of darkness where, voracious architect, Knowledge keeps watch."[88]

The Catalog Record as Historical Record

Little explicit discussion of the cataloging practices concerning the Delta Collection has survived, but a Delta shelflist was mentioned in a 1956 procedure memorandum labeled "Handling Customs Intercepts."[89] As of this writing, such a shelflist has not been unearthed. However, a search of the LoC online catalog using "Delta" in the call number field turned up 543 bibliographic records. An additional search using "delta" as a keyword anywhere and "problem" as a keyword in holdings turns up 467 more records, which reveal a "Problem location." The staff views of MARC records that direct patrons to this "Problem location" indicate that these were former Delta books. Another search for "Delta collection" as a phrase in a keyword anywhere brings up another thirty-nine records.[90] All together, precisely 1,049 bibliographic records describe items that were formerly part of the Delta Collection. This is relatively close to the last reported amount in the Delta Collection in 1962 (1,570 items) and may reflect the number of materials still in the Delta Collection when it was removed to the general collection. Perhaps some materials were mishandled and lost in the transition, or some items may have been mutilated or stolen. As mentioned above, a 2010 visit to the LoC in search of historical books on sex and sexuality revealed that many books are shelved in locations other than those listed in the online catalog or are missing. Books that indicated "Problem location" sent me on a chase in different reading rooms, searching card catalogs, filling out paper call slips, and sometimes ending up empty handed because librarians were unable to locate the items. Another possible explanation for the discrepancy of approximately five hundred items is that they may not have been processed or cataloged when they were added to the Delta Collection and thus did not have Delta marks to retain. Pictured in Figure 8 is a catalog card from the Delta Collection. This one contains the typewritten "Delta" in the call number, but other cards simply included hand-drawn triangles. This image is copied from mimeographed sheets that were processed by the FBI in its investigation of the mutilated Delta books.

Figure 9 shows the Library of Congress classifications to which these works were assigned within the Delta Collection. Many titles were consid-

GN27
.S33
1943
Delta

Schultze-Naumburg, Paul, 1869–
    Nordische schönheit, ihr wunschbild im leben und in der
kunst, von Paul Schultze-Naumburg. 2., verm. aufl., mit 190
abbildungen. München/Berlin, J. F. Lehmann, 1943.

    228 p. illus. 23ᶜᵐ.

    "Weitere bücher von Paul Schultze-Naumburg": p. 228.

    1. Beauty, Personal. 2. Teutonic race. 3. Human figure in art.
ɪ. Title.
    GN27.S33   1943   572   A F 47–1122
    Art Institute of Chicago.   Ryerson library
        for Library of Congress   (2,†

Figure 8. Catalog card from the Delta Collection. *Source*: Papers of the Keeper of the Collections, Manuscript Reading Room, Library of Congress, Washington, D.C.

ered fiction or literature, and we can probably assume that a good share of these arrived via the Customs Bureau. Most of the works that were classed as PZ3 or PZ4—once designated as the spaces for fiction at the Library of Congress—were published in France. Sixty-one titles from Olympia Press, including *Lolita* and *Naked Lunch*, which were both first published by Olympia in France, met with the censoring practices of the Customs Bureau, as did some of Olympia's more explicit and decidedly erotic/pornographic books.[91] Indeed, the archival record indicates that *Lolita* and other titles were seized and then delivered to the library. Perhaps unsurprisingly, most of the catalog records for the works of fiction and literature lacked subject headings, whereas most of the other books in the collection are more fully cataloged with descriptive headings. It turns out that the majority of the nonfiction books in the Delta Collection had to do with sex in marriage and what would have formerly been considered "normal" sex customs, and relatively few concerned sexual perversions (as they would have been categorized at the time). Many of these books contained illustrations, which would have been vulnerable to theft and mutilation. A good share of the books included collections of photography—mostly nudes. Books found in the medical section of the library mostly had to do with contraception or more generally gynecology.

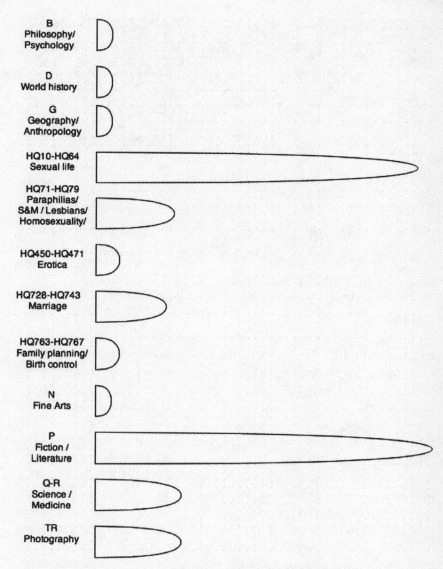

Figure 9. Books formerly in the Delta Collection, according to LC Classification.

It is a credit to the Library of Congress that the Delta label has been preserved in the catalog.[92] It is remarkable that these items still bear the marks of the Delta Collection, particularly because policy memoranda explicitly state that traces of the collection were to be removed: The Delta symbol was supposed to be erased from the spine labels and catalog cards.

Either this project simply was never completed, or the policy was changed at some point. Several books reviewed in 2010 still bear the stamp of the Delta symbol on their spines and pages, and the catalog clearly reveals at least 1,010 books that were formerly part of the Delta Collection. This trace of the Delta Collection serves as an affirmation of the value of the library catalog as historical record, as it is by way of this record that we are admitted entry into the complexities of the management of obscenity and erotica at different points in U.S. history. It gives voice to a history of texts that were once silenced by precisely this symbol.

CHAPTER 3

Mapping Perversion: HQ71, etc.

A nation's greatness lies in its possibility of
achievement in the present, and nothing helps it more
than the consciousness of achievement in the past.

—THEODORE ROOSEVELT, "American Ideals"

The problem with reason is that it works
in the service of passion.

—JOHN K. NOYES, *The Mastery of Submission*

Classification is often regarded as synonymous with categorization and taxonomies, but *bibliographic* classification in libraries has a distinct meaning
and purpose, which concerns the physical location of library materials, that
is, the placement of items on library shelves. Think of it as a geographical
code. A class determines the call number—the notation stamped on the
spine of the volume and in the corresponding catalog record, directing patrons to the book. A class also brings topically related materials together—
a process called collocation—ideally placing similar books in the same section, according to where they fit within a given discipline. Bibliographic
classification can be conceived of as a sorting mechanism—a way of drawing associations and relationships across methodologically or substantively
similar things. Whereas the previous chapters focused on the terminologies used for sexual perversion and labeling, this chapter interrogates the
spatial dispersal of subjects as well as the ways in which printed texts bear
the classification marks on their spines. Library classifications distribute
hierarchies along a linear path, arranging books in a shelflist order. A book
can only ever occupy one space in a library, so definitive decisions must be
made with regard to the discipline and topic of texts. Being anything but

arbitrary, classifications draw materials together and then divide them up by topic, carving out disciplinary norms and attachments.

Bibliographic classification presents particular challenges that other taxonomies don't necessarily face. While the acts of naming and cross-referencing are clearly political, the act of positioning a subject on a specific shelf in relation to other texts is decisively so. Although various classificatory processes are entirely enmeshed, at play in the hands of the same political and social mechanisms, there are particularities of shelf classifications that have their own histories and merit a distinct account and methodology.

It is this type of classification that resulted in the placement of Sedgwick's *Epistemology of the Closet* in the section on American literature with the class designation PS374.H63, as described in the first pages of this book. Figure 10 reveals how the cataloging practices enacted on Sedgwick's entire body of work has dispersed her books across the library. The list of subject definitions for the locations at which her works are placed provides a glimpse of some of the questions at play regarding how a classification functions. First, looking only to those books for which the LoC's catalog indicates Sedgwick is an author or editor, we see that her corpus is mostly spread across the language and literature section, with books in general literature, linguistics, American literature, and English literature. A few of Sedgwick's books reside in a section for individual authors within American literature (PS3569.E316), indicating that she is considered an author of literary works and that literature written by her, as well as critical works about her, should be placed there. It is a bit curious that of the books she has written, these items and only these items—*Fat Art, Thin Art* (a book of poetry) and two books of essays, *Touching Feeling: Affect, Pedagogy, Performativity* and *The Weather in Proust*—have been placed in the class created by and for her name. The secondary works *Eve Kosofsky Sedgwick* (Routledge, 2008), by Jason Edwards, and *Regarding Sedgwick: Essays on Queer Culture and Critical Theory* (Routledge, 2002), edited by Stephen M. Barber and David L. Clark, are also shelved in PS3569. E316, as they are considered literary criticism and are organized around Sedgwick's literature. Why are these and only these shelved at this location? One could certainly argue that it would make sense to shelve all of her books and many of the secondary books together under her name. Where Sedgwick's work is considered to be *about* literature rather than having the status of literature itself, we find her books distributed around the discipline, resulting in the spread of her work across the P, PN, PR, and PS sections.

BF531.T583—Psychology—Affection. Feeling. Emotion—Emotion—General works—English and American.

Shame and Its Sisters: A Silvan Tomkins Reader (Editor)

P95.55.P47—Philology. Linguistics—Communication. Mass media—Special aspects—Oral communication. Speech—Speech acts.

Performativity and Performance (Editor)

PN56.H57—Literature (General)—Theory. Philosophy. Esthetics—Relation to and treatment of special elements, problems, and subjects—Other special—Topics, A–Z—Homosexuality.

Tendencies

PR409.M38—English literature—History of English literature—By period—Modern—General—Treatment of special subjects.

Between Men: English Literature and Male Homosocial Desire

PR868.T3—English literature—History of English literature—Prose—By form—Prose fiction. The novel—By period—19th century—Special topics, A–Z.

The Coherence of Gothic Conventions

PS374.H63—American literature—History of American literature—Special forms—Prose—Prose fiction—Special forms and topics, A–Z—Homosexuality.

Epistemology of the Closet
Novel Gazing: Queer Readings in Fiction (Editor)

PS3556.I8135—American Literature—Individual Authors—1961–2000—F.

Gary in your Pocket: Stories and Notebooks of Gary Fisher (Editor)

PS3569.E316—American literature—Individual Authors—1961–2000—S.

Fat Art, Thin Art
Touching Feeling: Affect, Pedagogy, Performativity
The Weather in Proust

RC464. S43—Internal medicine—Neurosciences. Biological psychiatry. Neuropsychiatry—Psychiatry—Biography of mental patients and psychotherapy patients.

A Dialogue on Love

Figure 10. Eve Kosofsky Sedgwick's works.

We begin to realize her cross-disciplinary reach when we consider her essay in a book on breast cancer, shelved in medicine in the R section, and the placement of the Silvan Tomkins reader, edited by Sedgwick and Andrew Parker, in psychology, in the B section. I wonder what Sedgwick might think about the placement of *Dialogue on Love* (a memoir based on her psychotherapy sessions) in RC464. S43, the section for internal medicine, specifically defined as "Neurosciences. Biological psychiatry. Neuropsychiatry—Psychiatry—Biography of mental patients and psychotherapy patients." Why wouldn't this literary memoir be placed in the section that seems to be trying to collocate her work under her name? Surely, the placement in internal medicine is unlikely to facilitate discovery through browsing for most Sedgwick readers. This is not to say that a conversation is not to be had with medicine. I mean, rather, to point out that the library's choice is decisive and that it carries political weight and consequences and gives us important information about the disciplinary imagination. When we consider that only one choice is allowed, we necessarily have to think in terms of a "best" choice. Catalogers typically strive to anticipate the needs and information-seeking habits of readers, and potential readers of *Dialogue on Love* are likely to have varying interests or investments in the text. While some are interested in Sedgwick's body of work and might expect it to be found with her books in the literature sections, other readers might be more inclined to consider this a psychoanalytic text, which would mean that the book would be shelved in the B section, along with other books on psychoanalysis, psychology, and philosophy. It seems that this particular cataloger viewed this to be of interest primarily to people reading about medical psychiatry.

Figure 11 illustrates my attempt to gain a physical sense of where Sedgwick's books are located. To gather an understanding of the relations among the books in these ranges, I jotted down all the call numbers for her books and went hunting for them in the stacks. Retrieving all of Sedgwick's books from the University of Kentucky library proved to be a strenuous exercise: It involved traversing three floors of the library and a number of wings within those floors. (In another library, this exercise may be more or less daunting, depending on the size and scope of the collection and the layout of the stacks. *Dialogue on Love*, for instance, might be in an entirely different library building for the medical sciences.) My quest also revealed that the system is so hierarchically refined that it confuses. For as much as it aims to standardize and guide a logical placement of books on shelves for retrieval, the wide array of subdivisions within disciplines results in a system that fails to collocate. For example, special topics in American literature are

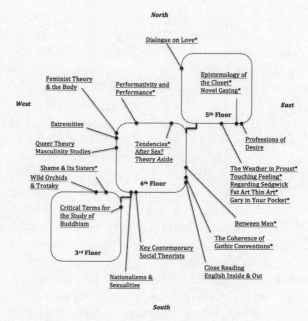

Figure 11. Map of Sedgwick's works in the University of Kentucky Library.

organized alphabetically, so books on homosexuality are housed between books on homicide and horror tales. The books in this section are quite a distance away from books on homosexuality in English literature and in general literature—at the University of Kentucky, for instance, those are on different floors of the library.

Given that Sedgwick protested the placement of *Epistemology of the Closet*, it bears asking whether it would fit better within another class. While I resist the idea that there can be one best choice, I would suggest that there were better alternatives available to catalogers at the time of the publication of *Epistemology of the Closet*. For example, PN56.H57, reserved for homosexuality within the section on theory, philosophy, and esthetics in general literature (and where *After Sex?: On Writing Since Queer Theory*, edited by Janet Halley and Andrew Parker, and *Tendencies* are located), is currently home to sixty-six works at the Library of Congress. The class was available at least as early as 1978, so a budding body of literature would have been present in that location when the book was first cataloged.[1] A class dedicated for the specific topic of homosexuality within modern English literature was not available at the time but was added five years later. This might provide a clue as to why *Epistemology of the Closet* was placed with American literature rather than English literature. While this is pure speculation, I like to think that perhaps the cataloger privileged the concept of homosexuality over geography, and as a subdivision for the special topic of homosexuality was available in American literature but not in English literature, the book ended up there. By contrast, Sedgwick's *Between Men*, published ahead of *Epistemology* in 1985, was placed in a category of general special topics within modern English literature.

Reading the library shelves invites a particularly fruitful conversation for doing the history of the development of queer theory. The history of scholarship on sexuality is made visible through the history of cataloging with Sedgwick's and her interlocutors' works. The changes in cataloging norms and the addition of classes over time reveal the discomfort and confusion inherent in the emergence of queer studies. This not only illustrates one way to do the history of queer theory; it also tells a story about the history of homosexuality in the United States—in American literature and in terms of how the nation was writing sexuality into its history. Indeed, the LoC's insistence on placing *Epistemology of the Closet* in American literature rather than English literature is a statement that says this book *belongs* in and to American literature.

Organizing a National History

Foucault tells us that the histories of madness, psychology, and sexuality were all made possible by the division between normal and abnormal.[2] The epistemic cut between reason and nonreason enabled a system of limits that designated what is allowed and desirable and what is prohibited and cast out of history. These divisions also made possible the construction of the history of nation-states, by setting up a grid upon which citizenries are organized. I take the Library of Congress Classification to be a frame upon which the United States has constructed its history. The classification totalizes the library's bibliographic world, rendering the library a "space of corporal reality, and space of social order."[3] It is in the bibliographic classification that organizes books on the shelves where we most acutely observe the disciplinary apparatus and its divisions at work. It serves as an architectural technique in carving out certain truths about American history and the history of sexuality.

I am drawing upon Foucault's analysis of disciplinary power, particularly as articulated in *Discipline and Punish*, the 1975/1976 lectures at the Collège de France published as *Society Must Be Defended*, and his research on governmentality to explain the place of the Library of Congress and its bibliographic classification in U.S. history and history making. While critics have argued that Foucault underestimates the significance of the state in his account of governmentality, I find his analysis indispensible for this project because the Library of Congress plays a unique role as both a state and cultural institution.[4] Foucault does not deny the significance of the state; rather, he insists that to privilege the state in analyses of power relations is a mistake and that "power in its exercise goes much further, passes through much finer channels, and is much more ambiguous, since each individual has at his disposal a certain power, and for that very reason can also act as the vehicle for transmitting a wider power."[5] An account of library classifications both deepens and challenges Foucault's claims about governmentality. The Library of Congress's role in the workings of the federal government seems to be overshadowed by the fact that it provides access to cultural objects and knowledge. Librarianship's claims to equity of access and freedom to read in the name of democracy mask the role of libraries in reproducing the dominance of certain discourses and groups.[6] And I imagine it is fair to say that most people who visit academic and public libraries do not give much thought to the fact that these places are state apparatuses. However, as members of the bureaucratic intelligentsia, the crafters of the classifications systems at the LoC not only propelled the high modernist ideology of scientific and technological progress, but they did so out of a sense of responsibility to the U.S. Congress and its public. Indeed, librarians of all types in the Progressive Era United States viewed their role to be vital in educating, protecting, and informing the citizenry, and libraries were sites that advanced social progress and reform.

I am not the first to note the library's resemblance to the model described by Jeremy Bentham as the Panopticon, a schema for obtaining the "power of mind over mind," but here I want to extend this model to convey the way in which institutions acquire and wear this mask of good will.[7] Panopticism extends far beyond prison walls to schools, factories, hospitals, and, of course, libraries. Foucault construes it as a model or "a diagram of a mechanism of power reduced to its ideal form."[8] Key to the functioning of the economy of a panoptic institution is a structure that places the eye of power and authority in the center, with a view of all of its subjects—keeping order and ensuring maximum efficiency of operations. Figure 12 reveals an uncanny resemblance between the prison and the Library of Congress, recalling images that appear in *Discipline and Punish*. Librarians are seated at the circulation desk in the center, with a view of all the readers as well as the books shelved in alcoves (cells). Bentham believed there was no risk that the power of the machine might become tyrannical because the prison was a public institution to which visitors were invited. The

Figure 12. Reading Room in rotunda, Library of Congress, 1901. *Source*: Library of
Congress Prints and Photographs Division (Washington, D.C.: Library of Congress).
Reproduction number: LC-DIG-det-4a08613. http://www.loc.gov/pictures/item/
det1994005030/PP/.

public would essentially keep things in check, assuring democratic rule.
This illusion of democracy sustains the power relation, further circulating sanctioned notions of disciplining, so that visitors will then carry such
ideas out into the world, repeat them, and reinforce and extend the reach
of the disciplinary apparatus. According to Foucault, Bentham envisioned

a way to "unlock" the disciplines so they would function throughout the entire social body, allowing the whole society to be "penetrated through and through with disciplinary mechanisms."[9] It is the articulation and distribution of the various dispositions and linkages of power in all the arms of government, populations, and political economy that gives it force.

Similarly, the Library of Congress views its mission as supporting democracy through the provision of information, and it promotes itself as a public cultural institution that works in the interest of the U.S. citizenry.[10] Libraries are held in the minds of the public to be a benefit to society, particularly because they promote egalitarian ideals with regard to access. And as they are open to the public there is a mostly unchallenged perception that they not only promote democracy but also operate democratically and justly. Studying the classification problematizes such a position: It reveals the various ways in which access is granted by systems that produce and sustain norms, margins, and exclusions. It ultimately reveals this institution to be circulating disciplinary discourses in ways that Foucault has identified in and outside of Bentham's panoptic prison.

The Library of Congress embodies, in a very real sense, the ensemble of discourses that contribute to modern governmentality, as it contains knowledge from all the disciplines and many parts of the world in one institution. Legal, political, literary, medical, technical, scientific, religious, and historical texts, as well as photographs and maps and art and sound recordings, are all centralized in this space. The extent to which its classificatory standards are repeated in libraries around the globe, numbering in the thousands of locations, means that a vast and powerful network of cultural and intellectual institutions reproduces these norms. Enacted in rulebooks and applied in the catalog, the terms for norms and their binary oppositions are reiterated over and over, naturalizing and normalizing discourses, creating a cycle of prohibition that authorizes certain ways of speaking and disallowing unacceptable speech and subjects. Seemingly nonpolitical institutions like our academic and public libraries provide access to information via these systems. At the same time, the Library of Congress is directly tied to the state, as the literatures it houses have been selected and organized so as to serve the U.S. Congress and the nation's interests. According to the website for the United States House of Representatives: "The Library's stated mission is to support the Congress in fulfilling its constitutional duties and to further the progress of knowledge and creativity for the benefit of the American people."[11] It must be understood as a state institution, and its classifications as state apparatuses. The Library of Congress is quite literally attached to the U.S. Capitol by an underground tunnel for efficient delivery of documents to members of Congress. Wendy Brown explains: "While governmentality in general includes the organization and deployment of space, time, intelligibility, thought, bodies, and technologies to produce governable subjects, the governmentalization of the state both incorporates these tactical concerns into state operations and articulates with them in other, nonstate domains."[12] Indeed, according to James C. Scott, one of the ways that the state made its categories stick was by embedding them in institutions that structure experience and daily life.[13] Brown argues that what is lacking in Foucault's analysis is the recognition that the state gives a certain legitimizing weight to the organization of subjects.[14] Such is the case in libraries, as the state has not only funded and supported the LoC, but the library serves the mission of the state, and arguably, it is the state that gives the Library of Congress and its standards the legitimacy and authority by which it has extended itself to this vast network of libraries and other information agencies around the world.

Foucault suggests that the selection, organization, and centralization of knowledge—as well as its division—brought about the possibility of the modern state. He locates the emergence of French universities at around the same time as the formation of the disciplines, in the early nineteenth century, and describes the processes by which the disciplines were used to construct a particular kind of historical discourse that fortified the state. In other words, the state acquired knowledge and used it in such a way that allowed "the State to talk about itself."[15] Foucault cites postrevolutionary France, a nation that had recently been unified, to illustrate the use of history to secure the universality of the state. In his analysis, this transition took form not in war but in civilian discourse and institutions. No longer was the state primarily driven by a will toward domination, but instead its primary struggle was precisely this "striving toward the universality of the State," and that struggle would take place in the economy, governance, and public institutions.[16] The parallels between Foucault's account of French history and that of the United States are too striking to overlook. Foucault's reliance on Augustin Thierry in his interpretation of postrevolutionary political conditions surely resonates with American Civil War historians: "We believe ourselves to be a nation, but we are two nations within one land, two nations which are enemies because of what they remember and because their projects are irreconcilable: one once conquered the other."[17] In the American context, one can look to Theodore Roosevelt's writings about American patriotism to find just how urgently felt was the need for a unified nation composed of an upright citizenry during the Progressive Era. One gathers the sense that the United States was on the brink of collapse in 1894 when Roosevelt proclaimed that the citizenry must be broadly American and national rather than local or parochial. He wrote in his essay "True Americanism" that "we must soberly set to work to find out all we can about the existence and extent of every evil, must acknowledge it to be such, and must then attack it with unyielding resolution. There are many such evils, and they each must be fought after a separate fashion; yet there is one quality which we must bring to the solution of every problem—that is, an intense and fervid Americanism."[18] Foucault marks the French postwar condition as bearing a grid of intelligibility upon which the construction of the national state relied. Similarly, in the years after the U.S. Civil War and Reconstruction and during the construction of the library's Jefferson building and creation of the Library of Congress Classification, unification under the banner of Americanism was the highest ideal.

The LoC moved into its new building, established collection development priorities, and created the scaffold upon which those collections would be organized not long after the American Civil War and precisely during the Spanish–American War. The country was undergoing its own transition in becoming a universalized state and expanding its empire, and the Library of Congress took on a new role in figuring the nation by organizing a national history. Foucault explains that in this kind of moment, the present becomes "the moment of the greatest intensity, the solemn moment when the universal makes its entry into the real."[19]

In the United States, the Library of Congress became the site where knowledge was disciplined and divided so that it could facilitate and secure the foundation upon which the nation was built, and the organization of knowledge into this universal system must be read as part of this process of constructing a history of the present in a particular moment. The library collected the world's knowledge in order to inform domestic and diplomatic relations, and its formulation of categories and standardized practice to get "a handle on its subjects" mirrors and records the state's broader project of regulating its citizenry and conducting foreign relations.[20] Foucault notes that the version of history created at the moment of the consolidation of the nation-state assembled a past that privileged the present, and I would argue that perhaps even more interesting is the way in which the classification froze that present and organized the future. We continue to build upon and expand that structure that reinforces and further embeds the divisions set forth 115 years ago. Imagined as exemplary of the Enlightenment ideal of a rational classification, the system confirms the universality of the state, unifying divisions of knowledge within this massive cultural institution. As this system was designed at the dawn of the twentieth century, it reflected not only the literature of the time but also the librarians' interpretations of that literature and the strivings of officers of the state. While it is important to situate the formation of the classification in the Progressive Era in the United States, it is equally important to consider the ways in which this point of view is reproduced over space and time and how this system figures into knowledge organization in the twenty-first century. It is necessary to consider how aspirations to uniformity have been part of a larger project intended to shape and monitor a citizenry, as well as how they have been an instrument of imperialism and domination, within and outside of the United States.

Diagramming the Library — "A Map of Destiny"

Discipline, according to Foucault, begins with the deployment of technologies to distribute individuals in space, or, in Jean-Luc Nancy's terms, a *"techne* of the creation of bodies."[21] The purposes of such mechanisms are to control and identify individuals most efficiently by transforming "the confused, useless or dangerous multitudes into ordered multiplicities."[22] First among these techniques is enclosure, "the protected place of disciplinary monotony."[23] Libraries, whether enclosed by walls or other restrictive measures, function to close off a protected space for the books.[24] But for discipline to operate, enclosure is not a constant or indispensable requirement. Rather, the cornerstone for disciplinary control is the act of partitioning: "Each individual has his own place; and each place its individual."[25] The purposes of partitioning a disciplinary space are many, including the provision of assessing, locating, knowing, and mastering individuals, and preventing their "diffuse circulation."[26] Partitioning also ensures that bodies are brought together in the most useful ways and prevents a dangerous mixing of types or ideas. What matters most for disciplinary power to work, though, is that each body is defined by its rank—"the place one occupies in a classification, the point at which a line and a column intersect."[27] Disciplinary classifications, in Foucault's view, distribute and derive as many uses as possible from the multiplicity of bodies by describing and analyzing individuals but also by ordering them within a collective body politic.

The operations involved in classifying perversion in the library are so layered and complex that it becomes next to impossible to comprehend the mechanisms and their effects without sitting down with maps and building designs and diagrams of bookshelves and networks, all with an eye toward the relations of power through which they are constructed and function and the configurations and conversations they make possible. Foucault admitted (after some resistance to his geographer interviewer) that geography is at the heart of his questions—he said that it acts as "the condition of possibility for the passage between a series of factors I tried to relate."[28] Not only are metaphors of territory and domains critical to Foucault's and my questions, but our analyses absolutely rely upon the conceptualization of power relations as the dispersal of knowledge and subjects over space.

To understand the mechanisms and reach of the classification, I rely on images in the forms of maps, diagrams, photographs, and drawings to illustrate the ways in which the Library of Congress, by constructing an assemblage of statements about sexual perversion, has produced peculiar bodies of literature. I lean on Foucault and Deleuze for guidance in displaying the social fields as drawn out by the classification by conceptualizing it as a diagram. For both Foucault and Deleuze, the diagram illustrates how lines cross through time and space and institutions and categories, all composing and providing the scaffolding that constitute and sustain power relations. The diagram is never complete and is always unstable and evolving, producing a model of truth. It is "a map of destiny" laying out the relations of forces and the possibilities for becoming.[29] Understanding a classification as a diagram that maps out possibilities for what bodies of literature can become helps us dismantle the illusions of disciplinarity.

Deleuze locates a critical distinction between discursive and nondiscursive formations in Foucault's *Discipline and Punish*, where the discursive elements involve statements and the nondiscursive has to do with environment. The environment and the statements speak back to one another, making the other possible. Or as Michel de Certeau might put it, the classificatory apparatus is needed to write the law onto bodies, to make those bodies "demonstrate the rule," transforming individual bodies into a body politic. A series of apparatuses works in concert to organize a social space by both separating and linking bodies and texts. By following the rule of law, bodies then demonstrate and reproduce the rule in an "epistemologico-juridical formation."[30] In the case of the library, we would speak of the books, the statements about the books, and the library architecture and space. The books on the shelves, arranged according to the classification system, demonstrate the rule, supplying the proof that it applies. The law is set by the disciplinary norms; the apparatus is the classification; the body is the corpus of books. The library environment provides the very public reproductive space for norms and deviations. The classification serves as a rulebook for librarians to follow, designating how a knowledge can be organized: "To tell the truth, they become bodies only by conforming to these codes."[31]

To classify is to make a statement. A library arranged according to a classification system is a series of statements: "___ book is about ___," and "___ belongs to ___ discipline," ad infinitum. The space, or environment, is defined by architectures, of which there are many in the library. Understood as an "ensemble of frames, vectors, and abstract lines," the function of architecture is connection.[32] The organization of the library building, the lines of library shelves, the information architecture that enables findability in the catalog and on the web, and the networks that connect libraries to one another and the public are each diagrammable. The map allows us to see "how we spatially organize our surrounding space and, by extension, how we organize our thoughts. . . . The map should be perceived as lines and traits that connect the mental landscape to the outside world in an interweaving network."[33] It also reveals the possibilities for encounters between books and their readers through the articulation and distribution of the various dispositions and linkages of power in the economy that gives it its force.[34]

One can diagram the Library of Congress Classification in a variety of ways, as there are seemingly endless angles from which to analyze it: its architecture—the hierarchies and lines; the collections it organizes; the time period during which it was created; its purpose; its uses—past, present and future; its technologies; the laws, codes, and notations through which the classification is comprised and articulated. To apprehend the extent and implications of the intermingling of forces and functions, one has to account for both the space and the statements. We might begin at the center of the Library of Congress Main Reading Room—the circulation desk, occupied by the librarian, who keeps watch over the reading room, where patrons place requests, ask questions, and put the machine into action. LoC patrons have always requested books at the reference or circulation desk, or "issuing desk," as it was called in 1900 (today requests can also be made online). A request sends a series of library workers on a quest to locate the desired book and present it to the reader. Behind the scenes are an astonishing 838 miles of bookshelves, holding a total of 36 million books and print materials of various forms.[35] The newer buildings—the Madison and Adams buildings—are connected to the Jefferson Building through underground tunnels, as is the nation's Capitol, and a number of facilities house materials offsite.

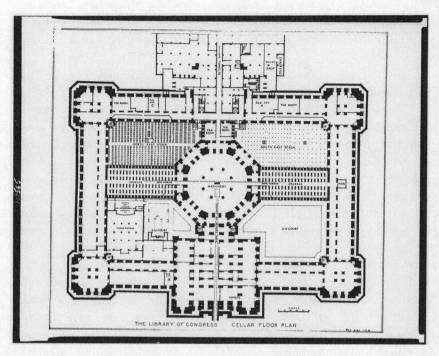

Figure 13. Library of Congress. Alterations to the Library of Congress, Thomas Jeffer-
son Building, Washington, D.C. Cellar floor plan. *Source*: Library of Congress Prints and
Photographs Division (Washington, D.C.: Library of Congress). Reproduction number:
LC-USZ62–109565. http://www.loc.gov/pictures/item/2002719566/.

Figure 13 is a representation of the Library of Congress's cellar floor as
drafted in an architectural plan. The reading room floor above this shares
the same basic outlines, with the seat of authority at the center, surrounded
by the books and patrons. Libraries of virtually all sizes and shapes imitate
the panoptic design of the Library of Congress, as they map knowledge
in nearly identical sequences along their shelves. Large universities will
have multiple library buildings specializing in particular disciplines spread
across campuses, and variations on floor plans abound. Still, the critical
disciplinary mechanism at work is the Library of Congress Classification,
which structures the possibilities for assigning works to a location. More
important, though, is how these architectures delimit and support the relationships among cataloged works. The diagram is repeated across localities, with some variation in form and content. In function, however, these
replications of the abstract machine organize and discipline knowledge,
operating as sites in the network where normative sexualities are distrib-

uted to the public. They are in every sense local extensions of the state and cultural apparatus.

Bibliographic classifications, subject headings, other classificatory techniques, and their attendant/enabling technologies operate in concert, by way of particularly insidious architectures that reside beneath the hood of the library catalog at the level of the database, and these techniques also govern how the books are displayed to the eye. The panoptic eye is simultaneously inside the system, disciplining and correcting subjects and seeing to it that authority headings and classes are in control, and outside looking in. Although the authority records do not perform the surveillance function in the way that algorithms and big data on the web do, authority control is happening at a series of levels, from inside the catalog, in the cataloging department, and at the Library of Congress, where the classifications and terms are designed and decided upon by the Policy and Standards Office. And though the control happens at every local point, the overarching control mechanism is far from localized: This function is repeated worldwide, and every instance is connected to the other through library networks. Standards ensure continuity across every system, but their deployment may vary from library to library, as each has its own multiplicity—its own collection, its own lines of shelves, its own purposes for which decisions about where to place materials may happen on a book-by-book basis. In other words, "among the discursive elements there are also whole families or formations of statements, whose catalogue is open-ended and subject to constant change."[36] The overall effect is to enforce equivalent statements about social norms through a vast network of knowledge organization systems.

A single catalog record is distributed and copied across a gigantic library network called WorldCat. The 72,000 member libraries can download to local systems complete catalog records produced by other member libraries. As of January 2016, WorldCat contained over 360 million records in 485 different languages.[37] In 2012, the number of LoC-produced records in the WorldCat database was over 11 million, and although the number of libraries using LCSH or LC Classification is impossible to know, we do know that they (along with the Dewey Decimal System) are the most widespread subject standards in libraries across the globe. The Library of Congress's Linked Data service is expanding the possibilities for adopting LCSH, LCC, and other standards. It is by way of this vastly powerful machine that the possibilities drawn by the Library of Congress are replicated across U.S. libraries and beyond.[38]

Diagramming Perversion

Gayle Rubin vividly diagrammed a "sex hierarchy" in her 1984 essay "Thinking Sex," drawing for her readers the lines and degrees between normal/natural/good sex and abnormal/unnatural/bad sex.[39] Inspired by her technique, this section will illustrate how libraries draw similar lines. To show how language maps onto the geography of the library, I have graphed the locations of books with the heading "Paraphilias," according to when they were published (Figure 14). The HQs are well represented, with most books in the HQ71s but books also distributed across the library—in BF (Psychology), HV (Social pathology), K (Law), P (Language and literature), and R (Medicine). I also draw attention to the temporal aspects of this graph. Some classes are only assigned to works on this subject during specific decades, some are fairly consistently assigned through the decades, and others come and go. For the rest of the chapter, I will focus on HQ71 as this is, in fact, the class designated for paraphilias, but it is important to note that perversion is distributed across various sections of the library.

The photograph in Figure 15 shows a line of books in the HQ71 section of the William T. Young Library at the University of Kentucky, but it could easily be a photograph of the HQ71 section of any research library in the United States. This single photo displays a small segment of a shelf arrangement, but it provides a wealth of information about the regulation of sexual deviance in libraries.

The first thing one probably notices is the titles stamped on the spines, with those in the sharpest contrast standing out among the rest: Roudinesco's *Our Dark Side* certainly catches the eye, as does Rosewarne's *Part-Time Perverts* (two of the books described in Chapter 1 as being ones that actively resist medical language). Upon closer examination, you will notice that *Our Dark Side* and *Part-Time Perverts* are nestled between books on child sexual abuse and incest, which sit between two copies of *Problems of Sex Behavior*.[40] A bit farther down is a book that actually includes the term "paraphilias" in the title—with wavy script, perhaps to signify disorientation or deviance—conjoined with sex crimes. Even from the titles we glean a variety of perspectives on sexual "deviance," including Rosewarne's reclaiming of "perverts," the associations across problems and crime and child molesters, the use of the terms "deviance" and "paraphilias," and the elusive "dark side."

What may be less obvious from this view of the static positioning of books is the intermingling of temporalities. *Problems of Sex Behavior* was

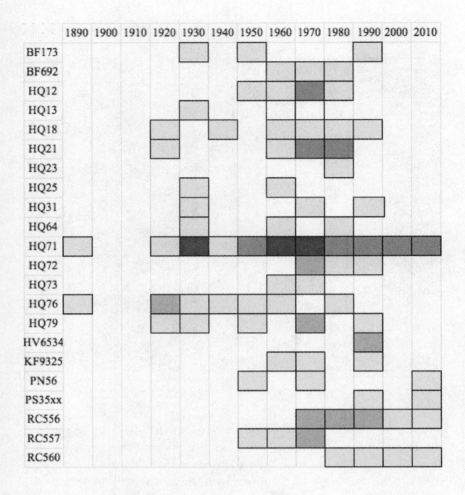

Key: number of books

☐ 1-5 ▨ 6-10 ■ 11-15

Key to subjects (as defined in the year 2014):

BF173—Psychoanalysis.
BF692—Psychology of sex. Sexual behavior.
HQ12—Human sexuality—History. Sex customs.
HQ13—Human sexuality—History. Sex customs—Ancient.
HQ18—Human sexuality—History. Sex customs—By region or country.
HQ21—Human sexuality—Sexual behavior and attitudes, 1801–
HQ23—Human sexuality—Sexual behavior and attitudes—General special.
HQ25—Human sexuality—Sexual behavior and attitudes—Curiosa.
HQ31—Sex instruction and sexual ethics—General.
HQ64—Sex instruction and sexual ethics—Other miscellaneous.

HQ71—Sexual practices outside of social norms. Paraphilias.
HQ72—Sexual practices outside of social norms. Paraphilias—By region or country.
HQ73—Sexual minorities.
HQ76—Gay men.
HQ79—Sadism. Masochism. Fetishism, etc.
HV6534—Social pathology. Criminology—Homicide, Murder, etc.
KF9325—Law—Sexual offenses.
PN56—Literature—Special topics.
PS35xx—American literature—Specific authors.
RC556—Internal medicine—Psychiatry—Sexual and psychosexual conditions.
RC557—Psychiatry—Sexual therapy.
RC560—Sexual and psychosexual conditions—Other special problems.

Figure 14. Books with "Paraphilias" as a subject heading, according to class and decade.

Figure 15. Section of shelving in the HQ71 section at the University of Kentucky.

published in 1968, two of the books were published in the 1980s, and the rest were issued more recently, in the twenty-first century. Other areas of the HQ71s include titles that date back to the nineteenth century, among which are texts that deal with inversion and homosexuality, and Krafft-Ebing's *Psychopathia Sexualis*. Attitudes from different eras are mixed with varying attitudes of the present, and all are lumped together in this section of the social sciences that was once called "Abnormal sex relations" and is currently defined as "Sexual practices outside of social norms. Paraphilias." The caption reflects the change in phrasing corresponding to the LC subject heading. The inclusion of the medical term "Paraphilias" to define a social science classification is problematic for a number of reasons, including those described in the previous chapters. The attitudes presented on the shelves derive not only from different temporal periods but from various disciplinary conventions. The classification reveals how the structure produces and controls certain subjectivities by attributing books to this singular category, reducing them to one particular vector of perversion.

One begins to understand this phenomenon through one of the foundational problems with the Library of Congress Classification: It relies on the myth of the possibility of a universal classification capable of organizing all bibliographic knowledge.[41] To be sure, at the Library of Congress, classifications were designed not for the entire bibliographic universe but for the knowledge held within the LoC's collection. But the language used by librarians indicates that they viewed it to be universal in scope and design, and the classification reflects this belief. Upon moving into the new building, deliberations began in 1897 to decide on the proper scheme for the LoC, and in 1901 Librarian of Congress Herbert Putnam gave the order to proceed with the Library of Congress Classification system, which remains the predominant classification among academic libraries.[42] J. C. M. Hanson was responsible for overseeing the creation of the Library of Congress Classification system, and his key contribution to the classification stemmed from his perception of the universe of subjects as a collection of specialized fields.[43] No overall logical principle of subject order was adopted, making it appear to be a conglomerate of smaller, more specialized classifications, with variations in logics and patterns. This broke with library tradition, as previous classifiers had tried to find a logical order inherent in the entire universe of subjects. Charles Cutter, for instance, had spoken of arranging subjects according to their "scientific relations."[44] Presently the Library of Congress system arranges all knowledge into twenty-one classes, each identified by a letter of the alphabet and subdivided by notations made of combinations of numbers and letters.

Hanson appointed subject specialists to create these discipline-specific systems, and he selected Roland P. Falkner, a statistician, to devise an early version of the H classification for the social sciences.[45] Prior to and after his appointment at the Library of Congress as director of the Division of Documents from 1900 to 1904, Falkner was a professor of statistics, statesman, and census taker. He was also editor of the *Annals of the American Academy of Political and Sociology*. While professor at the University of Pennsylvania he contributed to U.S. census sections on criminals and prisoners and compiled an 1890 *Statistics of Prisoners* from surveys he designed on the basis of categories he developed. He was also commissioner of education in Puerto Rico (1904–1907), chairman of the Commission of the United States to Liberia (1909), and a member of the Joint Land Commission of the United States and Panama (1913). In 1911 and 1912 he was assistant director of the Census Bureau.[46]

That the present H section of the LC Classification begins with Statistics (HA) and Economics (HB) is hardly a coincidence. Nor is the organization of subjects toward the end of the classification (HV), where we find criminals, people with disabilities, social welfare, and addiction. In

Falkner's original sketch there is no reference to sexuality at all, either in general specialties of Sociology or in "Classes of Persons," which is limited to "Blind and Deaf and Dumb"; "Feeble-minded"; "Indians"; "Criminals"; "Negroes, Freedmen"; and "Poor, The." Such categories resemble those in the census. In describing his method for devising a system for Economics, Falkner stated that the scheme should harmonize as much as possible "with the methods of presenting the subject which are familiar in academic work and which are followed somewhat by writers in general."[47] The classification does reflect much of the academic literature and how social scientists organized and understood its subjects, but more importantly, it reflects a nation as imagined by a census taker and agent of the state. The version printed in 1910 was worked over and expanded from Falkner's original draft by a number of Library of Congress catalog staff members.

The continued reduction of the human sciences to mathematics over the eighteenth and nineteenth centuries led to a particular form of population assessment and management—the statistical census, organized around various demographic categories, including race. Ian Hacking suggests that, although statistics itself is not a human science, its influence in determining norms within the social sciences has been "immense," as has its role as a "technology of power in a modern state."[48] Charging Falkner, a statistician, with the task of developing this classification supports Hacking's claim, and the placement of statistics in HA, at the front of the classification, signifies the primacy of statistics in social science research. As Benedict Anderson writes of the significance of census instruments of the late nineteenth century, it "was not in the *construction* of ethnic-racial classifications, but rather in their systematic *quantification*."[49] In fact, these observations speak directly to Anderson's thesis regarding the ways that the census, map, and museum "shaped the way in which the colonial state imagined its dominion."[50] We might substitute Anderson's museum with the broader concept of memory institution, a category to which libraries surely belong, and we can conclude that the ranking, ordering, and quantification of subjects across categories and mapped onto territories reflect and legitimate an imagined nation. The "fiction of the census"—that each individual can occupy one category—is certainly a problem of the bibliographic classification as well, and each illuminates the ways that the nation conceives of its domain.[51]

Initially, the printed version of the classification for the HQ section was quite simple, with rather broad categories (Figure 16). It is worth noting the insistence of the classification for "homosexuality" on the shelves and the concomitant absence of "homosexuality" as a subject heading in the

HQ   SOCIAL GROUPS: THE FAMILY. MARRIAGE   HQ

Abnormal sex relations.

71	General. Psychopathia sexualis, etc. Cf. RC 620.
73	Special. Woman.
76	Homosexuality.
79	Sadism, Masochism, Fetishism, etc.
	Prostitution.

Figure 16. LCC, 2nd ed., 1920. *Source*: Library of Congress (Washington, D.C.: Government Printing Office, 1920). https://catalog.hathitrust.org/Record/001163425.

catalog for the first half of the century. It is in this difference that we can begin to see the varying purposes of classifications and headings. Whereas headings are intended to foster accessibility by way of searching the catalog, the classification divides, sorts, and disciplines on the shelves. An absence of "homosexuality" in the catalog results in rendering the subject invisible, whereas the division on the shelves clearly delineates normal from abnormal and cuts the latter category further by specifying particular abnormalities. It marks a spatial difference, as well, as the abnormal is linearly subsequent to the normal, most likely on another shelf. Although classes have been added, the classification has changed little since its earliest inception. In fact the placement, notation, and wording used to define the class "Sadism. Masochism. Fetishism, etc." has remained unchanged since 1910. The text of the classification indicates Krafft-Ebing's *Psychopathia Sexualis* as exemplary of the types of materials that would be placed here. It seems reasonable to speculate that the Library of Congress would have drawn literary warrant for this structure from that and related works.

HQ73 was designated for the vaguely described class "Special. Woman" under the broader "Abnormal sex relations." One might surmise that inversion in women was shelved there, as well as other topics about perversion in women. Indeed, a variety of titles on women as sex criminals, perverts, and lesbians are housed in this section, even today. For example, the lesbian magazine *The Ladder*, first published in 1956, is there. The class was completely unused between the years 1974 and 2001, however, as the topic Lesbians was moved to HQ75 in the early 1970s, leaving the class intellectually empty for decades. HQ73 was renamed much later and is now home to works on "sexual minorities." The older works on "Special. Woman" assigned to HQ73 have not been shifted, so now the class is a mix of very outdated ideas about sexual perversion in women and much more recent works on sexual minorities, or what are commonly referred to as LGBTQ subjects. A perplexing mix of literature has accumulated in this section, with such titles as *Female Sex Perversion* (1935) and *Woman as a Sexual Criminal* (1934) sitting alongside *Positive View of LGBTQ: Embracing Identity and Cultivating Well-Being* (2012) and *That's So Gay: Microaggressions and the Lesbian, Gay, Bisexual, and Transgender Community* (2013). To add more confusion, some early works on sexual relations between women were shelved with the broader HQ71 or HQ76, and there they remain. One work on lesbians is still classed as HQ76, the former class for homosexuality and current class for gay men. And referring back to the graph in Figure 14 we see that a small number of texts assigned the heading "Paraphilias" were classed in HQ73 in the 1960s and 1970s, indicating that as late as the 1970s these classes were associated with sexual deviation and perversion.

In 1972, at the same time that the subject heading "Homosexuality" was removed from "Sexual deviation" (as shown in Chapter 1), librarians were also calling for a removal of "Homosexuality" as a hierarchically related term in the Library of Congress Classification system. The caption for the LC class HQ71 had been changed from "Abnormal sex relations" to "Sexual deviation" in 1966, and the indentation of the printed classification was changed in 1972 so that homosexuality aligned with but was not hierarchically under "Sexual deviation." This speaks directly to Mary K. D. Pietris's correspondence in the Introduction, in which she claims that the current placement of items on the shelves is simply an accident of classification. Homosexuality was classed under abnormal sex relations, right along with sex crimes. Removing the hierarchical relationship from the classification system did not change the arrangement of books on the shelves, and the legacy of the previous arrangement is not wiped away by changing the indentation in the printed classification. It is no accident that books on lesbians and gays are classed adjacent to HQ71. In fact, especially before 1946 but even into the 1980s, some materials about gays and lesbians were classed in the HQ71s and neighboring classes. Again, this pattern is repeated throughout libraries. A case in point is the placement of *Gayspeak* (Pilgrim Press, 1981), a book about communication styles of gays and lesbians, shelved between books on child molestation and sex abuse in HQ72, which is essentially an expansion of the HQ71 section.

When you peruse the HQ71 and HQ72 sections of a research library, you are likely to find shelves lined mostly with texts on child molestation, incest, and sex crimes; historical volumes on sexual perversion and inversion; and a few more recent titles on what some might consider perversions today—sadism, masochism, fetishism, and so. In the adjoining HQ73, HQ74, HQ75, and HQ76 sections, we find books on bisexuality, lesbians, homosexuality, and gay men. How did things come to be arranged the way they are? Some of this is a matter of history playing out on the shelves, and some of it is simply bad cataloging (as in the placement of biblical teachings about the sin of premarital sex in this category), but all of it is an illustration of inconsistently shifting American attitudes toward sexual perversion over the past 115 years. While it may be alarming and troubling to some patrons, it is no mistake that consensual practices like sadism, masochism, and kink sit beside criminal offenses, including the sexual abuse of children and rape. Nor is it an accident that homosexuality is a neighboring class residing just down the shelf.

The fundamental structure of the classification remains the same as the original, with new classes added and some removed. The content of the statements change over time, as do the terms used to define the classes. It has not always been the case that materials on sex crimes were placed within the category "Abnormal sex relations." This has something to do with the literature published on sexual perversion and sex crimes. When the classification was initially printed in 1910, there was no accounting for sex crimes within the classification.[52] There was, however, a cross-reference from HQ71 to RC620, enacting a relationship with medicine. RC620 was designated as "Moral insanity," citing *Psychopathia Sexualis* again as an example. Today that class is reserved for materials on nutritional diseases, but a smattering of titles on sexuality remain there, out of place and time.

It was not until the third edition of the H Classification, printed in 1950, that sex crimes entered the classification, under HQ71 and HQ72. Thirty years had passed between the publication of the second and third editions of the H Classification, so changes in nomenclature and class assignments are to be expected. But the marked indication that "Sex crimes" are to be classed with HQ71 and HQ72 beginning in 1950 is a clear reflection of the societal association between sexual perversion and criminal acts, reflecting the moral panic surrounding perversion stirred by J. Edgar Hoover in the mid-1930s and continued by Joseph McCarthy in the postwar era. The association between sex crimes and perversion was ostensibly removed again in 2007 when the "See also" reference from the Social pathology/Criminology section was removed. Nevertheless, as the photograph in Figure 3.6 so clearly shows, a majority of books in the HQ71 section are about incest, child abuse, and other sex crimes, and despite the removal of sex crimes from the actual hierarchy, catalogers have continued to place works on child abuse and incest here. A more appropriate fit for works on victims of incest might be R560.I53, designated for psychosexual conditions of incest victims. For criminal aspects of the topic, books would go into HV6570.6, specifically intended to hold books on "Incest. Sexual abuse of children" within the broader class of sex crimes. What we read in the HQ71 section is a series of statements regarding the relationships and equivalencies among perverse subjects.

This association between crime and perversion gained attention around 1937 when J. Edgar Hoover, director of the FBI, declared a "War on the Sex Criminal." In fact, the *New York Times* created the index category "Sex Crimes" to describe the 143 articles it published on the subject that year.[53] The growing climate of postwar homophobia, the fear of conspiracies and infiltration of uncontrolled sex perversion, led to the passage of laws to police perverted acts, and in 1947 Hoover stated that the most rapidly increasing type of criminals were degenerate sex offenders.[54] Estelle Freedman writes: "Each of the two major sex crime panics—roughly from 1937 to 1940 and from 1949 to 1955—originated when, after a series of brutal and apparently sexually motivated child murders major urban newspapers expanded and, in some cases, sensationalized their coverage of child molestation and rape."[55] She also notes that the literature published in and between these periods mapped out two new forbidden boundaries for men: sex with children or with other men. And she speculates that the increased attention to child molestation and homosexuality, along with the overlapping use of the terms like sex criminal, pervert, and psychopath, served as a sort of code for homosexuality.[56] According to Freedman, sexual psychopath laws did not "differentiate between violent and nonviolent or consensual and nonconsensual behaviors. Rather, they targeted a kind of personality, or an identity, that could be discovered only by trained psychiatrists. . . . The laws rested on the premise that even minor offenders (such as exhibitionists), if psychopaths, posed the threat of potential sexual violence."[57] From the 1930s through the 1950s, the sexual psychopath provided the focus for public discussions of sexual normality and abnormality, and the state played an increasingly important role in defining sexual deviance and in prescribing psychiatric treatment. The debates on the psychopath statutes did more than expand the legal authority of psychiatry; they also expanded the conversation and fears about sexual deviance to a wider public. The creation of the term "Homosexuality" in the subject headings just after World War II also coincides with the homosexual panic and the changes in the bibliographic classification.

Indeed, perversion lurks across the library in far more areas than one might expect, with a spread from the confines of the HQs into other disciplines beginning in the second half of the twentieth century. Postwar-era books mirrored the panic surrounding the preoccupation with subversive sexual behavior, and as homosexuality was considered among the most dangerous of the perversions, most of the literature from this time focuses on identifying and treating homosexuals.[58] For example, Paul De River's 1950 *Sexual Criminal* is a graphic account of sex crimes in the United States, complete with shocking photographs of murder and rape victims, including children. Aimed at criminal justice professionals, the book provides a telling glimpse of the perceptions and aims of law enforcement by placing homosexuals in the same category as murderers and rapists. In his introduction to the text, attorney Eugene D. Williams calls readers to take precautions against "sex perverts":

> Sex perversion, of course, includes many types which manifest themselves in the form of homosexuality, exhibitionism, and so on down the categories, until we reach the dangerous sadomasochist whose frequent terminal outbursts direct the attention of the world to the fact that sex perverts do exist.[59]

Williams cautions readers against thinking that perverts, including homosexuals, are harmless and argues that they pose a particular danger to young people. The introduction seems to imply that every homosexual should be considered dangerous and likely to commit violent crimes. This attitude was common, and it circulated widely in printed books and other media, supporting J. Edgar Hoover's fear-mongering and war against sexual perverts.

The Library of Congress Classification reproduced those fears by drawing lines between normal and perverse and directly associating the perverse with crime, and as the shelves were never reordered, these time-sensitive norms remain on display. Today, however, in addition to these texts are more recent ones that challenge normative notions of sexual perversion, and just by reading the spines and the catalog, we witness the changing debate surrounding definitions and attitudes about deviance, with overlapping and fuzzy lines of temporalities and boundaries between consent, violence, crime, perversion, pleasure, and freedom.

Strangely enough, investigating the development of the classification of abnormal sexual relations in the years 2013–2016 turned out to be a genealogy of blurred lines and shades of gray.[60] I am referring specifically to the ways in which two exceedingly popular cultural texts mirror the discursive statements on library shelves, as the Library of Congress Classification, which is ostensibly meant to erase such gray areas, enacts a similar tension on the shelves. Its disciplinary cuts place multiple forms and expressions of sexual variance—criminal and noncriminal—into one category. In HQ71 there is no difference between incest, pedophilia, rape, and kink. Being largely invisible to the general public in their effects, classification systems reproduce particular ways of knowing. Such systems are embedded not only in our libraries but also in our technologies for finding information on the Internet, websites, and databases of all kinds. Notions of normal and abnormal are circulated and repeated across various sites of popular culture, the academy, and institutions, reinforcing dominant attitudes and ideas.

Libraries are part of the entire network of discourses that Foucault talks about, which collectively repeat and reproduce dominant norms. Variations of these types of associations that I have identified persist in online technologies, with some still carrying messages that gay is dangerous. In 2009 Amazon.com infuriated LGBTQ people when they discovered that Amazon was categorizing books on LGBTQ subjects as "Adult," thereby rendering them invisible from sales ranks. On the list of "adult" books were titles such as Ellen DeGeneres's and Melissa Etheridge's biographies, Lesléa Newman's *Heather Has Two Mommies* (Alyson Wonderland, 1989), and Linas Alsenas's *Gay America: Struggle for Equality* (Amulet, 2008).[61] Even more troubling was the recommendation of sex offender apps for those who use and purchase Grindr, a mobile social application for gay men—implying that, if you like sex with gay men you might also be interested in sex offenders.[62] Google has also been exposed for censoring terms, as it blocks certain words from its autocomplete and Instant Search features so users cannot automatically see suggestions for resources or search terms on the topic. It's not that one can't retrieve resources, but they don't make it as easy as searching for other topics. "BDSM" is blocked, and even "bisexual" has been blocked to a certain extent. The *Huffington Post* reported in 2013 that, after a series of inquiries, Google unblocked the term, but for a number of months after that a search revealed that when you begin to type in "bisexual," no suggestions were offered. When I searched in January 2016, "Bisexual women," "Bisexual flag," "Bisexual definition," and "Bisexual quiz" were suggested. "Bisexuality" triggered the same suggestions. How decisions to block and control terms are made is unknown to the general public, as are the search engines' proprietary algorithms that generate the associations between search terms, but the question of who and why is less relevant to this discussion than the questions related to how all of these technologies and techniques coordinate to produce normative sexualities through categories and spatial sorting mechanisms.

Library classifications, globally distributed to a huge array of publics, are integral to this vast network of state and nonstate, public and private actors and institutions. Indeed, Ann Laura Stoler finds one of the most significant themes of Foucault's *Society Must Be Defended* lectures to be that it offers "an appreciation of historiography as a political force, of history writing as a political act, of historical narrative as a tool of the state and as a subversive weapon against it."[63] The Library of Congress played a key role in organizing and producing certain truths about sexuality and perversion. The hope is that unmasking the political agendas underlying the organization of subjects will open up possibilities for understanding how the LC Classification shapes the ways that we do history and acquire and create knowledge as well as ways that we can reconfigure library, history, and archival practices.

CHAPTER 4

Aberrations in the Catalog

> We dream of a library of literature created by everyone
> and belonging to no one, a library that is immortal and will
> mysteriously lend order to the universe, and yet we know
> that every orderly choice, every catalogued realm of the
> imagination, sets up a tyrannical hierarchy of exclusion.
>
> —ALBERTO MANGUEL, *The Library at Night*

Roderick A. Ferguson's *Aberrations in Black: Toward a Queer of Color Critique* (2003) is shelved at PS374.N4, just paces away from Sedgwick's *Epistemology of the Closet*. An important distinction between the two books' class assignments resides at the level of "special topics" within American literature. *Epistemology of the Closet* is assigned to PS374.H63, with the "H" standing for "homosexuality"; the "N" in the class for *Aberrations in Black* serves as shorthand for "Negro." As with all bodies of literature in the library, those that have grown in this and associated locations have particular histories.

I cite Ferguson's text not because its classification is exemplary (as we will see, it is, in fact, exceptional) but because his account of the necessity of a queer-of-color critique directly confronts one of the core challenges I encountered in conducting this research. I had originally written a manuscript that bore a near absence of discussions of race, and Ferguson's queer-of-color critique of canonical sociology brings to light some of the processes by which my own work was unwittingly participating in the reproduction of a particular version of the history of sexuality, one that left various dimensions unaccounted for. The history of the canonization of scholarship includes the history of the Library of Congress classificatory devices. The extensions of margins out from assumed and unmarked norms impede multidimensional analyses, and to gain a full understanding of the ways in which the classification functions, one has to cruise outside the confines of singular subjects.

Expanding upon the previous chapter, which mapped sexual perversion in the library, this chapter offers a critical geography of racialized queer subjects. Indeed, *cruising the library* is the only way to obtain books that address the intersectionality and complexity of sexuality and subjectivities, and such a technique also brings the limitations of the classification into full view. One has to venture away from the HQ section and visit other parts of the library, as the associations drawn up in the catalog and on the shelves cannot account for multiplicities of subjectivities and are unlikely to match one's own identifications with the works. I begin with a discussion of the cataloging of Ferguson's text and of how Ferguson's approach informs a critique of the Library of Congress Classification's universalisms and disciplinary divisions. I then examine the classes designated for the books described in the catalog as being about "African American gays" and the treatment of African Americans as a "special" topic in a range of disciplines. The analysis reveals the instrumentality of the Library of Congress and its classification system in the production and reproduction of ideas about race, gender, nation, and citizenship in the history of the United States and in continued projects in nation building and imperialism. I seek to understand the truth and consequences of Affonso Romano de Sant'Anna's suggestion that "libraries, especially national libraries, constitute what are known in the sciences as 'reduced models' of their country's social reality and ideological complexity."[1]

Cataloging Aberrations in Black

First, let us take a closer look at Ferguson's book. His prefatory remarks begin with a vivid description of a photograph housed at (of all places!) the Library of Congress. The photo was part of an exhibition about the history of the African American quest for citizenship, and, as Ferguson explains, it depicts four African American men waiting outside a railroad employment office, with signs behind them that read "Colored Waiting Room" and "Colored men." What is notable for Ferguson is the way in which the photograph figures particular faces in the history of exclusion of African Americans, thereby circulating a canonical sociological rendering of African American history. The picture elicits questions for Ferguson, some of which have to do with the positioning of the photograph in a national

exhibit, its location in a government archive, and the terms by which the
photo is deployed as representative of a moment in history in terms of liberal capital. Ferguson's overarching question is: "How do we speak of the
picture as part of a dialogical and polymorphous network of perversions
that contradicted notions of decency and American citizenship?"[2]

Ferguson recalls from memory the railroad station in the picture, as it
is located near his childhood home, and he notes important absences in the
photo (Figure 17):

> I know as well that there are subjects missing who should be accounted
> for—the transgendered man who wore Levis and a baseball cap and
> chewed tobacco; the men with long permed hair who tickled piano
> keys; the sissies and bulldaggers who taught the neighborhood children
> to say their speeches on Easter Sunday morning.[3]

Looking beyond the photograph to the catalog record by which it is in-
ventoried and made accessible, we witness more exclusions and regula-

Figure 17. Railroad station, Manchester, Ga., 1938. Photo: John Vachon. *Source*: LC-USF
3301–001172-M4, Library of Congress, Prints and Photographs Division Washington,
D.C. http://www.loc.gov/pictures/item/fsa1997003449/PP/.

tions. The image can be found in the LoC's digital library and belongs to the Farm Security Administration/Office of War Information Collection. Three headings by which to access the photograph have been assigned: "Segregation," "United States—Georgia—Manchester," and "Cities, towns—Georgia."[4] These headings are not from the Library of Congress Subject Headings discussed in the first chapter but are part of a nomenclature called the Library of Congress Thesaurus for Graphic Materials—a list of headings specifically created for images. It is a limited list, which, as a matter of policy, does not include headings for racial, ethnic, or social groups or organizations.[5] Any mention of race is veiled—it is only to be implied by "Segregation." Images in the Library of Congress's huge collection of photographs cannot be retrieved or found by way of subject headings that describe race or ethnicity.

Extending this line of analysis to the cataloging of Ferguson's book, we trace more silences. In spite of his explicit aim to bring visibility to subjects who have been effaced, beginning with the drag queen prostitute portrayed in Marlon Riggs's *Tongues Untied*, the catalog record does very little to bring noncanonical subjects into view. The headings are many and include the names of Richard Wright, James Baldwin, Ralph Ellison, and Toni Morrison. They also include "Gays' writings, American," "Gays in literature," and "African American gays—Intellectual life." But there is nothing in the record about drag or trans or lesbians (and certainly not trans or lesbian African Americans), although significant portions of the book are devoted to these topics. There are no references to Marx or Marxism, nor to sociology, despite that one could quite easily describe the book as a project in queer-of-coloring the sociological canon. At the time the book was published, the heading "Queer theory" had not yet been authorized, and it still remains absent from the LoC's catalog record for the book.

We might make some guesses as to where Ferguson would place his own book, but we'll find that this game necessarily leaves us unsatisfied. *Aberrations in Black* is currently shelved with books on African American literature, but it could easily fit with the section that includes more than ten thousand books on African Americans in the E section on U.S. history, sexuality in the HQs, or other sections of sociology or literary studies. It would be a good shelf companion for *Epistemology of the Closet*, in fact. The problem with the classification of *Aberrations in Black* is not merely a case of disciplinarity but of subject formation through certain processes of exclusion and marking and the singularity of particular spaces in the classification. Indeed, bodies of literature have been assembled into a body politic in the library and fit into spaces within a vast heteropatriarchal classification.

Aberrations in Black demonstrates not the rule but rather how the combinatory effect of sexuality and blackness and a queer-of-color critique provides an opportunity for a thicker analysis of the failures of universality. The book is shelved at PS374.N4, with other books on African American literature. This is the only book in this location that has been cataloged with the heading "African American gays." While the book shares certain common themes about blackness with its shelfmates, conversations and connections with books about queer authors and literature are suppressed. Surely, there are other books on James Baldwin or others that would speak to Ferguson's queer-of-color analysis, but that relationship is not expressed in the cataloging, and the effect of classification is to put distance between related texts. It turns out that the book is, in fact, an aberration in cataloging, as the vast majority of books that have been assigned the subject heading "African American gays" are organized according to their sexual deviation rather than their racial difference.

The book cannot be at more than one place at once, however, and here the necessity of the demarcation of discrete subjects becomes painfully apparent. The division into subjects is fundamentally problematic and always presents a challenge to catalogers and seekers of texts, but it also illustrates quite vividly a paradox central to discussions about subjectivity and access. Various markings in subjects are added so as to make works accessible via the catalog, but each is created through different kinds of power, possesses a different history, and derives from different mechanisms with their own particular regulatory schemas. In the case of library classifications, we can read these dimensions as part of a national history. The analysis of the various classes devised by the Library of Congress provides a window into the essentializing histories and regulatory mechanisms enacted on subjects: Various parts of the E section account for the history of racial, ethnic, and religious groups in the United States; the HVs house the history of social pathology; the HQs contain the histories of women, family, and sexuality. The classification presents these subjects as unified within discrete categories, as if these histories are separable and distinct. As Wendy Brown explains, however, the various kinds of powers "do not operate on and through us independently, or linearly, or cumulatively, and they cannot be radically extricated from one another in any particular historical formation."[6] The Library of Congress Classification divides the bibliographic universe into subjects in relation to heteropatriarchal norms, rendering certain subjects illegible or invisible or at the margins within this "universal" bibliographic classification. Analysis calls notice to exclusions and silences, the display of discourses that have attained the status of being knowledges worth authorizing, and the privileging of certain disciplines over others. Library classifications cannot adequately account for the complexities of subject formation, and although we know that race, class, gender, sexuality, able-bodiedness, colonialism, and religion are interwoven into subjects and subjectivities, a classification can only recognize one of these dimensions at a time, sometimes writing in another dimension in the form of a subdivision, but always locating only one position at a time on the shelf.

While Ferguson observes the disciplinary machinery at work in the history of sexuality and race, he does not locate the Library of Congress as a critical site in the network of apparatuses and institutions. Rather, it seems to be taken for granted that the LoC would house the photograph of the men at the railroad station, and the role of the LoC in circulating not only the photograph but also the infrastructure for maintaining and administering the machinery are overlooked. Materials found at the LoC are often used as examples—entry points into scholarly conversations, but little regard is paid to the library itself. In his more recent book, *The Reorder of Things*, Ferguson situates the American academy as central to setting the archival agenda of the state and capital by way of the disciplines, which incorporate certain minority subjects into a neoliberal order and exclude others. Ferguson's readers confront difficult questions about the academy, as he frankly and persuasively explains certain limits to ethnic studies and women's studies in the context of neoliberalism. He very effectively describes the United States as "the archival nation par excellence" and refers to an ensemble of institutions and techniques that have given rise to the emergence of the academy as the "model of archtonic power," but again, the Library of Congress and academic libraries in American universities are not figured as part of that ensemble.[7]

I attribute the relative absence of critical scholarship about the institutional practices of the Library of Congress to a certain invisibility of the classificatory mechanisms and to a faith in the benevolence of libraries as protectors of knowledge. Nicholson Baker has suggested a similar notion in his assessment of the LoC's preservation techniques: "It is a strangely secretive place, underscrutinized by comparison with other federal bureaucracies, its maladministration undetected by virtue of its reputation as an ark of culture. The library has gone astray partly because we trusted the librarians so completely."[8] Bowker and Star have argued that the invisibility and naturalization of classificatory infrastructures makes them more potent and secures their ground.[9] As they become entrenched in information systems, it becomes more difficult to resist or change them. For these reasons, critique of the Library of Congress must foreground its role as a connector and support for the vast network of national, academic, political, economic, and cultural institutions and projects. It is incredibly important as a site that collects discourses from all disciplines and regions of the world, organizes them according to a universal system, and passes its standards along to a huge number of libraries and organizations. It must be pointed out that the definitions of the classes that I describe throughout this and the previous chapter are not readily visible to the public, but rather, they are written into the classification like a set of instructions to be used by librarians to assign books to classes. The hierarchies and labels are not likely to be encountered by anyone other than catalogers. I wish to make that hidden infrastructure visible so that we can read it as a historical document that illustrates how subjects are viewed in the eyes of this state institution and how the classification participates in epistemic violence and oppression.

Ferguson's queer-of-color critique provides a methodology for analyzing the ways in which "liberal ideology occludes the intersecting saliency of race, gender, sexuality, and class in forming social practices."[10] He argues that the universalization of heteropatriarchy has been produced and reinforced in sociology and in the state. Heteropatriarchy has served as a model for rehabilitation and regulation in the sociological canon, and sociological critiques of capital conveyed it as a site of pathologies and perversions through its production of surplus populations and imagining "African American culture as the site of polymorphous gender and sexual perversions."[11] African Americans, gay people, and other deviant subjects have stood in contrast to the ideal citizen. This helps us understand how the Library of Congress, by using the principle of literary warrant, would have created classifications that reflected and universalized the sociological and literary canons.

Recall from earlier chapters that the Library of Congress during the Progressive Era was imagined to be a universal library, and its classification was derived from Enlightenment-era classifications, with ties most specifically to a Baconian system. Theodor Adorno and Max Horkheimer identify classification as a primary technique of the Enlightenment's rationalization of dominance. For them, thinking has been abandoned to categories, mathematics, rationalism, and universalism. One of the mechanisms of universalism is the excision of incommensurability, or the erasure of subjects that don't conform to the dominant system.[12] Adorno goes so far as to suggest that this kind of universalism is violent and "has no substantial reality for human beings."[13] The divergence between the universal and the particular is at the heart of morality for Adorno. Judith Butler, reflecting on Adorno's conceptualization of universalisms, takes care to note that the problem is not with universality itself but rather in "an operation of universality that fails to be responsive to cultural particularity and fails to undergo a reformulation of itself in response to the social and cultural conditions it includes within its scope of applicability."[14] The universal is not always necessarily violent, but where universals produce norms, they have the power to install or disinstall recognizable subjects. The universalization of heteropatriarchy plays out in our libraries and serves as the justification of the special treatment of subjects who deviate from a universal norm.

Cruising for "African American Gays"

Returning to the catalog record for *Aberrations in Black*, I turn our focus to one of the subject headings assigned to the book: "African American gays—Intellectual life." This heading provides a point of entry into a discussion of privilege and marginalization in the bibliographic classification. I searched the subject fields of the Library of Congress catalog with the keywords "African," "American," and "gays" to see where books described in these terms are located. My 2015 query resulted in eighty-eight unique titles that include all of these terms.[15] Of these, many are novels or poetry and are organized by author within a type of American literature. Forty-three are unique nonfiction titles, and what is immediately striking about their organization is that they are almost all filed according to sexuality before (or instead of) race. In fact, out of the forty-three titles, thirty-five (more than 80 percent) are shelved with books about homosexuality. Titles like *Black Like Us: A Century of Lesbian, Gay, and Bisexual African American Fiction* (2002/2012), *Black/Gay: The Harlem Renaissance, the Protest Era, and Constructions of Black Gay Identity in the 1980s and 90s* (2012), and *Queer Pollen: White Seduction, Black Male Homosexuality, and the Cinematic* (2011) are all shelved with homosexuality in various sections of American literature (as is *Epistemology of the Closet*). *Aberrations in Black* is a remarkable exception to this practice, as it is one of two books that are placed in a section on African American literature. The other is *Carry the Word: A Bibliography of Black LGBTQ Books*, by Steven G. Fullwood (2007).

The other class in which some of the books are placed is HQ76, designated for homosexuality within the social sciences. Here are titles such as *The Greatest Taboo: Homosexuality in Black Communities* (2001), *Homophobia in the Black Church: How Faith, Politics, and Fear Divide the Black Community* (2013), and *Nobody Is Supposed to Know: Black Sexuality on the Down Low*

(2014). A few of these books are assigned to a more specific category hierarchically embedded within homosexuality—HQ76.27.A37—the class designated for African Americans as one of a few "Special classes of gay people." This is the only place in the classification where "gay" and "African Americans" explicitly intersect.

A handful of books about "African American gays" have been placed in other locations, and each informs the story of the classification of African American gay subjects and an understanding of the logics of the library. For example, *Butch Queens up in Pumps: Gender, Performance, and Ballroom Culture in Detroit* is placed in GV1749.5—a section reserved for "Gay and lesbian dance parties, Including drag balls" within the topic "Recreation. Leisure." Here the dance or ball is the privileged subject, and the category of gay and lesbian dance parties is squeezed in with a range of other types of dances, such as "Mask and fancy-dress balls." It is refreshing to see this category driven by something other than an identity category, with the gay and lesbian dance parties operating simply as a type of party, rather than a special topic set apart from a norm. That class is far removed from other books on gender and drag, however, and in fact, there are only five books in the LoC collection shelved at this location. Indeed, most of the books on drag balls are shelved in HQ77 for transvestism. In both the HQ and GV sections, race is ignored completely with regard to this topic. These books can be about gay and lesbian dance parties, or drag, or transvestism, but they can't be about African American expressions of any of these.

In contrast, two titles on homosexuality and African American churches are placed in the B section (Philosophy, Psychology, Religion), this time driven by their association with theology or churches rather than with dance parties. Those books are both arranged into subtopics on African Americans, and the classification does not in any way offer representations of the topic of homosexuality in these spaces.

One book on "African American gays"—*Mind Your Own Life: The Journey Back to Love* (2011)—is placed in E185.97.A57—within a very large class reserved for African Americans as "Elements of the population" in U.S. history. This "Elements" category is defined as "Including racial, ethnic, and religious groups that have significance in the history of the U.S.," and the range of classes reserved for African Americans contains over ten thousand books. The division for the African American "element" is an exceptionally expansive section, which is divided into many topics about African Americans, including slavery, emancipation, rights, and biographies. This class is not subdivided into any category for gay African Americans, however.

Finally, four books include "AIDS" or "HIV" in the title. Three of these are in sections on public health or internal medicine. While one title in the medical section is produced by the Work Group on Health Care Access and seems to be well situated within the public health field in method, substance, and audience, the other two are arguably better placed with sociology or another area, as they are primarily about social, cultural, personal, and political aspects of HIV/AIDS. *My Rose: An African American Mother's Story of AIDS* (1997) offers a personal account, and *North Carolina and the Problem of AIDS: Advocacy, Politics, and Race in the South* (2011) deals with political and social issues surrounding HIV/AIDS, but both are medicalized by being placed in the R section of the library, reserved for books on medicine and public health. One title is shelved in HV1449.H58, a class whose place within a hierarchy is rather halting: "Social pathology. Social and public welfare. Criminology—Protection, assistance, and relief—Special classes—Gay men and lesbians." For each of these books on HIV/AIDS, the driving content for determining where the book is classed is the disease, meaning that they all are blatantly rendered socially or medically pathological in the stacks.

Now, having found ourselves in the HV class, we find that cruising this section brings into view the vastness of the field of subjects arranged within "Social pathology. Social and public welfare. Criminology." This class resembles the nineteenth-century census categories, a feature that is likely attributable in part to the fact that Roland Falkner, the original designer of the H classification, was also a census taker and statistician. HV is placed near the end of the H classification, with HA set for statistics, HB and HC economics, HD for industries, and so on. We see quite plainly how subjects determined to be pathological and criminal rank in relation to topics like economics and industry. The only class farther removed than HV is HX, defined as "Socialism. Communism. Anarchism." The HVs are home to subjects that were formerly named "Defectives" and "Degenerates," as well as to criminals, crimes, and prisons. Today the class "Defectives" has been renamed and includes topics related to people with disabilities. However, the hierarchies remain essentially the same, with added classes fitted in. For example, HV1568, a location that is likely to be familiar to any scholar working in disability studies, is found in this section. Again, the force of history has rendered the legacy of the rhetoric of dependence and inadequacy inescapable. While the caption for the subject class is presently "People with disabilities," in place of the former "Defectives," "Cripples," and "Imbeciles," the location within the broader class of social pathology on the margins of the social sciences sends troubling signals about attitudes toward the position of people with disabilities in relation to others. Emerging works in the humanities that critique such pathologizing associations are shelved here as well.[16]

Subcategories within the HVs are divided into all sorts of special classes, a phenomenon that began with the creation of the classification. In 1910, the scope of the category "Defectives" was defined as "General works on the blind, the deaf and dumb, the feeble-minded, and the insane." It was also subdivided by race, nationality, and occupation: "Seamen"; "Shop women, clerks, etc."; and "Other, A–Z". Next to "Defectives" were "Poor in cities," "Pauperism," and "Protection of animals." And following that was the class "Degeneration," which was divided into types of degeneration—physical, mental, and moral—as well as related issues and practices: "Inbreeding," "Sterilization," and "Child study." Next in the shelf arrangement were books on alcoholism and drugs, and then the section on criminology and prisons. It is in this section of the library that we see the disturbing intersections across histories of disability, race, and sexuality—all dimensions formerly defined and regulated in terms of degeneration. It is also in the HVs where books on eugenics reside, and so works on regulatory policy and practices would be conveniently shelved near books on "defective" and "degenerate" classes. The continued placement of all these materials within related ranges not only reminds us of that legacy, but it also suggests that these relationships still hold in the American imagination. With every item added, these ideas and norms are reproduced and further embedded, thereby contributing to systemic racism and anxieties.

The dizzying dispersal of books across disciplines serves as concrete evidence in support of Ferguson's claim about the canonization of both sociology and literary studies. In most cases, if blackness is visible at all in relation to homosexuality, it is as a subcategory—a "special class." Let us not forget that homosexuality is already on the margins, in a rather peculiar setting within a broader category defined by its deviance from a heteronormative universality. The erasure of race is not accidental but instead a repetition and reinforcement of the canon and of a particular kind of accommodation and folding of subjects into the archive. Where the classification is driven primarily by a topic like churches or dances, there is only one axis upon which the field can be subdivided, thereby erasing other axes. In those spaces, the national imagination is brought to bear, as we see the association of churches with African Americans and of drag with white. As Jasbir Puar would argue, this shows how cultural productions figure the sexual other as white and the racial other as straight.[17]

The fact that there is only one point in the classification where gays and African Americans intersect, "Special classes of gay people" at HQ76.27. A37, is worth pondering further. First, it is interesting that only six titles are shelved in this location, as of November 2016. Works that don't clearly belong to other disciplines or are determined to be sociological studies reside here. A book like *Aberrations in Black* isn't in this space because it has been classed in literary studies, for instance. What is perplexing about this class is the choice to privilege gayness, effectively relying on the order African American gays rather than gay African Americans, a label that might result in a placement as a subtopic of African Americans in E185.5. The label for this class, set within its entire hierarchical chain, is this: "The Family. Marriage. Woman—Human sexuality. Sex—Sexual minorities— Homosexuality. Lesbianism—Special classes of gay people, A–Z—African Americans." As with most classes subdivided into the final subtopic of African Americans, it is delineated as a special topic in a series of markings and erasures. The act of naming this special class brings a heightened visibility along with its marked removal in degrees from the universal norm. At the same time, it is rendered invisible to those seeking texts in the sections that house much larger bodies of literatures on African Americans. Even on the shelves in the HQ section, this particular grouping would be separated off from other texts in the more general HQ76. Linearly, it would follow that section. In contrast, the instructions indicate that we should look to the HVs for "Deaf gays," so that in that case "Gay" serves as a subtopic of "Deaf" over in the section for works on people with disabilities. There the disability is privileged, and the category is marked by sexual difference. The rabbit hole is tempting: One can easily get lost chasing down subjects and trying to make sense of it all.

With regard to the classification of books on "African American gays," I have arrived at a few possible explanations for choices that have been made regarding the HQ location. Wendy Brown's theory of how tolerance discourses play out, depending on the subject category in question, is instructive. According to Brown, in France, women have been talked about in terms of equality, whereas Jews are tolerated, and she argues that this is the result of particular histories playing out in ways that shape how difference is variously viewed by and incorporated into society. One explanation has to do with a distinction between private and public life. Questions of religion and nation and how to assimilate Jewish people into the fabric of French society resulted in making Jews as French as possible, disavowing their heritage and their Jewishness. The critical axis on which this turned was that of nation building and understanding Jews as part of France and the French character. Women, by contrast, have been marked by their sexual difference, and their significance was in the home, "underneath the nation."[18] So whereas Jewishness played a very public role in building the nation, women's difference and their role in building the nation through domestic labor and reproduction played out in private. The same lens applies to the question of sexuality and race in the Library of Congress Classification. Indeed, most works on African Americans are held in the E section, devoted to U.S. history. They are a subtopic within the category of "Elements in the population," which includes a large section on Jews and many other racial, ethnic, and religious categories. The implication is that these groups are integral to the nation and national identity. Women, and anything that concerned the family, marriage, or sexuality, on the other hand, were organized in the H section, within the HQs. The classification has quite clearly sequestered women and the family in a taxonomical domestic sphere. Rather than being considered part of nation building in a public sense, women were associated with family and marriage in the private realm.[19] In Brown's analysis, women's access to equality has been granted on the basis and assumption that their difference was acted upon in certain ways that confirmed and protected their domestic role and upheld reproductive norms.[20] When women deviate from expectations, the discourse quickly turns to tolerance. Lesbians are tolerated; women are equals. Again, the classification illustrates this distinction: Lesbians are not organized as a subset of women but rather, according to sexual practices, in a class formerly within the broader "Abnormal sex relations." The "Abnormal sex relations" class sets queer people not only within the private sphere and outside of national history but also outside of the home. Here we see a remarkable series of marginalizations that symbolically excludes people from public life, which challenges familiar notions of equity of access in libraries.

This casting out of the public sphere may help us understand the placement of African American gays in the HQs, which effectively distances works shelved in that location from any other books on African Americans. It can't quite be explained as a consequence of the early twentieth-century attitudes, as the class HQ76.27 A37 was first created in 2004 and applied to a book in 2006. There are only six books in this location at the present time, and it remains to be seen whether a body of literature will grow in this space. Is there an implicit disavowal or discomfort with black sexuality? Is it the case that gayness trumps blackness? Or is it that homosexuality and, by extension, black homosexuality are not understood as part of U.S. history? Is it a question of disciplines—method or content? Are African American gays viewed as objects of sociological inquiry rather than history? In a sense there is an erasure of African Americans by removing this particular section to works on sexuality, but we would likely be observing the same problem in reverse if the class had been assigned as a subtopic within E185; one might wonder if there are reasons for or consequences of such a location, as it would pull texts on African American gays away from other books in queer studies. Where the question gets even more strained is the recognition that most works (over one thousand) on African American women are, in fact, located with E185.86, in U.S history! Most are not located with women in the HQs. Is it the case that African American women are not imagined to be of the domestic sphere—that they are not to be read as integral to the reproduction of the citizenry in the family? I would wager that answers to these questions will forever be open to speculation, but I contend that these cases begin to illustrate the ways in which American discourses around race and sexuality have given form to subjects and how difficult it is to navigate across the disciplines. It serves as a mirror of American society and the imagined citizenry in the eyes of a federal cultural institution. It reflects the literature, to be sure, but it reflects a particular reading and interpretation of select literatures, which are sometimes at odds with one another, and it is a reading performed in the interest of the state. It reveals the ways in which subjects are differently relegated to the margins, depending on their relation to the heteropatriarchal design. We see the racialization of sex and the sexualization of race, and we witness simultaneously the essentialization of subjects and the impossibility and absurdity of placing texts and subjects in discrete (even discretely subdivided) categories. The refinement of categories into special topics within already marginalized topics is fraught with this paradox that renders subjects visible while hiding them in particularly troubling ways.

Some classificationists regard the LC Classification as mostly nonhierarchical and have suggested that it was never exactly intended to be a tool to enable browsing because the vast majority of books are held in closed stacks, retrieved upon request.[21] The system is meant to be very practical, enabling retrieval by expert librarians on behalf of their patrons. It is sometimes viewed to be a list of subjects in order of importance, rather than a co-locative device. This approach to thinking about the classification relies upon the supposition of its universality: The orderings and rankings within the Library of Congress system almost always refer to a special class or a margin of exception—particularly when it classifies human subjects.

Racialized Subjects and the State

To apprehend the weight of this problem, to understand how this classification system operates by and through this concept of universality, how it relies upon heteropatriarchy, and how it collapses under critique, I think of this project as a genealogy of the disciplines in the library—or rather—the library in the disciplines. If the primary mechanism by which discipline operates is normalization, where "the perpetual penalty that traverses all points and supervises every instant in the disciplinary institutions compares, differentiates, hierarchizes, homogenizes, excludes," then we must inquire into what happens when subjects fail to conform to a norm.[22] The key to upholding a norm is to specify a delinquency against which to compare and uphold acceptable behaviors and materialities. Butler asks us to inquire into "how bodies which fail to materialize provide the necessary 'outside,' if not the necessary support, for the bodies which, in materializing the norm, qualify as bodies that matter."[23] It is in the binaries of normal/abnormal, the universal American/"elements in the population," and the universal heteronormative/queer-of-color subjects that norms are sustained. The negative relation is in fact made plainly visible: The traits that belong to the universal require no mentioning, but the abnormal and the racialized and the perverse are marked and made to stand out—always at a distance from the center. Nowhere is this more apparent than in the literature concerning African Americans. While the vast majority of texts on African Americans are shelved in the section on U.S. history, a huge array of topics within other disciplines have been subdivided into a class on African Americans as a special topic, and so these books are dispersed across the library, always in a class set aside on the margins as exceptional. Most of these sections house small bodies of literature, sometimes with only two or three works, but they range in size. None are nearly as comprehensive as that which resides around E185. To call the list of classes extensive is a bit of an understatement, and in it we see not only which disciplines identify African Americans as objects of study but how they are contained and specified within those disciplines.[24] In contrast to the thousands of books described and classed with labels specifying African Americans or Blacks or Negroes, extremely few indicate that they are about Whites. Hundreds of classes established as special topics related to Blacks, Negroes, or African Americans across the disciplines, but only about ten classes are subdivided into "Whites" or "White," and these are in the fields of literature or art or are in histories of Africa and Asia. They are not in U.S. history because whiteness is assumed.

Whereas the previous chapter argued that the LC Classification must be read as an instrument of nation building and history making, the analysis of racialized subjects speaks specifically to Foucault's discussion of biopolitics. Key to the functioning of the state and the discourse of universality was and is a fundamental state racism, according to Foucault. He construes war as a battle of races—groups battling other groups. With the focus shifting from war to domestic relations, race took on a different kind of significance, racism became domesticated and institutionalized within the state, and biopolitics was born. Foucault looks to techniques and apparatuses of spatial distribution and regulation to understand how racism has materialized, and he finds that the concern over the regulation of populations arose out of scientific and political processes. Bioregulation was enacted by the state and reinforced by disciplinary apparatuses and institutions like schools, hospitals, police—and libraries. Biopolitics operates through a norm that circulates across the population and its members. And so begins the systematic hierarchizing of race through classification, observation, and documentation, and the anxieties about racial difference would come to fuel discussions of sexuality and class, driving discourse about degeneracy and the state-sanctioned practices of sterilization of humans based on fitness within the nation's population. Arguably, nowhere is this transition of focus to race more prevalent than in the United States during the Progressive Era, and the sexological and sociological taxonomies on which library classifications were based reflect the prevailing attitudes and methods by which sexuality and race were conceptualized in research and nation building. The United States is unique for its history of slavery and reconstruction and the ways in which the state has used racial figurations to expand its domestic and imperialist projects. Michael Omi and Howard Winant assert that racial myths have been essential for the maintenance of social order and political life in the United States and that those myths are supported by a racial system that has grown out of social-historical processes.[25] Ann Laura Stoler has argued that a racial grammar has underwritten sexual regimes far more than Foucault recognizes, and in her work she draws connections across domains that had been previously treated discretely in colonial discourses.[26] The task of reconnecting these and other domains is far too vast for this space and is one that can continue indefinitely. The key is in finding a way of speaking about the forces of history and relations of power that have produced these subject divisions, to give voice to and recognize the extent to which our libraries sustain the "education of desire" to support an imagined nation.

The arrangement of subjects in the library displays, with remarkable precision, how scholars and librarians have viewed objects of study in relation not to one another but to the project of nation building. In fact, this is the key to understanding how subjects are situated in the library and the logic that drives their placement. The histories of race, sexuality, class, and notions of normal and abnormal have been written into this classification on the basis of how they inform the history of the United States. And so it is a sort of metahistorical document—a history of the histories of subject formations within the disciplines. Such a reading foregrounds the extent to which knowledge and power and nation building are interlocked; indeed, knowledge structures in our libraries have and continued to contribute to racist, imperialist projects and state violence.

Reports of the Library of Congress show how tightly connected its collection and classification practices were tied to U.S. agendas. In 1898, just after the Library of Congress moved into its current Jefferson Building, Librarian of Congress John Russell Young expressed a special passion for increasing the LoC's collection, and he imagined the library as a critical component in supporting U.S. national interests. In that year's annual report he provided an overview of the LoC's priorities: "Special attention has been given to the political, social, and religious movements attendant upon the development of the Republic."[27] He went on to set an agenda for collecting foreign materials, as well:

> The Library would be justified in spending as much money on continental literature as upon that of Great Britain. This is the home of many races coming and still to come, who are welcomed with undiminished hospitality to our ultimate citizenship. A national library can have for them no feature of more enduring interest than that which tells them of their history, literature, and ancestry.[28]

This was the rationale for arguing for increasing the collection of literature from Germany and France. Young continued:

> The same might be said of Italy, the literature of Russia with its recent strenuous advance, that of Scandinavia as well as of the vanished and vanishing tongues which remain as fragments of dissolving civilizations. There are the realms of research in Arabia, India, China, and Japan, whose frontiers we are but approaching.[29]

The project of collecting literature from foreign lands was just beginning to take shape, with the cooperation of the U.S. secretary of state and an appropriation of funds from Congress. Dreams of a new universal classification for this universal collection had begun to stir in 1897. The structure and primary divisions of the emerging Library of Congress would be based on the collection initiatives formed at the dawn of the twentieth century. Young said of the classification:

> As an inflexible rule, no method of classification should be favored which would disintegrate the general collection. The Library of Congress must ultimately be the universal library of the Republic. To that end the most magnificent library edifice in the world has been erected and is destined to be, it is hoped, the home of America's literary and artistic genius, supplemented and strengthened by that of all lands and all time.[30]

As the priority was U.S. history and diplomatic relations, the first classification to be established (after the Zs were arranged for Library Science and Bibliography) was the E section, on the United States, the "preliminary and provisional" version of which was printed in 1901.[31] That quite simple version was mainly organized around geographic locations and the histories of wars and presidents. There was a space for "Slavery controversy" at E441, but in that edition there was not yet a classification of "Elements in the population." It wasn't until the second edition of the E section, published in 1913, that subject classes became much more precise, including an expansive section around the topic of "Negroes" at E185.[32]

In the Progressive Era United States, bureaucratic techniques served to achieve cohesion and ultimately alleviate national anxieties. Robert H. Wiebe argues that this moment in U.S. history was profoundly shaped by a "search for order" to control conditions and populations, and well before Foucault arrived at his theory of biopolitics, Wiebe argued that the most elaborate devices of control was exclusion through a "compound of biology, pseudo-science, and hyperactive imaginations," which divided the world by race and organized groups along an evolutionary scale.[33] There is no question that the triangulation of science, politics, and capital gave extra legitimacy and potency to racialized militarism, and as Jackson Lears and others have argued, rituals of white supremacy "fueled imperial ambition."[34] Indeed, scholars point to the years in which the Library of Congress moved into its new building and began writing its subject headings and its classifications as a critical moment in the "rebirth" of the United States. Lears suggests that a language of regeneration and rebirth permeated American discourse. After the failure of Reconstruction, the disenfranchisement of African Americans and purification became central to regeneration on the domestic front, and white supremacy and American frontier myths laden with racialized violence were essential for acquiring an overseas empire.

Hannah Arendt might have regarded the Library of Congress as a particularly essential institution not only for managing knowledge about and for American domestic relations but also in colonial and imperialist programs. She argued that two devices for political organization emerged in early stages of imperialism: "One was race as a principle of the body politic, and the other bureaucracy as a principle of foreign domination."[35] According to Arendt, colonial bureaucracy gave institutional form to ideological notions of racial difference. It is worth considering whether the Library of Congress has been an ideal place to construct and organize colonialist/imperialist agendas in the United States. In fact, Alfred McCoy locates libraries and their classifications within the United States' development of documentation and information control for surveillance and imperialism.[36] The organization of the world's knowledge in this huge government bureaucracy to serve the U.S. Congress and produce an informed citizenry must be read with a view toward thinking about what the classifications of race does to serve the state.[37] Additionally, we need to understand that the export of the classification and other bibliographic standards into catalogs around the world has been one channel by which American ideology and culture has become dominant. Regarding the catalog as a colonized space brings the analysis of sexualized and racialized categories to significant new depths.

The LC Classification was not initially intended to be used by libraries other than the Library of Congress, but it nevertheless became an instrument of cultural domination. With the practice of copy cataloging and calls for uniformity and efficiency, the classification was adopted by a number of American research libraries in the early part of the twentieth century. Today it is the most widely used classification in American college and university libraries. Additionally, by the middle of the twentieth century it was being used in libraries around the globe, along with a variety of other Western cataloging technologies and standards. During the post–World War II era, the Library of Congress and its classifications came to possess a status of cultural authority around the world and arguably facilitated imperialist aims, as the reach and influence of the classification increasingly extended beyond U.S. borders. The internationalization of Anglo-American librarianship was made possible by the LoC, in partnership with the American Library Association, UNESCO, and other organizations, through the exportation of bibliographic tools, techniques, and expertise, especially after World War II. It was believed that the sharing of cultural texts and objects would bring and sustain peace, and bibliography was considered to be an essential component of an international program to increase and exchange knowledge. Luther Evans, who held the post of director general of UNESCO beginning in 1953 (and was the only American ever to hold this post), just after serving as librarian of Congress, declared the LoC to be "a Universal library with a national duty," which included acting as an "international servant of enlightenment."[38] With such a mandate the LoC became a leader and partner in programs to bring modern librarianship to "underdeveloped" nations—particularly in initiatives that required technical expertise and coordination. Library extension projects during and after World War II varied in scope and purpose, as U.S. librarians and State Department information agencies contributed to the installation of American libraries in locales all around the world and provided support and training in developing nations for modern libraries to serve their public and academic communities. While these programs were variously conducted in the interest of preserving an international cultural record, saving books from war-torn countries, and enhancing democracy by getting reading materials into the hands of a vast public, there was also an underlying belief that the spread of American culture through books and other cultural products was a powerful and necessary instrument in winning the Cold War.[39]

One of the lasting results of post–World War II and Cold War library and information programs has been that various library cataloging and metadata technologies developed by the LoC have become ubiquitous. For example, the encoding scheme—Machine Readable Cataloging (MARC)—in which online catalog records are written was developed at the LoC in the 1950s and 1960s.[40] Additionally, either the Library of Congress Classification or the Dewey Decimal System (also currently housed in the LoC) serves as the classification for the majority of academic and public libraries worldwide.[41] Library of Congress Subject Headings are used in libraries everywhere, either in English or in translation—according to the LoC's website, "Library of Congress Subject Headings (LCSH) is the only subject headings list accepted as the worldwide standard."[42] The extent to which the Library of Congress provides infrastructural technologies for libraries virtually everywhere is indeed astonishing. This means that LoC and American library leaders were among those who "determined the intellectual agenda of and the perspectives of influential sectors of the government and academy" and participated in the expansion of American empire through ideological and cultural production.[43] Racialized subjects are constituted and framed in catalogs across continents and locales, and categories and spatial arrangements are transmitted along a vast transnational network. The scripts that underwrite conceptions of racial categories in the United States are deeply entwined with those that delineate and authorize racialized subjects abroad. It is beyond the scope of this project to investigate the consequences of this reality, and continued work must be done to understand fully American library techniques and standards as instruments of cultural imperialism.

Metadata or Metafiction?

Each category in the Library of Congress Classification has its own history, and reading the various editions, from 1901 to the present, reveals how librarians have organized objects of study and how bodies of literature and research have grown or shifted over time. But this bibliographic classification, as I hope I have shown, presents a particular interpretation of the world's literatures—one that relies on universalist discourses that assume whiteness and heterosexuality from a Western point of view. I want to press this point and suggest that we take this classification as both a fiction and a metafiction—one that was first drafted in a particular time and place and for a particular audience and purpose. The Enlightenment, in Adorno and Horkheimer's view, is a myth, and the principles of universality and rationalism that undergird the Enlightenment have circulated and repeated over time and space to uphold illusions of equality and justice. In their estimation, the Enlightenment, in spite of its reliance on reason to dispel the myths that came before it, has itself attained mythical properties, as it "allows no determination other than the classifications of the societal process to operate."[44] The very notion that a universal classification is possible relies on fantasy and serves projects in mastering nature and others. And the idea that creating a unified, rational system divided into discrete subjects is desirable begins to provide clues into the formulas and tropes through which this fiction has been constructed. The idea of a universal collection depends upon the exclusion and marginalization of certain knowledges and rule out the possibility of existence for those who don't conform to an ideal or fit into a category. A universal system in effect supports imperialism and makes institutionalized racism and heterosexism possible by recognizing subjects in terms of their legibility as normal or abnormal according to scientific categories. Literary criticism offers tools for interrogating the mythical claims to order, authority, neutrality, and equality of access. Having more than a century between the creation of the classification and the present critique means that we can recognize the extent to which those sexological, Africanist, historical, and medical works upon which the classification is based were advancing positions and policies that we have come to dispel and even abhor. So many of these eugenicist, regulatory, racist, and phobic policies were propelled in the interest of the state and derived from a national imaginary based on rationalist notions of citizenship and national interests.

Toni Morrison looks to literature written by white novelists to unveil the ways in which Africanism, arising out of the U.S. imaginary, has permeated American literature and extended racial ideology. For Morrison the fabrication of an African or nonwhite presence is a critical vehicle through which cultural hegemony operated. She argues that it was for reasons of state that "the process of organizing American coherence through a distancing Africanism" was crucial to a sense of Americanness.[45] Whereas Morrison critiques novelists, we can similarly look to the white crafters of the Library of Congress Classification to begin to unravel ways in which libraries figure into processes that make intellectual domination possible. Morrison feels it necessary to look to white writers to understand how racial ideology plays out in cultural forms and what it does in the imagination of masters. If we consider the ways in which works by and about African Americans have been classified under U.S. history and in other disciplines, almost always as a "special topic" or "special class," we can begin to think about how Africanism actually supports this classification, American racial ideology, and notions of universality and citizenship. As Adorno and Horkheimer have said, the tools of the Enlightenment—a totalitarian system of thought—are constructions that manage others through science by those who are free. Similarly, Morrison suggests that the American rhetoric surrounding the rights of man is tethered to Africanism, which was the mechanism by which the American knew himself to be free, and that this has inflected American literature written by white people.

As it is impossible to divorce attitudes and beliefs that carry a national character from the literature of any age, it is necessary to do a similar kind of critique of other kinds of cultural products. The Library of Congress Classification can be distinguished from other works of art and literature for its direct connection to the state, in its positioning as a federal agency. Whereas the national imaginary plays out largely unconsciously in the authors of literature, and most authors would not have claimed to be writing for or of the state or any of the state's missions, librarians of Congress—particularly those in positions of authority—were writing policies and reports that explicitly placed the Library of Congress as the central bureau of knowledge in the United States. The prioritization of the collection of materials that informed national interests and the classification of those materials before all others demonstrates that knowledge was selected and organized for the state. And as Morrison writes, "Knowledge, however mundane and utilitarian, plays about in linguistic images and forms cultural practice."[46]

Considering the ways in which the privileging of the present was critical to the formation of the nation-state, as suggested by Foucault, the LC Classification has had a tremendous shelf life. It has secured the vision of Progressive Era librarians into the twenty-first century and probably for years to come. And that means that the national character continues to play out on library shelves and that the positioning of racial, sexual, and all subjects in the margins against a white, male, Christian, U.S. norm will also have an enduring shelf life, too. As Morrison tells us, racism is as strong as it was during the Enlightenment, and it stands to reason that the continued use of the Enlightenment-inspired classification serves to embed, refine, and reify further those margins and norms. When we add books to our collections using the Library of Congress system, are we not strengthening the power of this tool by reproducing and affirming dominant ideas about American subjectivity? The master narrative continues to be held intact and reinforced through practice.

Although marking off race and devoting a chapter to the topic may seem to be at odds with the contention that subjectivities cannot be sectioned off, I have done so to demonstrate how discipline is enacted in libraries. The Library of Congress Classification was produced at a particular moment in U.S. history—one that inscribed racialized and sexualized difference in opposition to norms and in support of a national agenda of imperialism and protection. It was in studying the library's classification of books about African Americans that I became convinced that the classification must be read first as a history of the United States and a technology of government. Where it classifies other nations and territories around the world, it must be viewed it as a history of how the United States has studied, fought with or against, and colonized other parts of the world. In other words, the classification organizes countries and peoples as objects of research. That the LoC's systems are used in catalogs around the globe means that American-centric views are spread to libraries, rendering the catalog a colonized space.

I have only touched on a small range of questions regarding the classes associated with African Americans, and much remains to be explored with regard to how the Library of Congress classifies people that live or have lived in parts of the world other than the United States. I have merely brushed the surface of the vast literature that resides in the section once reserved for degeneracy and defectives. Religion, class, and nonhuman animals are all subjects that deserve attention, as well. But my hope is that this chapter has begun to underline the logic and mission upon which our libraries' knowledge is organized and indicate some of the ways in which we can understand a classification to be productive of knowledge and imagined communities.

CHAPTER 5

The Trouble with Access / Toward
Reparative Taxonomies

The point is not just to read the webs of knowledge
production; the point is to reconfigure what counts
as knowledge in the interests of reconstituting
the generative forces of embodiment.

—DONNA HARAWAY, "A Game of Cat's Cradle"

The perverse dynamic challenges not by collapsing
order but through a reordering less tolerable, more
disturbing, than chaos. Its difference is never the
absolutely unfamiliar, but the reordering of the already
known, a disclosure of a radical interconnectedness
which is the social, but which present cultures can rarely
afford to acknowledge and must instead disavow.

—JONATHAN DOLLIMORE, *Sexual Dissidence*

Eros can make of ontology, after all, something improper.

—DEBORAH BRITZMAN, "Theory Kindergarten"

Just how relevant to reading and library practices are the critiques in this
book, given the changing nature of information retrieval systems? Knowledge seekers tend to choose Internet browsers and websites, even for information about books, far more than library catalogs, and in library catalogs,
people generally tend to search by keywords rather than subject headings.
Browsing the library stacks is becoming a lost and forgotten pastime, except for a few. What's more, in the face of demands for library space and
shrinking book budgets, libraries are increasingly purchasing electronic
books, which dramatically alter the way we read and search. And so it may
seem that one should conclude that this project is purely historical and
theoretical, with limited practical application in the present. To this line of
thinking I have a few responses.

First, I want to distinguish public and academic libraries from commercial websites and search engines. I regard libraries as special places

that should be protected as much as possible from some of the forces that power the Internet. It is now widely acknowledged that corporations like Google are more interested in profits than privacy. Their search technologies rely upon the commodification of users, information, and knowledge, and the algorithms that drive relevancy and page rankings are based on profitability and popularity. These algorithms are also secret and proprietary. In the case of Google, knowledge and information seekers are delivered to sites that may or may not be the most appropriate to the reader's interests but that, rather, are based on a "rapid calculation of a web page's 'PageRank,'" which involves the counting of citations and backlinks to a page to determine its "importance or quality."[1] As Anna Lauren Hoffmann puts the point, people who look for information using Google "are no longer situated as free and equal citizens, but, rather, as mere consumers."[2]

"Metadata" became a household term when Eric Snowden made public the surveillance techniques enacted by information and communication technologies in 2013. What many people don't realize is that libraries have been creating metadata for centuries for inventory and access. The catalog entry should be considered the earliest and most ubiquitous form of metadata, and librarians were the first to create standards and schemas, like classification and rules for description, for how metadata is produced. Only recently did metadata become a tool for collecting and storing data about users for profit and surveillance. Commercial search engines work as effectively as they do in large part because they rely on data generated by users, and search engine companies also use that data to reap huge profits from otherwise "free" services. Nanne Bonde Thylstrup cites this as a key problem particularly because the private sector has no obligation to the public with regard to how they access or control the digital traces left behind by their searches.[3] Libraries, on the other hand, don't collect user information that way. One of the primary tenets of librarianship is that privacy is essential to the exercise of free speech, free thought, and free association. Whereas search engine companies purposely integrate user data and behaviors into their product development and marketing programs, the American Library Association regards the sharing of personal information with vendors or other third parties as a violation of privacy and confidentiality. Many librarians actively work to ensure and protect the values of intellectual freedom, the freedom to read, and social justice. With the advancement of linked data across libraries and across information systems, the reach and influence of library vocabularies and classifications is yet to be known.

Perhaps the most important point to be made, however, is that, whether they are made visible or not, classifications and categories are at the heart of any information retrieval system. The methodology for analyzing the history of categories that I've been using throughout this book can be applied to all kinds of settings that index and organize information.[4] In the online world, where the categories truly are hidden deep beneath the hood and shrouded in mathematical formulas, it is particularly important to recognize that classifications are functioning in ways that we don't fully understand. For a case in point, I conducted a series of experiments with Google searches using different combinations of terms. The most striking set of results derived from my searches for "black lesbians" and "african american lesbians."[5] The difference between the respective retrieval powers of "black" and "african american" tells us a lot about perceptions and the power of words (or strings of text). The top results retrieved by "african american lesbians" included sites about coming out, dating, and celebrities—for the most part, these sites seem to be targeted toward African American lesbians and provide information, some type of community engagement, or entertainment. At the top of the list is a page from Autostraddle.com, which describes itself as "an intelligent, hilarious & provocative voice and a progressively feminist online community for a new generation of kickass lesbian, bisexual & otherwise inclined ladies (and their friends)."

The set retrieved by "black lesbians," however, is entirely different. Each and every entry in the first page of the list links to a pornography site. Also worth noting is the fact that "african american lesbians" retrieved 3,270,000 links whereas "black lesbians" brought 16,700,000 results. This is more than a fivefold difference, suggesting that in some regard the string "black lesbians" has a much higher market value. How this all happens is a mystery to me, but Safiya Noble has been documenting the ways that Google retrieves pages about black women and girls.[6] She concludes that large commercial search engines, with their mathematical formulations and market-driven search technologies, fail to accommodate social and cultural contexts at the peril of those who seek information. She also observes that the ways that search engines index the web is critically different from the ways in which librarians curate and catalog their collections for their publics. Indeed, other search engines operate by different formulas, and results within any engine will also vary according to time and place. The reasons for these results don't simply reside with Google but have much to do with the keywords and metadata in the websites themselves and with web traffic. And although the observations above are applied to general web searches, related conclusions can be drawn for the Google Books product, which provides full-text access to books in the public domain and limited access to books still in copyright. The service has been extremely controversial for a variety of reasons, mostly concerning issues around privacy and the commercialization of knowledge and the public sphere. Also under fire has been the quality of metadata and digital copies, as the Google Books service is known to include inaccuracies.

I use these examples of Google searches to illustrate the danger of equating or comparing commercial services with those of the library. It is important to see what happens when control is given over to algorithms that govern the search and retrieval of full-text documents, rather than relying on the human interpretation of texts and the application of bibliographic techniques. Robert Darnton has explained that academic and public libraries do a much better job in digitizing, preserving, and making books accessible than Google, and one of the reasons is that libraries are most interested in preserving the cultural record and serving the public good.[7] Resource accessibility in libraries does not depend on market trends but on bibliographic control techniques applied by subject specialists. We might think of librarians as curators of knowledge. As the Library of Congress reference librarian Thomas Mann writes, the appropriate goal of research libraries "is to be found in an academic rather than a business model: research libraries are funded to promote scholarship."[8] Research libraries are also meant to serve the specific needs of scholars in all subject areas and disciplines, and those needs must be recognized as being distinct from quick, everyday information seekers. Mann points out several aspects of scholarly information seeking that demand a kind of bibliographic care that commercial search engines can't accommodate: the concern with doing an exhaustive search so as not to overlook important sources, the need to find both current and historical sources, the quest for rare or marginally used books, and the need for materials written in languages other than English. Scholars tend to be more inclined to understand that what is most relevant to their needs might not appear at the top of a list of retrieved items—nevertheless they don't want to sift through lists of hundreds or thousands of loosely relevant titles that might arise from basic keyword searches.[9] For Mann, the LC Subject Headings and Classification are two devices that serve scholars well, as they facilitate exhaustive and relevant retrieval of documents according to topic. And although he recognizes certain shortcomings of these standards, he suggests that they are much more adequate to the task of serving scholars than commercial search engines are.[10]

I would add that losing sight of the fundamental necessity of slow information seeking for scholarly practice might be read as part of a wider turn toward the troubling marketization of the academy. The demands for quick information retrieval go hand in hand with increased scholarly production and the economization of academic units. My concern is that the values of intellectual freedom, privacy, and access to information that libraries aim to uphold become threatened when we pretend that commercial search engines perform the same functions as library catalogs and databases. In an era when libraries and education institutions are being subsumed into a neoliberal apparatus while the Internet offers the illusion of a free and democratic public space, there is an urgent need to interrogate our own contradictions, investments, values, and desires. The ideals for which libraries strive are aligned with the ideal of the public sphere. At the same time, I believe that it is imperative that we as scholars, readers, and members of different publics understand the ways in which the knowledge we seek is structured by history and politics and made available in certain contexts. I take it for granted that our public institutions are situated in and serve political and economic interests. Libraries are incredibly paradoxical spaces for the way they promote ideals of democracy through the provision of information while deploying disciplinary techniques. We should strive to understand them in their complexity and work through some of the paradoxes by engaging in dialogue about the role of libraries in history and history making. Library classifications provide a point of departure for talking about some of the most critical social and political issues.

Given the account that I've provided so far, it bears reiterating the significance of the position from which these classificatory apparatuses are produced. As the United States' oldest federal cultural institution, the Library of Congress serves as the nation's library. By creating and standardizing the rules by which libraries analyze, select, and organize knowledge, the LoC not only produces knowledge in and through power but also plays a crucial role in mapping the field of scholarship and research. It ensures that knowledge organizing techniques are reproduced and normalized across disciplines throughout the entire network of libraries, including the local main street public library in small towns, digital libraries in cyberspace, academic libraries of varying types and sizes, and libraries of all varieties around the globe.

Whereas access for all is touted as a central tenet of libraries in their efforts to promote democracy, I would argue that this vision is undermined by the apparatuses, processes, and parties involved in authorizing and providing access. Indeed some scholars have pointed out that libraries do not live up to the democratic ideals so readily attached to them and that they are further threatened by librarians' complicity and engagement with neo-liberal models for library development.[11] Looking to the technologies and policies developed by the LoC provides insight into some of the forces that impede libraries' capacity to provide access to all and into some of the costs associated with access. It reveals that library classifications are in fact among "hegemony's handmaids," serving and supporting the state by imposing an infrastructural knowledge organization system that sustains dominant norms.[12]

Of utmost importance are the questions of how access is granted, and for whom. These types of considerations begin a number of debates, including those surrounding human rights and the digital divide, where the first step toward bridging the gap has been to work toward equity of access to hardware, software, and networks. Most digital economy scholars recognize the short-sightedness of viewing access to information technologies as a singular solution. In the library classifications under scrutiny in this book, we have seen how access is controlled by specific terms and rules. For "perverse" subjects, to be accessible is to be medicalized or cast off to a section of "abnormals" or branded "obscene." To be recognized is to be named and classed in terms not one's own and in ways that render subjects legible in the eyes of the medical/juridical disciplines and the state. Legibility is conferred by a series of techniques, and as James Scott warns, "legibility is a condition of manipulation."[13]

Dean Spade, who is concerned with administrative categories and their effects, notes: "We have to carefully consider the limitations of strategies that aim for inclusion into existing economic and political arrangements rather than challenging the terms of those arrangements."[14] I agree with Spade's contention that, for transformative change that is more than symbolic, "we must move beyond the politics of recognition and inclusion."[15] Emily Drabinski seems to be of a similar position when she "challenges the traditional approach of activist librarians who see as paramount the task of correcting classification and cataloging schemes until they become unbiased and universally accessible structures." Rather than relying on corrective tactics (a decidedly impossible project), according to Drabinski we should be attentive to the "contested ideological work performed by catalogers who must make these decisions every day."[16] While increased access by way of added and corrected headings and classes might attenuate the violations inherent to these heteropatriarchal systems, it does not free subjects from them. Indeed, the classifications reinscribe their subordinated and marginal designation as they provide access. And so we have a critical paradox—increased access by way of identity categories serves and fortifies a knowledge organization system based in universalisms that justify violence toward "special" topics and subjects.

According to Roderick Ferguson, the academy became the model of "archtonic power" in the United States, using texts to regulate and instruct the nation on difference, and thus the academy paved the way for the administrative regulation of queerness.[17] He cautions: "If the condition for sexuality's absorption into power's archive is the managing and disciplining of sexuality so that it conforms to institutional legibility, then the story allegorizes how various forms of sexual agency become the detritus of complex systems of intelligibility."[18] The practice of adding headings may actually contribute to what Ferguson and Lisa Duggan have described as the incorporation of queerness into a neoliberal political economy. They both suggest that the promise of hope brought by social movements of the 1960s and 1970s, with the creation and legitimation of ethnic studies and women's studies, has been stymied by the state and the academy. In the academic library the practice of admitting approved sexual practices into the range of normal has reproduced and reinforced normalizing discourses that regulate sexualities. One finds a striking resemblance between the move toward inclusivity in the subject headings by adding and refining headings and classes and the mainstreaming and integration of LGBTQ people in the American political marketplace.

The library gives a certain presence to the arguments presented by Ferguson and Spade and others. The arrangements and the names given to bodies of knowledge mirror the administrative categorizations and hierarchies in our universities, social services agencies, and hospitals, and by reading the catalog and the shelves we read social structures at large. The disciplinary divisions of and within bodies of literature produce a particular materiality that brings texts from all over the globe under one roof and one universal system, unifying the disciplines and arranging how we come to knowledge, making visible the ideological mappings of the world.

The Schema and the Soul

> These ambiguities, redundancies and deficiencies remind us of those which doctor Franz Kuhn attributes to a certain Chinese encyclopaedia entitled "Celestial Empire of benevolent Knowledge." In its remote pages it is written that the animals are divided into: (a) belonging to the emperor, (b) embalmed, (c) tame, (d) sucking pigs, (e) sirens,

(f) fabulous, (g) stray dogs, (h) included in the present
classification, (i) frenzied, (j) innumerable, (k) drawn with
a very fine camelhair brush, (l) et cetera, (m) having just
broken the water pitcher, (n) that from a long way off look
like flies.

JORGE LUIS BORGES, "The Analytical Language of John Wilkins"

Foucault tells us that Borges's fictional Chinese classification first inspired
laughter and then *The Order of Things* for the way that it breaks up "all the
ordered surfaces and all the planes with which we are accustomed to tame
the wild profusion of existing things."[19] The classification brings to light
the limitations of knowledge organization systems, their instability, their
apparent randomness, and their relation to any particular community or
society's way of organizing the world. It illustrates the very possibility of
grouping things together in an "unthinkable space." And for Foucault, this
passage led him to wonder about the implications of a kind of disorder
that brings together fragments of a large variety of possible orders within
the same dimension or, in other words, "in such a state, things are 'laid,'
'placed,' 'arranged' in sites so very different from one another that it is
impossible to find a place of residence for them, to define a *common locus*
beneath them all."[20] Foucault's reading of Borges's Chinese classification
helps us realize the disciplinary effects of the Library of Congress Classification system, bringing into view how the boundaries and placement of
books on library shelves, while seeming logical and natural, in fact designate an impossible arrangement.

One could argue that to perform a genealogy of the material effects of
disciplinary power is to inquire into the genealogy of the soul. Jean-Luc
Nancy draws from Aristotle the notion that the soul organizes the body
and makes it a whole: "The soul is the fact that a body exists, in other
words, that there is extension and exposition."[21] A body occupies a given
area, a space that articulates the limits of the body and distinguishes it from
others. In fact, Foucault writes at the beginning of *Discipline and Punish* that
his project is a "history of the modern soul," adding that the "soul is the
prison of the body" and that it is *this* prison that he is interested in, "with
all the political investments of the body that it gathers in its closed architecture."[22] According to Foucault, the soul is produced around, on, and
within bodies as a function of power-knowledge systems: "It is the element
in which are articulated the effects of a certain type of power and the reference of a certain type of knowledge, the machinery by which the power relations give rise to a possible corpus of knowledge, and knowledge extends

and reinforces the effects of this power."[23] It is out of this process that domains of analysis as well as scientific methodologies and technologies are constructed. The soul brings a body into existence, but as it is produced and constrained by power, the soul in fact functions as a prison of the body. The regularization of knowledge results in the creation of "soul-subjects," which are to be extracted from subjugated bodies. Extending these lines, then, a classification system should be understood as a power-knowledge technology that brings bodies of literature into existence, giving birth to certain knowledges, where being born means to be findable and intelligible and usable in the universe of knowledge—a *birth to presence*.[24] At the same time, these systems are inherently confining and constraining, functioning as a technology of power that operates on the soul, imprisoning the body of literature.

Judith Butler reads the Aristotelian *schema* through Foucault's notion of the soul: "The soul is taken as an instrument of power through which the body is cultivated and formed. In a sense, it acts as a power-laden schema that produces and actualizes the body itself."[25] The Greek *schema* means "the shape given by the stamp," or "form, shape, figure, appearance, dress, gesture, figure of a syllogism, and grammatical form." Information professionals can't miss the association to present-day metadata schemas—a concept that has become ubiquitous in organizing knowledge in libraries and on the web, all but replacing the language of library cataloging. Indeed, there is now a vast array of metadata schemas differently designed to describe and provide access to resources of various types (audio, images, videos, architecture, websites, etc.) for different audiences, and classifications are among these. We can think of the process of subjectification—of a subject in relation—as an effect of a schema, an instrument of power that puts a subject in its place, "forms and frames the body, stamps it, and in stamping it, brings it into being."[26] The call number, for example, is quite literally stamped on the *spine* of the book, indicating the discipline to which it is assigned and designating its place in the library space.

Butler asks how we "can think through the matter of bodies as a kind of materialization governed by regulatory norms in order to ascertain the workings of heterosexual hegemony in the formation of what qualifies as a viable body. How does that materialization of the norm in bodily formation produce a domain of abjected bodies . . . ?"[27] The task that has been set before us here is to locate the mechanisms by which norms are produced and reiterated in libraries, find the excluded and marginalized voices, and determine how unintelligible and unviable bodies of literature are banished and hidden through policies, oversights, and indecision, all of which are enacted from positions of power to produce effects of dematerialization and abjection. The preclusion of abnormal or illegible subjects from participating in discourse serves in support of a norm, providing space against which normative subjects come into being. Normative sexualities can only be produced by "barring from cultural intelligibility—and rendering culturally abject—cultural organizations of sexuality that exceed the structuring purview of that law."[28] The implications reach far beyond access to information and must be understood as being a part of a matrix of discourses, a "carceral" network, even. The "judges of normality are present everywhere," and libraries are just one site where judgment is obviously embedded in practice. But it is in everyday spaces—schools, medicine, on the playgrounds, and in the library—where the "universal reign of the normative has taken hold and reproduces itself."[29]

Scholars have long recognized LCSH and the LC Classification as active agents in marginalizing identity-based exceptions to rules. For instance, LCSH includes a heading for "Students" as well as for "Lesbian students," "African American students," and a wide of variety of types of students. But we won't see "Heterosexual students" or "White students" or "African American heterosexuals" or "White lesbians." The blatant marginalization of nonnormative subjects is obvious. My concern is that, in the present universal system, subjects associated with race and sexuality can only be added to the margins. An additive approach to access by way of subjects embraces a politics of recognition, which Nancy Fraser identifies as problematic for the way it both reifies identity categories and displaces economic redistributive efforts. Fraser argues that the present politics of recognition risks promoting the very exclusionary results it purports to be working against and may in fact promote inequality and sanction violations by reinforcing notions of who and what cultural categories are of value. Efforts to remedy misrecognition by way of identity politics may "serve less to foster interaction across differences than to enforce separatism, conformism and intolerance."[30] In the library the authorization of subjects signals recognition and indicates what counts as knowledge. As Fraser suggests, equal participation in social and political life "is also impeded when some actors lack the necessary resources to interact with others as peers. In such cases, maldistribution constitutes an impediment to parity of participation in social life, and thus a form of social subordination and injustice."[31] Clearly, such a conclusion brings to bear the significance of the perception that libraries facilitate equity of access to resources. Following Fraser, who argues that a politics of recognition inadequately addresses the social and institutional milieu out of which economic inequalities are born and perpetuated, I suggest that a sort of politics of redistribution of knowledge in the library is in order.

I would also suggest that one of the purposes of this project is to articulate a need—a lack or void that universalisms fail to address. The paradox we've identified with access to information cannot fully be resolved within existing discourses and structures, but ongoing discussions of equity of access can begin to identify a vision for how we want to see things take shape. Echoing Wendy Brown, I believe these kinds of conversations offer a political richness and validation by affirming the impossibility of fairness in the present while imagining the possibility for a field of justice and equality in the future.[32] "Perverse" subjects provide a particularly fruitful lens through which to begin to articulate a new vision based on more just conceptualizations of the richness and relations among subjects and subjectivities—one based on localized and lived experience rather than on the state's regulation and incorporative model.

The Interdisciplines

Disciplinary territorialization is not limited to perverse or queer subjects, but in fact, the questions of who does the naming, how bodies of literature are rendered intelligible for access, and to whom access is granted shoot through all of the humanities and posthumanities. Where there is a body of literature, there is a question of categories. In particular, the critical interdisciplines that bring together human and posthuman accounts of animals and disability and race and class and gender and sexuality—fields formerly under the purview of the sciences—are all similarly disciplined, and the intersectionality among the interdisciplines illustrates the limitations of library classifications. Some of the processes of coming of age for each of these categories have been similar, as each has been and is subject to policing and disciplining by the state, othering by a dominant group, and depersonalization. They have been marginalized by the academy, been named and categorized by external authorities, and been the subjects of experiments. Each of these groups has struggled to be heard and represented in their own terms. Halberstam argues that perhaps we should strive for antidisciplinarity, or knowledge practices that refuse form and content of traditional canons: "We may in fact want to think about how to see unlike a state; we may want new rationales for knowledge production, different aesthetic standards for ordering or disordering space."[33] In the academy, as evidenced by classification, various knowledges are disqualified, rendered illegible, and subjugated. Foucault calls for bringing those knowledges from below to light. We might consider resisting mastery and seek ways to invest in other modes of knowing, recognizing ways in which those knowledges that fail to live up to norms open up opportunities for creativity and cooperation through critical pedagogy, listening, and dialogue. Halberstam proposes that we consider alternative ways of thinking about success and that perhaps not knowing, undoing, and failing ought to be privileged. Failing to live up to society's expectations, what it means to be a citizen, or what it means to do research in any particular discipline can bring about growth and new knowledge. Perverse subjects confront all kinds of normal and begin the undoing of the disciplines.

Ferguson asks what might happen if we do find ways to free texts in the critical interdisciplines in the academy:

> Are there other ways to disseminate and circulate minority culture and difference that do not place them within dominant systems of value? What happens when the texts that engage minority difference disturb the expectations and systems of intelligibility put in place by disciplines and institutions? What happens if those texts are used to imagine how minoritized subjects and knowledges might inhabit institutional spaces in ways dominant institutions never intended?[34]

The academy as we know it needs the disciplines, according to Michael Ryan. And by their very nature, the disciplines are biased and exclusionary, with their methodologies, theories, and subjects, and "the purity of the internal arena is always already contaminated by what it seeks to exclude. . . . All knowledge operates through acts of exclusion and marginalization."[35] He suggests that the institutional divisions between disciplines reflect and promote an ideological structuring of the social world: "The division of the academy into disciplines . . . reflects a metaphysical conceptuality which would classify a world that denies the possibility of such classificatory divisions." Ryan argues that the very system of disciplinary divisions is a false mirror of the universe of knowledge. In other words, one cannot wrest the political from literature, language from economics, or gender from science, and the construction of disciplinary divisions denies crucial metaphysical realities. The world is not so simply divided up, but rather, everything is entangled.[36]

We can apply Ferguson's, Halberstam's, and Ryan's ideas and questions to library praxis, with particular regard for the ways in which we organize minority knowledges. Might we imagine ways for scholar librarians to work in partnership with academics to create and organize spaces in which subversive ways of knowing circulate and grow? Might we be able to advance this conversation by working from the place where the academy's knowledge is collected and stored? And would a restructuring in the library have an effect on the structure of the academy such that the oppressive techniques observed by Ferguson, Ryan, and others might be altered for the better, in ways that challenge the incorporation of subjects into state apparatuses?

This project would fit within the growing movement to turn libraries into "maker spaces" for students, artists, scientists, historians, librarians, and theorists of all sorts. As libraries are often considered the center of knowledge in the university, they provide the perfect space to carry out creative, interdisciplinary projects in making meaning, exhibits, connections, and texts. What would happen if we all came together to make and unmake readings in the library at the levels of knowledge organization and intertexuality? What if we collectively and individually created new ways of mapping and organizing knowledge by assuming different universalisms and different frames?

Creative Critique

Throughout this book I have tried to demonstrate various ways in which perversion exposes the limits of and exceeds the classificatory apparatuses in the library. In the first chapter we witnessed a variety of ways in which texts exceed the name "paraphilias." Chapters 3 and 4 perhaps best illustrate the irregularity and precariousness of the classification systems, particularly as applied to locating racialized and sexualized subjects spatially on the shelves. These subjects cannot be collated in any single section of the library, and where there are attempts to do so, as in HQ71, the result is a very strange mix. The Delta Collection eventually met its end, as it became clear that librarians were unable or unwilling to confine the Delta books or their contents. Indeed, the subjects and texts in question manage to escape the apparatuses in various ways. Their intertextual relations and their readers do not conform to any particular discipline or name. They traverse the bibliographic universe by way of citationality and interpretation. Nevertheless, I believe that we can do more in libraries to facilitate interdisciplinary conversations.

This project might be considered an example of "critique as creativity," which processes the negativities and "carves out active trajectories of becoming."[37] Critique and problematization in this view are creative undertakings, ones that inhere freedom by seeking forms of resistance that carry possibilities for creating ways of being that escape power's hold. It is by dissecting the apparatuses that we come to recognize our positions in relation to power. To refine classifications of queer and perverse subjects by adding more names and classes to the existing hierarchies is also to make more precise the instrument by which they are rendered objects of knowledge. Exposing the limits of the systems, however, can change the terms of the games of truth. The very mechanisms by which we find and access information—the route to knowledge and how that knowledge is conveyed—are bound to the state. Critique reveals the perversity and ten- uousness of the apparatus that upholds and enforces the law that sets the rules for inscribing the bodies in the library. Perverse readings constitute a process of de-formation and provide entry points into safe spaces for start- ing again, for uncertain, partial readings, and for entirely new relation- ships and interpretations. One way to theorize knowledge organization is through the concept of nomadic subjectivity, which, for Rosi Braidotti, "is a new figuration of subjectivity in a multidifferentiated nonhierarchi- cal way."[38] Such a frame honors the multiplicities of readings and enables a new way of thinking about how to organize bodies of literature, freeing them from their static positions on the shelves and from the names that might confine them and opening them to perverse readings and relations. Similarly, toward the end of his life Foucault wrote: "We must invent with the body, with its elements, surfaces, volumes, and thicknesses, a nondis- ciplinary eroticism—that of a body in a volatile and diffused state, with its chance encounters and unplanned pleasures."[39]

No normative system can ever exhaustively capture or delimit the com- plexities inherent in the social relations in which subjects are formed. A system that operates through categories can only fail to accommodate and position subjects, which is why working from action rather than a category might open up ways to redraw lines of connection and meaning. A project like this must not be limited to a reappropriation of terms, as there will always be an excluded entity upon which any category operates. Citing the case of "queer," Ferguson warns that insofar as "queerness seeks to attain status as a modern and normative mode of difference . . . queerness becomes the engine for a series of exclusions and alienations, particularly around class, gender, and race."[40] Given these conditions, it bears recon- sideration of the charge against the Library of Congress in its resistance to authorize "queer" as a subject heading. Indeed, it may be that the en- try into the system would mark its status as a normalized subject, and as Butler tells us, "normalizing the queer would be, after all, its sad finish."[41] Some would argue that queer is already finished: It has gotten caught in the trap of identity politics, strangely overdetermined and stuck. I still think that queer theory and queer as a verb are important and possible, but part of the reason I use the concept of perversion is that it seems to me to resist identity work. I feel no need to reappropriate or reclaim "perversion," as such a move would serve to reterritorialize it, but thinking about perversion in terms of action means we are always in motion and drawing new lines of connection and meaning, while perpetually challenging normative concepts, frames, and definitions.

Although I have been working toward a theoretical dismantling of LoC systems, I would not suggest we do away with them completely. The large-scale standards have a function in large general collections, and they allow libraries to communicate and share resources. But local and community-based taxonomies written from various points of view can augment and/or replace or even invert the universal classifications, depending on the site and context. The Lesbian Herstory Archives in Brooklyn, New York, serves as a good example. The archive contains 11,000 books and countless archival materials. It also houses a wall of subject files, which are described on the Herstory website:

> Our 1,569 fascinating Subject Files fill the drawers of four, five drawer
> horizontal file cabinets plus overflow boxes. Think of these files as
> "Lesbians and . . . ." The first file is "Abortion" and the last is "Youth."
> In between are such topics as "African-Ancestral Lesbians," "Bars,"
> "Health Care," "Marriage," "Music Festivals," "Publishers," "Religion,"
> "Theatre," and "Violence."[42]

Rather than a male heterosexual universal against which to arrange all other subjects that deviate from that norm, lesbians are the universalized norm and are assumed to be central to the entire system of categories. The thesaurus and subject files system radically reorient conceptualizations of universality and norms. The Herstory Archive inescapably relies on categories but moves them over and actively inverts assumed norms. This kind of practice, performed in various localities in different ways, can foster connecting, diverging, and meandering paths to reading and desire. What's more, the archive also includes a note on describing identity in each of its special collection descriptions:

> It is Lesbian Herstory Archives' policy to acknowledge cultural, sexual,
> and gender identity in donor descriptions whenever it is known. This is
> both to aid researchers who are undertaking projects on lesbians with
> a particular self identification and to combat universal assumptions of
> whiteness and dominant cultural definitions of sexuality and gender.[43]

The Herstory Archive clearly states its policy with regard to identifying cultural associations for the purpose of access, disavowing universalisms and emphasizing the importance of self-identification. It also invites participation from the community so that it can be accurate and precise in assigning donors and their collections to categories. The ways that the Lesbian Herstory Archives rewrites certain archival and library practices by foregrounding and universalizing lesbians' desires and positionalities can serve as one model for organizing knowledge about sex, sexuality, and human subjects.

Indeed, many archivists and librarians are doing this kind of work: creating new indexing systems, building terminologies for queer materials, and revising existing classifications, all while acknowledging and wrestling with the challenge inherent to classifying materials that refuse to be classified.[44]

Reparative Taxonomies: Sedgwick's Loom Book, *a Rhizomatic Taxonomy, and a Perverse Cat's Cradle*

With Sedgwick's call to "become perverse readers" in mind, I have drawn from her textile artwork, Haraway's use of the cat's cradle game, and Deleuze and Guattari's rhizomatic taxonomies to begin to envision alternative ways of drawing connections across texts and readers. Each of these theorists suggests that we should seek new connectivities, ones unrestrained by existing hierarchies. By opening up the possibility for connections drawn from a variety of perspectives, we can collectively arrive at a range of truths that challenge the singular version from the perspective of the Library of Congress.

I propose that we think of the designs described below as *reparative taxonomies* that reflect and facilitate queer and perverse readings. Sedgwick's turn toward reparative reading as critical practice is particularly relevant here.[45] Indeed, paranoid critique that resides in negative space is important and necessary work. But Sedgwick suggests, drawing upon the psychoanalytic frame as articulated by Melanie Klein, that by occupying a depressive position one can move from a paranoid position to perform reparative work.

> This is the position from which it is possible in turn to use one's own resources to assemble or "repair" the murderous part-objects into something like a whole—though, I would emphasize, not necessarily like any preexisting whole. Once assembled to one's own specifications,

the more satisfying object is available to be identified with and to offer one nourishment and comfort in return. Among Klein's names for the reparative process is love.

As Ellis Hanson explains, "faced with the depressing realization that people are fragile and the world hostile, a reparative reading focuses not on the exposure of political outrages that we already know about but rather on the process of reconstructing a sustainable life in this wake."[46] A reparative taxonomy can do this kind of reconstruction work. The aim is not to fix the existing systems but rather to reconfigure relations according to local and personal vantage points.

Indeed, Sedgwick finds taxonomies in all kinds of places—in Proust's long sentences, in Sylvan Tomkins's theory of affect, in J. L. Austin's *How to Do Things with Words*, and in Foucault's *History of Sexuality*. But she views these classifications as undoings, which "open and indicate new vistas" and reveal new "kinds of possible entailments in any generalization."[47] In fact, much of her work can be considered taxonomic, insofar as she questions and revises existing structures and reorganizes knowledge by way of axioms and categories. In *Epistemology of the Closet*, she explains why she privileges nonce taxonomies, which arise out of devalued knowledges. For her Proust and Henry James are the exemplary nonce taxonomists, in their "making and unmaking and *re*making of and redissolution of hundreds of old and new categorical imaginings."[48] What is clear from her description is that this process of making and unmaking taxonomies has no end. As soon as a category is made it becomes situated and risks reification and fixity. There must always be movement, a constant questioning, an unmaking and remaking. It is through the process of always becoming a perverse reader that we can continue this practice of imagining new categories and connections across them.

In the last decade and a half of her life, Sedgwick developed a practice of textile arts and crafts, inspired and influenced in no small measure by Buddhism and her travels to Japan and other parts of the world. Using a range of techniques and materials drawn from a variety of traditions and eras, nearly all of her artwork could be described as suggestions of new ways of seeing. Of these projects, her "loom book" strikes me as a marvelous model upon which we might reformulate connections across readings and texts (Figure 18). This loom book, constructed from string and text and acetate, weaves lines from Proust in layers, so as to convey the nonlinear, alternate dimensionality of the phrases and clauses in Proust. For Sedgwick, this piece provided an opportunity to express her own identifi-

Figure 18. Sedgwick's *Loom Book*. *Source*: Eve Kosofsky Sedgwick, *Loom Book* (detail), board, thread, text, and acetate; 11 × 17. Photo: Kevin Ryan.

cations with the relatedness between Buddhism and Proust, their mystical meditations on the dailiness of life, and the ways that they contributed to her own sense of reality.

I would love to extend this piece and weave through it all of Proust's interlocutors, those texts that cite his lines and cite one another. We could then weave those texts together with texts that cite and recite their lines, as well. We would find what might seem like some of the most unlikely connections, and we may gather a better sense of the strength of textual and authorial connections with which we are already familiar. The beauty of this concept is that an end to such an intertextual, citational weaving is impossible to locate.

Donna Haraway's cat's cradle similarly involves complex interstitial relationships. Taking this as a model allows a resituating of knowledges that the library has put disciplinary distance between, and it encourages not only an intersection of lines but also their interknitting and entanglement.

Cat's cradle is about patterns and knots; the game takes great skill and can result in some serious surprises. One person can build up a large repertoire of string figures on a single pair of hands; but the cat's cradle figures can be passed back and forth on the hands of several players, who add new moves in the building of complex patterns. Cat's cradle invites a sense of collective work, of one person not being able to make all the patterns alone. One does not "win" at cat's cradle; the goal is more interesting and more open-ended than that. It is not always possible to repeat interesting patterns, and figuring out what happened to result in intriguing patterns is an embodied analytical skill. The game is played around the world and can have considerable cultural significance. Cat's cradle is both local and global, distributed and knotted together.[49]

Play becomes the most productive and interesting when it involves multiple hands, and the game can go on indefinitely, changing as it passes across those hands. The cat's cradle is a web made of "interknitted discourses," and to illustrate how it works, Haraway uses cultural studies, feminist, multicultural, antiracist science projects, and science studies. She emphasizes that these fields are not outside or clearly distinct from one another, that they don't simply confront one another along disciplinary lines, but rather, as the cat's cradle reveals, they interact and knot themselves up in one another. For Haraway the tangles are the sites of a critical practice, a "nonhomogeneous, nonexclusive, often mutually constitutive, but also nonisomorphic and sometimes mutually repellent webs of discourse."[50] Again, she seems to agree that some order must be followed, directed by critical scholarly thinking, as without it, one would end up with a useless tangled mess.

Deleuze and Guattari would agree that the existing classifications inhibit relations among books and that part of the problem is that the very attribution of a book to a subject confines the text and its readings: "To attribute the book to a subject is to overlook this working of matters, and the exteriority of their relations. . . . In a book, as in all things, there are lines of articulation or segmentarity, strata and territories; but also lines of flight, movements of deterritorialization and destratification."[51] They argue for a reorganization of bodies into a rhizome, which maps multiplicities and endless flight of ideas. A rhizomatic taxonomy, in contrast to a treelike hierarchy (like the existing library taxonomies), allows growth from any point—from the middle, rather than the roots—and it provides a plane upon which connections and relationships are forged. "Unlike trees or their roots, the rhizome connects any point to any other point, and its traits are not necessarily linked to traits of the same nature."[52] Like the loom and cat's cradle, the rhizome is ongoing, starting points can happen anywhere, and its path is impossible to trace. The rhizome gets entangled in everything it crosses in its development.

Deleuze was particularly fascinated with classifications, and his books on cinema are regarded as new cinematographic taxonomies, designed to facilitate movement and relationships that other classifications of film foreclose. Elizabeth Grosz describes Deleuze's philosophy as being a seeking of "outlines, contours, and methods of a new way of conceiving ontology, new ways of thinking and conceptualizing the real as dynamic, temporally sensitive forms of becoming."[53] Deleuze and Guattari relentlessly point out that a deterritorialization always risks giving itself over to a reterritorialization. I would argue that a classification and the invention of concepts are in fact always reterritorializations and reclaimings, but necessary ones, without which texts would be unretrievable, lost in a mass with every other text. The key is always to keep the categories moving, always to be open to possibilities for unmaking and remaking—not to keep adding to existing structures but to undo them and start again. By locating those spaces and concepts that escape and defy the existing systems, perhaps we can create a desiring ontology that draws the kinds of connections and ways of relating that Deleuze seems to be calling for.

It comes as no surprise that these scholars, whose work extends across and between a huge range of disciplines, are interested in the force and weight of categories. Sedgwick, Deleuze, and Haraway are each skeptical of systems and would likely agree that designing a new system is not the answer. Rather, they would all side with the notion that partial knowledges derived and viewed from multiple points, whether assembled in a rhizome, a loom, or a cat's cradle, provide us with ranges of new possibilities for embodiment and relating. Indeed, bringing these three techniques together with a variety of others already and yet-to-be invented would allow for continually expanding opportunities for engagement.

One way we might draw connections is by showing how perversion and its related concepts travel through texts through processes of citationality, exploring ways that theory and literature and science have collided, comingled, expanded, and given birth to bodies of literature by wrestling with questions of what it means to be perverse. The possibilities for the kinds of connections we could draw across historical and spatial and scholarly and personal aspects of perversion are without limits. The library has drawn a particular set of connections, and reading the library as a map tells us much about the formation of sexuality studies. It begins to reveal how bodies of literature have contributed to the becoming of queer and perverse readings. Indeed, we can extend this methodology to all the disciplines and interdisciplines. Collectively creating new readings from a variety of perspectives might contribute to ways of advancing and thinking about sexuality in interdisciplinary work if we consider how the perverse extends to the far reaches of the library. Addressing the spatial and historical dimensions at play, such a project could trace how sexuality studies has taken shape in and through texts and scholars and students and the public. It would also convey the intertwining of sexuality with disability studies, animal studies, class, race, ethnicity, philosophy, literature, science, art, and politics. If we map these literatures by way of citationality and intertexuality, we will surely find shared histories with dissonance, conversations, violence, misunderstanding, and missed opportunities in space and time. It would show how the perverse runs through it all.

Epilogue: Sadomasochism
in the Library

Franz Kafka's "In the Penal Colony" elaborates the rise and fall of an apparatus—a horrifying device that, over the course of six hours, inscribes a condemned man's body with a sentence, deepening the inscription in the body until death. The officer who carries out the sentencing spends most of the story explaining and demonstrating the apparatus to an explorer who has been invited by the Commandant of the penal colony to review and advise on the efficacy of the machine.

> "I'm chattering, and his apparatus stands here in front of us. As you see, it consists of three parts. With the passage of time certain popular names have been developed for each of these parts. The one underneath is called the Bed, the upper one is called the Inscriber, and here in the middle, this moving part is called the Harrow."
>
> The Traveler wanted to raise various questions, but after looking at the Condemned Man he merely asked, "Does he know his sentence?" "No," said the Officer. He wished to get on with his explanation right away, but the Traveler interrupted him: "He doesn't know his own sentence?" "No," said the Officer once more. He then paused for a moment, as if he were requesting from the Traveler a more detailed

reason for his question, and said, "It would be useless to give him that information. He experiences it on his own body."[1]

The prisoner does not speak the officer's language and cannot comprehend the sentence until the sixth hour, at which point enlightenment is his: "'Nothing else happens. The man simply begins to decipher the inscription. He purses his lips, as if he is listening. You've seen that it is not easy to figure out the inscription with your eyes, but our man deciphers it with his wounds.'" Upon reaching enlightenment, the condemned man is pierced all the way through and is delivered to a pit.

The notion that a body is inscribed and reinscribed with a sentence declaring a person's crime, in a language foreign to the condemned and that is rendered intelligible only by way of the wounds the body bears, provides a powerful (albeit damning) metaphor for the acts of classifying, naming, and labeling bodies of literature that carry subjects or methods that deviate from accepted norms. By way of the disciplinary apparatuses of subject headings, classifications, and restrictive labeling policies, the Library of Congress has effectively condemned certain bodies of literature and, in some cases, sentenced them to certain death. The irony is that, like the penal colony, the library inscribes these classificatory marks in the name of enlightenment—to provide access to knowledge. Some of these classificatory acts are to be considered what Sanford Berman calls "bibliocide," where inadequate, incorrect, and biased cataloging practices render a range of effects: Entire classes of literature may be ghettoized, with the clear indication that the contents within include deviant topics; they may be made invisible and inaccessible, hidden by a lack of meaningful description and subject headings; and by way of labels, entire collections may be designated as restricted, closed off from the public. In the most extreme cases, the sentence is the flames of an incinerator. I invoke Kafka here because, as Jane Bennett writes, he "gives shape to a political stance that is skeptical of established ideals, capable of self-satirical laughter, and available for the 'spiritualization' of public life."[2] In those instances where the absurdity of the systems inspires laughter, the classifications break down. Indeed, the library is Kafkaesque.

Toward the end of the story, the explorer informs the officer that he cannot abide by his request to proclaim the brilliance of the machine publicly. "No," he says, "I am opposed to this procedure." Upon hearing this news, the officer first remains silent, then releases the condemned man from the apparatus and enters into it himself. The apparatus goes haywire, cruelly devouring the officer, jabbing at his flesh rather than inscribing any kind of sentence. No enlightenment would come to the officer. But for readers and the explorer the officer's death is anything but a meaningless sacrifice. It demonstrates the absurdity and perversity of the apparatus and the law as well as their failure to bring into being what they command.

Kafka wrote his story in 1914, within a decade of the publication of the list of LC headings and parts of the Classification. Rather than refiguring his characters as particular officers and commanders and subjects of the library, I take his actors to be models—of the state, its apparatuses, and its subjects. Hannah Arendt writes of Kafka's characters: "Given that these protagonists created by Kafka are not real persons, that it would amount to hubris to identify with them, and that they are only models left in anonymity even where their names are mentioned, it seems to us as though every one of us were being addressed and called."[3] The fact that any particular person might occupy a variety of roles in the story of the penal colony renders the rewriting of the story by refiguring the characters even more difficult. For instance, although my own role might at first most closely resemble that of the explorer, I am not at all external to the machine. I am not a foreigner in a strange land. I am, in a real sense, a cog, having been trained and employed to deploy the apparatuses. I currently teach practicing and aspiring librarians to use the myriad tools, skills, and principles underlying the classifications and their operations. And, while imploring students to think critically about its limitations and problems, I nevertheless find myself proclaiming something like, "It's a remarkable apparatus!" I encourage reluctant students to find comfort in the fact that learning cataloging is like learning a foreign language. The practices of encoding, classifying, and describing all adhere to separate codes and schemas. I have classed works, added subject headings (even when they fail to capture), and I have placed valuable books in a locked case. It would be dishonest to claim that all of these acts didn't bring a degree of satisfaction, a sense that I am protecting, conveying books to their readers, and bringing them to life through control. I have even maintained authority headings in a library's database (all the while taking notes on the more infuriating ones). At the same time, I have experienced the disorientation caused when trying to find books in the catalog and on the shelves. Perhaps it is the masochist in me that finds no place on earth to be as quite as thrilling as the Library of Congress. But it was precisely the training and on-the-job experience, colliding with these subject positions, that delivered me to my research.

Arendt seems to be taking a stance similar to Foucault's ethics of the care of the self—that we are all in the machine, but freedom is possible if each of us answers Kafka's call to break the system down in order to imagine and enact a better life. She writes: "In order, at least in theory, to become a fellow citizen of such a world freed from all bloody apparitions and murderous magic . . . [Kafka] necessarily had to anticipate the destruction of the present world."[4] Freedom in the penal colony only becomes imaginable with the destruction of the apparatus, which not only reverses relations of power but devours itself. It is at the moment that the command "BE JUST" is ordered that things fall apart. It would seem that the illegibility and impossibility of this particular command is what leads to the machine's breakdown.

The library classifications, along with library personnel and all of the technologies and policies, comprise a certain kind of perverse machine—an assemblage that disciplines and sometimes condemns its subjects. We can compare the Library of Congress's classifications with the diagrams designed by the deceased Commandant and carried by the officer as instructions about the apparatus. They map and instruct librarians in how to apply and inscribe terms and classes on the bodies in the library. The explorer, foreign to the country in which the penal colony resided, could not make any sense of the diagrams, frustrating the officer, who had been hoping to impart the beauty of their logics and design. In part the problem was that the set of instructions was a palimpsest, like the LC Classifications, written over by many people over time. The archaic formulation retains its control over those who are operating it even during a time in which it has become illegible. According to Butler, this is Kafka trying to "grapple with experience of time and space that is no longer organized legibly by progress or redemption."[5] In the same vein, patrons visiting the library may be at pains to decipher the intricacies of the rules that guide subject heading and classification creation and applications—a task made more confusing given that it was produced with Progressive Era notions of universality and the state.

One of the joys of reading Kafka springs from his endless trajectories. Deleuze takes Kafka to be an exemplar of nomadic writing, and Kristeva counts Kafka among the great modernists who collapse the Other.[6] In his foreword to Deleuze and Guattari's book on Kafka, Réda Bensmaïa notes that the book brings to light the fact that the compulsion to categorize Kafka's body of work can lead only to failure—"an always excessive reduction of his work."[7] And for Bennett, Kafka evokes a sense of "uncanniness: the Officer's penal system, which aims at closure, impartiality, moral transformation, and responsibility, is disquietingly familiar. Kafka doesn't so much describe a Justice gone horribly wrong as exaggerate the moral ambiguities inherent in an ideal that is always made up of more elements than any one invocation or execution can express."[8] Indeed, it is precisely this problem of trying to unify and capture bodies of literature with a single class or name that effaces multiple meanings and ambiguities.

On the library shelves we find that nearly all of Kafka's work and critiques are brought together in PT2621.A26—the section designated for Kafka within German literature—blatantly territorializing and disciplining a body of literature that extends far beyond any nation or language or author's name.[9] Kafka's struggles with his own sense of place and time as a German-speaking Jew in Prague are well documented in his own diaries and in scholarly analyses. According to Deleuze and Guattari, one of the ways we might define Kafka's body of work derives from his identifications and disidentifications with the German language, and they describe Prague German as a "deterritorialized language, appropriate for strange and minor uses."[10] Thus, it is with Kafka's body of work that we witness a further perverse effect of the system—an erasure of these nomadic, strange, polymorphous aspects of his literature.

I read "In the Penal Colony" as a parable that speaks to my study of the Library of Congress as a state bureaucracy and its apparatuses and that helps undo, so as to remake, a vision of a utopian library. The condemned man, when released, is free but not free. The explorer flees the penal colony, leaving the condemned men to life in the colony. That the former Commandant and his disciple (the officer) are no longer in control might offer reason for hope. There is a new Commandant who has doubted the efficacy of the apparatus all along. But before the explorer leaves (cutting his visit short), he views the dead Commandant's grave, upon which is inscribed: "Here rests the Old Commandant. His followers, who are now not permitted to have a name, buried him in this grave and erected this stone. There exists a prophecy that the Commandant will rise again after a certain number of years and from this house will lead his followers to reconquer the colony. Have faith and wait!" Here is the suggestion that, although the Commandant and his old methods of torture may themselves have been condemned and laid to waste, one might hold out hope in the belief that these techniques will be reborn. It may be the case that the human tendency for violence and control is so great that, although this particular apparatus is no longer functional, another equally menacing disciplinary mechanism will take its place. And as long as relations of power are present such as they are in the penal colony, apparatuses will be necessary to enact and inscribe the rules of the law.

It is for this reason that I am not so quick to find a solution by creating another system. I am skeptical of claims that the digital realm enables the lines of flight. Indeed, the Internet has become another battleground for claims to territory and authority. Far from the democratic space that we might imagine it to be, it has become a scene of surveillance and the advancement of capitalism. And battles over who speaks for whom and for what purposes access is granted and denied will only continue to unfold. I am not willing to relocate the library to the digital universe, nor am I quite able to endorse technologies like tagging and the semantic web. Whereas some scholars view such advances as holding great promise for access to information, I accept them with great reserve and cannot help viewing such technologies as another arrival of the devices of control and discipline.

Kafka's story is not only a great allegory for the library; it is an expression of polymorphous perversity on a particularly artful scale. Plenty of scholars have examined the sexual perversions in Kafka's oeuvre, but Anna Katharina Schaffner argues that part of Kafka's greatness has to do with the way it resists classifications and delineations and the ways in which it exposes the perversity of all desire. For her, Kafka's polyvalence destabilizes anything we think we know about the perversions. She points to his personal study of psychoanalysis—with Wilhelm Stekel's work being among those with which he was most familiar. Kafka also read Sacher-Masoch, Sade, and Freud, and he had a personal collection of pornography. Schaffner describes "In the Penal Colony" as a "homo-erotic torture-redemption fantasy" and marvels in its reversal of social and sexual hierarchies.[11] And Clayton Koelb points out that the apparatus in the penal colony is an explication of a machine that enacts disciplinary power through a sexualized ritual:

> The condemned prisoner is laid out, naked, on a platform covered with
> a layer of cotton and named "the Bed," while the Harrow, a mechanism
> shaped exactly like a human body, is placed in contact with him. In
> this copulation of man and machine, however, the male sexual role is
> reserved entirely to the machine. Not only is it covered with hundreds
> of penetrating and spraying organs, but it also performs a grotesque
> parody of sexual excitement . . . rigid discipline, is thus both sexual
> and authoritarian.[12]

The apparatus is perverse, as is, I would suggest, the desire to control the entire bibliographic universe through the practice of inscribing names and classes. But it the kind of perversion that does harm and stands in opposition to the kind of perversion I seek to embrace.

Similarly, drawing upon Deleuze, Margot Norris reads "In the Penal Colony" as an intensive study of sadism—one that reveals the perversity and absurdity of the law. She suggests that there may be no better source for a textual analysis of sadism than Kafka. "In the Penal Colony" so beautifully illustrates law with no content—one that is upheld by an apparatus that is meant to inscribe and demonstrate the rule but that is so easily blown up in the face of the explorer's gaze and critique. Norris argues that the diagrams and machinery combine to render the torture and execution impersonal, reducing them to pure reason, and, citing Deleuze and Barthes, she writes: "The subordination of personal lusts and passions to a sham rational system, the phenomenon of 'reasoned crime' is the violence behind the violence in sadism."[13] The officer's failure to convince the explorer of the efficacy of the rational system results in a reversal of the processes by which we come to view pain as acceptable. Following this line of argument, I suggest we consider the classificatory apparatuses of the library similarly, as order and reason necessarily rationalize suffering. To organize by class and name is to exclude and silence certain bodies. It is the justification of violence by necessity of the law that I wish to undermine. It is through perverse subjects that we can pierce through such rationalizing explanations of the inadequacies inherent in our present bibliographic control systems. And it is by way of this particular group of subjects that we see how flimsy the machine is, even with its multiple efforts to ensure disciplinary effects.

Let us not forget that the condemned man's crime was that he did not honor authority and that what is in question in this project are the rules of authorized subjects, names, and classes. It was precisely this body that refused the law that turned the machine on itself. Indeed, the body that challenged the law exposed that law's injustices. Deleuze and Guattari suggest that language is made to be obeyed; "order-words" give orders and order/organize the universe: "Language is not life; it gives life orders. . . . Every order-word, even a father's to his son, carries a little death sentence—a Judgment, as Kafka put it."[14] Perverse bodies and readings subvert the law, subjecting it to its own violence. To be sure, the reasoning behind such adherence to standards is an argument founded on the ideal of access: If all libraries use the same terms, the databases will communicate with one another, shared catalogs are possible, efficiency abounds and duplication of effort is eliminated, and the uniformity ensures searchability across systems. Among the libraries there is a shared language, but that may or may not be legible to the members of the public who visit them. There is a great sense of the necessity of the apparatuses and the standards, which, in turn, justifies their violence and sustains the belief in the efficacy of the systems.

We do not know the crimes committed by the members of the penal colony. The only evidence we have is the sentence imposed on the condemned and the word of the report about the prisoner who failed in the completely ridiculous task to which he was set, resulting in the inscription "HONOR YOUR SUPERIORS." The crime that resulted in a death sentence was that he did not submit to authority. But we don't know why he was in the penal colony in the first place. Let us assume that the residents are perverse in some way; they have perverted, rejected, or attempted to subvert a law, and they are being punished for it. Likewise, we have no evidence that the machine ever really brought enlightenment. We have to take the officer's word for what was read on the faces of the condemned. In truth, for all we know, the enlightenment viewed on the faces of the dying may have been the recognition of the injustice of the entire apparatus and the system.

So again, we can return to the question of legibility and recognition. For Andreas Gailus, Kafka's apparatus strips the body of life through the act of inscription:

> It stages a scene of ideological recognition: the moment of transfigura-
> tion is the one when the prisoner deciphers, and recognizes himself
> in, the Law that is being inscribed onto his body. . . . The Law is
> inscribed through a process of repetitive writing that hollows out the
> body and evacuates its corporeality. The writing of the Law is therefore
> not, as the officer believes—and wants others to believe—a miraculous
> fusion of body and meaning. Rather, it is a mechanical operation for ex-
> tracting the body's vital energies. Thus the radiating image of compre-
> hension on the prisoner's face is the product of a terrifying exchange;
> it is the chiastic transfer of a meaning whose vitality is brought about
> through the extraction of life from the body.[15]

We might ask when and where recognition happens. There seems never to be any recognition of the subjects in this story. Rather, it is by way of the inscription that the body's life is expelled. And it is only through that inscribing/condemning/killing that the subject recognizes its position in relation to power. Ultimately, it is this incapacity to recognize or signify that makes the system break down, and without the support of the apparatus, we might assume the colony will crumble along with it.

Jane Bennett writes: "The term 'Kafkaesque' is conventionally applied to situations involving an organization that is in principle highly complex and relentlessly efficient—but in fact so obese that it is anarchic, so thorough in aspiration that it is inefficient, so comprehensive in aim that it is incomprehensible, so rational in design that it is idiotic."[16] If we relocate this plot to the Library of Congress, an arm of the state, with its current organization having been designed at a time when bureaucratic expansion and technological efficiencies reigned, we immediately recognize the possibilities for freedom that come with the undoing of the apparatus that inscribes the bodies that escape recognition.

The Masochistic User

Early on I said that any reference to a library "user" would be deferred to the end of the book. Ron Day has suggested very convincingly that the construction of the user in library and information science has failed to point to the processes by which users and user needs are produced by the systems they use. Day calls for moving beyond the "user" as generally conceived by information science toward a conceptualization that views subjects and objects as co-constitutive and co-emergent within "in-common zones for affects between bodies."[17] More precisely, for the purposes of this particular analysis, subjects and objects can and do use one another. Having analyzed the power structures in the library and how those structures produce subjects, we can see not only where the system breaks down and opportunities for creating new paths for knowledge discovery, but with this critical work we can assume a position of power within the existing mix. In such a scene, the life of a user in the erotics of the library takes on entirely new depths. By removing violence from the contexts in which it is used to encode unjust laws and uphold relations of power, and then appropriating it for bodily pleasure, sadomasochism dissolves the foundations upon which those laws are built.

In contrast to the interpretations of sadism in the penal colony, I would like to end with the suggestion that it is in viewing the user as a masochist that we find freedom in the library. Masochism remains a great mystery, with wildly diverging theories and interpretations that entertain and frustrate the mind. I am being deliberately selective in my positioning the user as a masochist, and, no doubt, there will readers who will disagree with my decision to conclude on this perverse note. This is intended to be playful and not at all a final interpretation. It is my own attempt at a perverse reading. I speculate that the masochistic user is, in fact, the necessary agent for gaining freedom in knowledge/power/pleasure relations because, as Noyes puts it, "the struggles we have come to associate with masochism are struggles for a technology of control."[18]

I dare to side with the Marquis de Sade—or at least particular readings of his work and life. Jean Paulhan, writing in 1946, actually viewed Sade to be a masochist, and in spite of the fact that he found the masochistic position of deriving pleasure from pain completely incomprehensible, Paulhan determined that Sade, with his repeated imprisonments that so neatly paralleled the virtuous Justine's subjection to brutality and abuse, must be read as a masochist.[19] What Sade did, in Élisabeth Roudinesco's and Paulhan's views, was to expose the fact that people derive pleasure from destroying and brutalizing others—even those we love. His writings are a refusal of lies and cover-ups, a refusal of the law, and an exposure of the evil that underlies nature and humanity. Roudinesco says that Sade "distorted the Enlightenment Project to such a degree that he turned it into its antithesis."[20] Indeed, he created a universal system based on the logic of pleasure, and his writings promoted a pleasure economy that exchanged in power and destruction and cruelty. I would argue that the brilliance of Sade is the way in which his system revealed the absurdity of universalisms. His "catalogue of sexual perversions"—*120 Days of Sodom*—might best be read as system akin to Borges's Chinese classification, as it reveals the extent to which a "rational" system is, in fact, politically and socially situated and motivated, serving those for whom it is designed.[21] A man who belonged to the age of encyclopedists, he was a steadfast collector and cataloger (and even applied for a position as head librarian at one point). Sade parodied the sciences, abolished the Law of God, and turned jouissance into a discipline. In Roudinesco's interpretation, Sade's writings realized a utopia where the Law was inverted. And it is with Sade that perversion made a mockery of the "natural order" and laws of procreation. Ironically, while the censors locked his books away, Krafft-Ebing consecrated Sade's categories in his sexological taxonomy. This is why it is important to view Sade's work for its power to draw attention to the ways in which a universal system, based on Enlightenment ideals, can easily be used as justification for violence and subjection. Sade revealed the perversity of positivist ethics that sought to control the human passions.

For that (and other reasons, to be sure) the Marquis de Sade was imprisoned for much of his adult life. Nevertheless, Paulhan viewed Sade to be the freest spirit, even while his body suffered confinement. Relatedly, Slavoj Žižek argues that a masochistic staging is the first act of liberation: In order to be freed of our subjection, we must invest the body in a redemptive violence.[22] According to both Žižek and Michael Uebel, masochistic violence is rooted in a desire for interbeing. For Uebel, the violent act denies the unbearable necessity of interdependence and contravenes shame and the fear of alienation.[23] For Žižek it brings a certain connection between the masochist and the dominant.

According to Deleuze, we must rethink the notion that the sadist is complementary to the masochist. Instead, he construes the masochist in relation to a dominant—one who is not a sadist but who derives pleasure from supporting the masochist's desires in power play. As Amber Musser explains, "Deleuze's masochist cannot be thought as a singular entity—s/he requires a symbolic dominator to be complicit in the illusion of powerlessness."[24] I part ways from Deleuze where he says that an encounter between the sadist and masochist is impossible because they are organized around entirely different orientations. But I would agree that masochism is a cultural practice—one of the imagination and aesthetics—whereas the sadist is a systematizer. And I would suggest that Sade illustrates a profoundly sadomasochist being—one who drew up a great system based on a logic of perversion, but one who must first be read as a creator of fictions and a cultural figure—a masochist who upset social norms through writing "the most indefinable body of work in the entire history of literature."[25] There certainly is a masochistic side to Sade—one that aligns quite nicely with the masochistic library user. Sade's work has a life that far exceeds him, and we as readers encounter a truth of ourselves and our world in Sade. Nature and man and laws are cruel. We face the deeply unsettling experience of simultaneous arousal and disgust, precipitated by what Sade understood to be a universal condition of humankind. While our first response may be to write his work off as the product of a madman, we eventually come to the realization that the world is mad and perverse and that we are, too.

The necessary interrelation between the masochist and the dominant becomes clear in the library. As Day suggests, systems and their users must be understood as interdependent and coemergent. For Deleuze, masochism has several formal characteristics. For one, the fantasy is of "primordial importance" for the masochistic scene to commence. It is always a contractual relation, but the masochist pushes the contract to its extremes by dismantling its machinery and exposing it to mockery. The masochist is not weak, nor does s/he aim toward self-annihilation, but rather, citing Theodor Reik, Deleuze finds the masochistic traits to be "defiance, vengeance, sarcasm, sabotage, and derision."[26] The mockery of the Law of the Father is manifested in a submission to that law in order to obtain a forbidden pleasure. Deleuze suggests that by "scrupulously submitting" to the law that seeks to separate us from pleasure, we are subverting it. There is a "masochistic form of humour" that demonstrates the absurdity of the law. The masochistic contract always positions punishment as primary—not that the masochist necessarily enjoys being punished (s/he may or may not) but that it is required as a sort of rite of passage in order to obtain pleasure.

Masochism illustrates the possibility for agency in acts of subordination, in a desire to submit. It is not that the masochist loves submission for its own sake, however. John Noyes explains this so well:

> Within this network of bodily spaces and mediating machines, masochism is not the love of submissiveness. It is not the purity of unpleasure or humiliation. It is a complex set of strategies for transforming submissiveness, pain, and unpleasure into sexual pleasure. But over and above this, it is the appropriation of the technologies that our culture uses in order to perpetuate submissiveness, an appropriation that plays a subtle game with the machinery of domination. As such, masochism is the eroticism of the machine, or . . . "An erotics of discipline."

Noyes also reveals that masochism as we know it is a nineteenth-century invention. Or rather, the pathologization of the erotic acts made famous by Leopold von Sacher-Masoch's fiction, the person for whom Krafft-Ebing named the condition, is a specific (and, arguably, perverse) form of disciplining. In reducing a suite of expressions to a category within his taxonomy of perversions, Krafft-Ebing erased the historical and cultural contexts in which masochism is required and thrives. Indeed, Sacher-Masoch's *Venus in Furs* and other stories each displaced the scenes of subjection, humiliation, and violence of social and political conflict in mid-nineteenth-century Eastern Europe into the sexual realm. Writing about sexual power was effectively a dramatization of political power. Like the Marquis de Sade, Sacher-Masoch depicts a struggle between reason and nature in the bedroom, to formalize wider political and social conflicts. Foucault's description brings this together neatly: Sadomasochism, according to him, is "the eroticization of power, the eroticization of strategic relations. . . . It is an acting-out of power structures by a strategic game that is able to give sexual pleasure or bodily pleasure."[27] It also appears to Foucault that sadomasochism is the "real creation of new possibilities of pleasure." Given that he viewed the invention of new possibilities to be the highest form of resistance within relations of power, the masochist in the library might actually have the greatest capacity to create new possibilities for knowledge and self-discovery.

It is hardly surprising that Sedgwick mentions her own encounters with the library catalog in her essay about beating fantasies. Recall her words from "A Poem Is Being Written": "The wooden subject, author, and title catalogues frustrate and educate the young idea."²⁸ We enter into a library, seeking pleasure in books, and submitting to the laws as written in the classification and in the terms of use. For many of us, the entire of suite of encounters—entering the building, searching the catalog, inquiring with the reference librarian, checking out books—is simultaneously thrilling, intimidating, and fearsome. The first step toward obtaining pleasure in perverse readings is to submit oneself to the library's disciplinary techniques. The threats of punishment and shame are real. And the shelves, with their separation of subjects from one another and the placement of sexualized and racialized subjects in the margins, reflect one's alienation. Take, for instance, Lillian Faderman's account of first discovering a book about lesbians in the library:

> So I'm in the stacks of the English Reading Room about to be seduced. I'm looking for a novel by E. M. Forster, and it's not there. . . . But in the spot where the book is supposed to be sitting is another book, not by Forster, but by Foster. Jeannette Foster. With the title *Sex Variant Women in Literature*. . . . Is "Sex Variant Women" really a euphemism for what I think it is? It is! And that spectacular revelation knocks the breath out of me. . . . Standing there in the stacks, I devour the opening section, even forgetting to look over my shoulder to see if I'm being observed. I read for twenty minutes or half an hour, and no one comes by to frighten me away. But I mustn't press my luck. I place the book back in its slot, vowing to visit again as soon as I can, praying I'll have no rival for my devoted attention to it.²⁹

This tale is charged with a magnificent erotic tension deriving from the pleasure obtained after submitting, and the threat of being caught, with the continued worry of a rival. She will return to this spot repeatedly, subjecting herself again to gain forbidden, secret pleasures.

The dominant library and its systems must be viewed in relation to the user, as it is by submitting to the law that users find their books and their pleasures, in spite of the disciplinary lines. In order to use the library, users must subject themselves to these dividing practices and participate in the denial of intertextuality and intersubjectivity by seeking texts in various spaces, as determined and disciplined by the rules. But we must also consider how the user is used by the library and how the constitution of subjects is integral to these relations between the library and its users. One might argue that the enmeshment of human subjectivity in technologies of control begins with categories. Of course, the trick, as Žižek points out, is in knowing how to draw the line between redemptive violence and the kind that "confirms one's entrapment."[30] This, in my view, is the purpose of critique, and I would argue that it is by first submitting to the rules and cruising the lines of shelves, and then through defiance, curiosity, perseverance, and mockery of the laws of classification, that perverse readings and pleasures become possible.

Perverse subjects expose the library classifications to their own weaknesses, or to the extent to which the condition of the apparatus is one of "being in force without significance."[31] The inability of the system to signify or enforce a law via the inscription of categories means that the rationally ordered hierarchies quite easily collapse under their own weight. The authority with which they are created and enforced is then called into question, and we have to ask whether and how we can consent to the terms by which we engage in the relations of power when we enter a library, peruse its catalog, and browse the shelves. I would suggest that, as long as we do the kind of work that examines how the machine functions, take it apart, and interrogate the mechanisms by which knowledge is produced and circulated, we are able to move toward a more just way of producing knowledge. Relations of power are always present, but we are, in fact, free in the library if we understand what is going on. We can consent to playing the power games. Through the act of dismantling the system, even if only in theory, we can open the library up to other possibilities, particularly in the ways that we figure and refigure the self in relation to the system and its subjects.

Acknowledgments

The most challenging part of finishing a book might be finding the words to convey the depth of my gratitude to all of the people who helped make it possible. There are certain people without whom I am quite sure this book would never have been imaginable, much less a real thing, and there are many others who have provided invaluable opportunities, feedback, and emotional support.

This book started out at the University of Wisconsin–Madison. I am especially grateful for Christine Pawley's mentorship and continued support. I also thank Greg Downey, Finn Enke, Helen Kinsella, and Louise Robbins, for encouraging me to reach. Thanks to friends and colleagues who supported me in those years—especially Nathan Johnson, Michelle Caswell, Michelle Besant, Anjali Bhasin, Rebekah Willett, Kristin Eschenfelder, Katie Zaman, Ethelene Whitmire, and Brenton Stewart.

The research was supported by a Social Science Research Council fellowship. That program not only funded a good deal of my research, but it also brought me into a rich interdisciplinary group led by Samuel Lucas and Lisa Materson. Thanks also to Trevor Hoppe, Kate Jirik, and Stephanie Hinnershitz. I conducted most of my archival research at the Library of Congress and have many people to thank for their assistance, including Cheryl Fox in the Manuscript Reading Room; Thomas Yee, Beecher Wiggins, Mary K. D. Pietris, and Paul Weiss in the Policy and Standards Division; and Thomas Mann and David Kelley for their reference help. I also thank Melissa Salrin and the staff at the American Library Association Archives at the University of Illinois, Urbana-Champaign.

My first three years at the University of Kentucky have been more fruitful than I could have imagined, in part because of a few extraordinary individuals. Carol Mason has been priceless in affirming my voice and catalyzing a major turning point in my writing, and I am grateful for Marion Rust and Lisa Cliggett for welcoming me to the Committee on Social Theory. Thanks to my Lexington colleagues and friends, each of whom has uniquely supplied emotional and/or intellectual support: Jeff Huber, David Nemer, Shannon Oltmann, Ellen Riggle, Rusty Barrett, Ashley Ruderman, Sean Burns, and Amy Sharland.

I also must thank those who have invited me to speak and work through pieces of the project. I am especially grateful to Jens-Erik Mai and Joseph Tennis for asking me to take part in a 2015 knowledge organization forum in Copenhagen. Thanks also to Emily Drabinski and Patrick Keilty for including me in the 2014 Gender and Sexuality in Information Studies colloquium and reader and for their work in building this field. Thanks to the Library and Information Science faculty at the University of Missouri and the College of Communication and Information at the University of Kentucky for inviting me to speak. I am grateful to the participants at the 2016 LACUNY Institute, the 2014 Deleuze Studies Conference in Istanbul, the 2014 Document Academy meeting, the 2016 LGBTQ* Archives, Libraries, Museums, and Special Collections conference in London, and the Classification Research group of the Association for Information Science and Technology. Thanks to Grant Campbell, Barbara Kwasnik, and Jonathan Furner.

It is an honor to have Richard Morrison as an editor and new friend. This book has been greatly improved by his insight and care. Gratitude goes to the Fordham University Press staff—especially Eric Newman and Robert Fellman, whose curiosity helped unearth pieces of a puzzle that I didn't even know were missing. Thanks to Janet Francendese for seeing the potential of this project when it was still very new. Thanks to Katie Kent and Polly Thistlethwaite for their readings and feedback. And I am indebted to Ron Day for his generosity, encouragement, and attentive readings.

I am grateful to the publishers who granted permission to reproduce content for publication here. Material has been borrowed from an article produced in the early stages of the project: "PARAPHILIAS: The Perversion of Meaning in the Library of Congress Subject Headings," in *Feminist and Queer Information Studies Reader*, ed. Rebecca Dean and Patrick Keilty (Duluth, Minn.: Library Juice Press, 2014); reprinted from *Advances in Classification Research Online* (2011). Chapter 2 is expanded and revised from "The Keeper of the Collections and the Delta Collection: Regulating Obscenity at the Library of Congress, 1940–1963," *Interactions: UCLA Journal of Education and Information Studies* 12, no.1 (2016). Thanks to Hal Sedgwick for allowing me to reproduce Eve Kosofsky Sedgwick's *Loom Book*.

I must extend heartfelt gratitude to librarians everywhere—especially those who fiercely guard intellectual freedom, promote equitable access, and protect the cultural record. Thanks to the catalogers who will catalog this book. I can't wait to see its bibliographic record and to find out where it will be shelved.

Thanks to Valerie Adler, grandma and catalog librarian at Marshfield Public Library, and my parents, Dick Adler and Peggy Michalski. I carry each of your spirits with me always.

A very special thanks goes to Stella and Gabe Guralski, who have been with me on this journey since they were very small. Stella, your bravery and strength and talent inspire me beyond words. Gabe, your compassion and courage and cleverness amaze me every day. More than anyone, you have had to bear the madness of it all. You are two of the most remarkable people I know. I cherish you both.

And Sharon Sliwinski, thank you for being a heart and a safe harbor, for seeing and being seen, but, most of all, for keeping the dream alive.

PREFACE

1. Lauren Berlant, "Two Girls, Fat and Thin," in *Regarding Sedgwick: Essays on Queer Culture and Critical Theory*, ed. Stephen M. Barber and David L. Clark. (New York: Routledge, 2013), 71.

2. Queer Theory: Lesbian and Gay Sexualities, University of California at Santa Cruz. Proceedings published in a special issue of *differences* 3, no. 2 (1991).

3. "Review of *Epistemology of the Closet*, by Eve Kosofsky Sedgwick," *Publishers Weekly* (1990), http://www.publishersweekly.com/978-0-520-07042-4.

4. Library of Congress catalog record for *Epistemology of the Closet*, http://lccn.loc.gov/90035697/marcxml.

5. Not all research libraries use the Library of Congress Classification, but the vast majority of American research libraries do, as do many libraries on all continents. I did verify that university libraries in Hong Kong, Toronto, Sydney, and Kentucky use the LoC system to organize their collections. Other classifications include the Dewey Decimal System and the Universal Decimal System (based on Dewey and used widely in Europe).

6. Libraries certainly can change the classification, but most of the time they retain the class provided in the original catalog record. The libraries I looked at kept the classification given by the LoC to *Epistemology of the Closet*. For the current descriptions of classes within the Library of Congress Classification, I relied on Classification Web, a cataloging tool used by librarians and produced by the Library of Congress Catalog Distribution Service, copyright Minaret Corporation and Library of Congress.

7. Ronald E. Day, *Indexing It All: The Subject in the Age of Documentation, Information, and Data* (Cambridge, Mass.: MIT Press, 2014), 41.

8. José Esteban Muñoz, *Cruising Utopia: The Then and There of Queer Futurity* (New York: New York University Press, 2009).

9. Ibid., 15.

10. There are hundreds of controlled vocabularies similar to the Library of Congress Subject Headings. They are often topic specific, as with the Medical Subject Headings or the Getty Thesaurus for Art and Architecture,

and they tend to be used among particular communities of interest or on a very local level. For those, the terms are authorized by experts in the fields. The Library of Congress Subject Headings are in used in almost every public and academic library in the United States as well as in many digital libraries and libraries in countries other than the United States.

INTRODUCTION: A BOOK IS BEING CATALOGED

1. Eve Kosofsky Sedgwick, "A Poem Is Being Written," *Representations* 17 (1987): 132.

2. Eve Kosofsky Sedgwick, *Epistemology of the Closet* (Berkeley: University of California Press, 1990), 3.

3. Umberto Eco, "De Bibliotheca," in *Sette Anni di Desiderio* (Milano: Bompiani, 1983); quoted in Michael F. Winter, "Umberto Eco on Libraries: A Discussion of 'De Bibliotheca,'" *Library Quarterly* 64, no. 2 (1994): 120.

4. Eve Kosofsky Sedgwick, "Queer and Now," in *Tendencies* (Durham, N.C.: Duke University Press, 1993), 4.

5. Patricia MacCormack, "Perversion: Transgressive Sexuality and Becoming-Monstrous," *thirdspace: a journal of feminist theory & culture* 3, no.4 (2004), para. 9.

6. Deborah Britzman, *Lost Subjects, Contested Objects: Toward a Psychoanalytic Inquiry of Learning* (Albany: SUNY Press, 1998), 69.

7. Roderick A. Ferguson, *The Reorder of Things: The University and Its Pedagogies of Minority Difference* (Minneapolis: University of Minnesota Press, 2012), 232.

8. Lauren Berlant and Michael Warner, "What Does Queer Theory Teach Us About X?" *PMLA* 110, no. 3 (1995): 344; Eve Sedgwick, "Shame in the Cybernetic Fold," in *Touching Feeling: Affect, Pedagogy, Performativity* (Durham, N.C.: Duke University Press, 2003), 118.

9. MacCormack, "Perversion," para. 8.

10. Julia Kristeva, *Powers of Horror: An Essay on Abjection*, trans. Leon S. Roudiez (New York: Columbia University Press, 1982), 4.

11. Ibid, 16.

12. Michel Foucault, *The History of Sexuality*, vol. 1. (New York: Vintage, 1990), 81.

13. Michel Foucault, "Ethics of the Concern for Self as a Practice of Freedom," in *Essential Works of Michel Foucault, 1954–1984*, vol. 1: *Ethics: Subjectivity and Truth*, ed. Paul Rabinow (New York: The Free Press, 1997), 288.

14. Ibid., 285.

15. Deborah Britzman, "Theory Kindergarten," in *Regarding Sedgwick: Essays on Queer Culture and Critical Theory*, ed. Stephen M. Barber and David L. Clark (New York: Routledge, 2002), 128.

16. Foucault, "Ethics of the Concern for Self," 284.

17. Ian Buchanan, "The Problem of the Body in Deleuze and Guattari, Or, What Can a Body Do?" *Body Society* 3 (1997): 76.

18. Ronald E. Day, "Diagrammatic Bodies," in *Organized Worlds: Explorations in Technology and Organization with Robert Cooper*, ed. Robert C. H. Chia (London: Routledge, 1998), 99.

19. Gilles Deleuze and Félix Guattari, *A Thousand Plateaus: Capitalism and Schizophrenia* (Minneapolis: University of Minnesota Press, 1987), 257.

20. Eve Kosofsky Sedgwick, *Touching Feeling: Affect, Pedagogy, Performativity* (Durham, N.C.: Duke University Press, 2003), 124.

21. Adam L. Schiff, *SACO Participants Manual* (Washington, D.C.: LC Catalog Distribution Service, 2001), 10. http://www.loc.gov/catdir/pcc/saco/sacomanual.pdf.

22. This is what cataloging staff at LC said to me in conversation in 2010.

23. Marla S. Nonken to Betty Bengtson, January 8, 1989, Box 26, Library of Congress Subject Cataloging Division Papers, Library of Congress Manuscripts Division, Washington, D.C.

24. Mary K. D. Pietris to Maria [*sic*] S. Nonken, March 1, 1989, Box 26, Library of Congress Subject Cataloging Division Papers.

25. For a defense of retaining catalog cards for the historical record, see Nicholson Baker, "Discards," *New Yorker* (April 4, 1994): 64–86.

26. Patrick Wilson, *Two Kinds of Power: An Essay on Bibliographical Control* (Berkeley: University of California Press, 1968), 4.

27. Samuel Gerald Collins, *Library of Walls: The Library of Congress and the Contradictions of Information Society* (Duluth, Minn.: Litwin, 2009), 27.

28. There are far too many to name, so I supply a few select examples: Michelle Caswell, *Archiving the Unspeakable: Silence, Memory, and the Photographic Record in Cambodia* (Madison: University of Wisconsin Press, 2014); Kate Eichhorn, *The Archival Turn in Feminism: Outrage in Order* (Philadelphia: Temple University Press, 2014); Ann Laura Stoler, *Along the Archival Grain: Epistemic Anxieties and Colonial Common Sense* (Princeton, N.J.: Princeton University Press, 2010); Diana Taylor, *The Archive and the Repertoire: Performing Cultural Memory in the Americas* (Durham, N.C.: Duke University Press, 2003); Geoffrey Bowker and Susan Leigh Star, *Sorting Things Out: Classification and Its Consequences* (Cambridge, Mass.: MIT Press, 1999); Ann Cvetkovich, *An Archive of Feelings: Trauma, Sexuality, and Lesbian Public Cultures* (Durham, N.C.: Duke University Press, 2003).

29. Michel Foucault, *Society Must Be Defended: Lectures at the Collège de France, 1975–76*, ed. Mauro Bertani and Alessandro Fontana, trans. David Macey (New York: Picador, 2003), 224.

30. Ibid., 212.

31. Rory Litwin, "Interview with Barbara Tillett," *Library Juice* blog, August 9, 2006, http://libraryjuicepress.com/blog/?p=115.

32. In fact, both "Aliens" and "Illegal aliens" would be cancelled according to this plan. "Aliens" will be replaced by "Noncitizens," and "Illegal aliens" would be replaced with both "Noncitizens" and "Unauthorized immigration," depending on the contents of the book being cataloged.

33. Lisa Peet, "Library of Congress Drops Illegal Alien Subject Heading, Provokes Backlash Legislation," *Library Journal* (May 24, 2016). http://lj.libraryjournal.com/2016/05/organizations/ala-organization/library-of-congress-drops-illegal-alien-subject-heading-provokes-backlash-legislation/#_.

34. Lamar Smith, Jeff Sessions, Ted Cruz, and John A. Culberson to David S. Mao, Letter to Library of Congress re Illegal Alien (May 19, 2016), https://www.scribd.com/mobile/doc/313551827/Letter-to-Library-of-Congress-Re-Illegal-Alien?skip_app_promo=true.

35. Diane Black, Quoted in Peet, "Library of Congress Drops Illegal Alien Subject Heading."

36. Margot Canaday, *The Straight State: Sexuality and Citizenship in Twentieth-Century America* (Princeton, N.J.: Princeton University Press, 2009), 53.

37. Giorgio Agamben, *"What Is an Apparatus?" and Other Essays*, trans. David Kishik and Stefan Pedatella (Stanford, Calif.: Stanford University Press), 14.

38. Ibid., 14.

39. For a Foucauldian reading of the culture of fear and stereotypes of librarians, see Gary P. Radford and Marie L. Radford, "Libraries, Librarians, and the Discourse of Fear," *Library Quarterly* 71, no. 3 (2001): 299–329.

40. Giorgio Agamben, *The Open: Man and Animal*, trans. Kevin Attell (Stanford, Calif.: Stanford University Press, 2004).

41. Michel Foucault, "The Fantasia of the Library" [1967], in *Michel Foucault, Language, Counter-memory, Practice: Selected Essays and Interviews*, ed. Donald. F. Bouchard (Ithaca, N.Y.: Cornell University Press, 1977). See also Gary P. Radford, "Flaubert, Foucault, and the Bibliotheque Fantastique: Toward a Postmodern Epistemology for Library Science," *Library Trends* 46, no. 4 (1998): 616–634.

42. Michel Foucault, "Preface to Transgression," in *Language, Counter-Memory, Practice: Selected Essays and Interviews*, ed. Donald F. Bouchard (Ithaca, N.Y.: Cornell University Press, 1977), 50.

43. Ronald E. Day, "Death of the User: Reconceptualizing Subjects, Objects, and Their Relations," *Journal of the American Society for Information Science and Technology* 62, no. 1 (2011): 78–88; Ronald E. Day, *Indexing It All:*

The Subject in the Age of Documentation, Information, and Data (Cambridge, Mass.: MIT Press, 2014).

44. Day, *Indexing It All*, 41.

45. John Cole, Henry H. Reed, and Herbert Small, *The Library of Congress: The Art and Architecture of the Thomas Jefferson Building* (New York: Norton, 1997), 59.

46. William Warner Bishop, "Thirty Years of the Library of Congress, 1899 to 1929," in *Essays Offered to Herbert Putnam by His Colleagues and Friends on His Thirtieth Anniversary as Librarian of Congress* (New Haven, Conn.: Yale University Press, 1929), 26.

47. Francis Miksa, *The Development of Classification at the Library of Congress*, Occasional Papers 164 (Champaign: University of Illinois, 1984).

48. Wayne Wiegand, "Tunnel Vision and Blind Spots," *Library Quarterly* 69 (1999): 4.

49. Roosevelt to Putnam, October 6, 1902. Roosevelt Papers, quoted in Paul T. Heffron, *Index to the Theodore Roosevelt Papers* (Washington, D.C.: Library of Congress, 1969). http://memory.loc.gov/ammem/trhtml/trfaid .html#eight.

50. Heffron, *Index to the Theodore Roosevelt Papers*.

51. Speech to Theodore Roosevelt Memorial Association, October 27, 1929, quoted in Heffron, *Index to the Theodore Roosevelt Papers*. It seems that, without Roosevelt's support, the Library of Congress might look very different today. The relationship between Putnam and Roosevelt would be a fascinating topic for further study.

52. Herbert Putnam, quoted in David C. Mearns, "Herbert Putnam and His Responsible Eye—A Memorial Tribute" in *Herbert Putnam, 1861–1955: A Memorial Tribute* (Washington, D.C.: Library of Congress, 1956), 38.

53. At the same time that Roosevelt was actively supporting and funding the Library of Congress, he also was a key player in social purity campaigns and spoke of race suicide and the patriotic duty of women as mothers, thus advocating proper gender and reproductive roles for citizens of the United States. See Jennifer Terry, *An American Obsession: Science, Medicine, and Homosexuality in Modern Society* (Chicago: University of Chicago Press, 1999), 100.

54. Library of Congress, *Report of the Librarian for the Fiscal Year Ending June 30, 1902* (Washington: Government Printing Office, 1902), 80.

55. Jane A. Rosenberg, *The Library of Congress and the Professionalization of American Librarianship* (Ph.D. diss., University of Michigan, 1988), 121; Francis Miksa, *The Subject in the Dictionary Catalog from Cutter to the Present* (Chicago: American Library Association, 1983), 179. In 1902 the Library of Congress also agreed to publish the ALA Catalog. This involved close working relationships between Herbert Putnam and the ALA in editing and

publishing. That year the ALA appointed a Committee on Cataloging Rules, and Hanson was appointed chair. One of the reasons for the establishment of the committee was the plan to catalog the eight thousand recommended titles in the ALA Catalog. The Library of Congress began work on a printed list of subjects in 1909 and published the first edition in 1914, at which point the American Library Association ceased publishing a separate list of headings. Mary W. MacNair, "The Library of Congress List of Subject Headings," in *Proceedings of the Catalog Section: American Library Association*, Washington, D.C. Conference, May 13–18, 1929 (Chicago: Catalog Section, American Library Association, 1929), 54–58.

56. Miksa, *The Subject in the Dictionary Catalog*, 332.

57. David Judson Haykin, *Subject Headings: A Practical Guide.* (Washington, D.C.: U.S. Government Printing Office, 1951).

58. Miksa, *The Subject in the Dictionary Catalog*, 365–366; The LoC also produced the National Union Catalog, Pre-1956 Imprints, from card files from the previous seventy years. The National Union Catalog is a list of holdings from libraries across the United States and Canada. The total number of volumes for the pre-1956 imprints amounted to 754 and took thirteen years to complete.

59. James C. Scott, *Seeing Like a State: How Certain Schemes to Improve the Human Condition Have Failed* (New Haven, Conn.: Yale University Press, 1998), 2–5.

60. Richard von Krafft-Ebing, *Psychopathia Sexualis with Especial Reference to the Antipathic Sexual Instinct: A Medico-Forensic Study*, 12th ed., trans. F. J. Rebman (New York: Rebman, 1939), 1.

61. John K. Noyes, *The Mastery of Submission: Inventions of Masochism* (Ithaca, N.Y.: Cornell University Press), 56–58.

62. Michel Foucault, *Abnormal: Lectures at the Collège de France, 1974–1975*, trans. Graham Burchell (New York: Picador, 2003), 168.

63. Sedgwick, *Epistemology of the Closet*, 49, 73.

64. Ibid., 11.

65. This is my central critique of Wikipedia, as well: Melissa Adler, "Wikipedia and the Myth of Universality," *Nordisk Tidsskrift for Informationsvidenskab og Kulturformidling* 5, no. 1 (2016).

66. Hope Olson has discussed a similar problem in terms of a universality/diversity binary. See Hope A. Olson, "The Power to Name: Representation in Library Catalogs," *Signs* (2001): 639–668.

67. Foucault, *Society Must Be Defended*, 9.

68. Michel Foucault, "The Will to Knowledge," in *Essential Works of Michel Foucault, 1954–1984*, vol. 1: *Ethics: Subjectivity and Truth*, ed. Paul Rabinow (New York: The Free Press, 1997), 12.

69. Donna Haraway, "Situated Knowledges: The Science Question in Feminism and the Privilege of Partial Perspective," *Feminist Studies* 14, no. 3 (Autumn 1988); Michel Foucault, *Society Must Be Defended*. For an application of this perspective in LIS, see Melanie Feinberg, "Hidden Bias to Responsible Bias: An Approach to Information Systems Based on Haraway's Situated Knowledges," *Information Research* 12 (2007): 1–13.

70. Foucault, *Society Must Be Defended*, 10.

71. Donna Haraway, "A Game of Cat's Cradle: Science Studies, Feminist Theory, Cultural Studies," *Configurations* 2, no. 1 (1994): 60.

72. https://www.routledge.com/products/9780415903875.

73. Derrida, *Archive Fever: A Freudian Impression* (Chicago: University of Chicago Press, 1996), 10.

74. Scott, *Seeing Like a State*, 7.

1. NAMING SUBJECTS: "PARAPHILIAS"

1. The catalog has since been updated with revised and new headings. As of 2016 the LoC's record supplies the following headings:

"Gay men's writings—History and criticism—Theory, etc." and "American fiction—Male authors—History and criticism."

2. WorldCat is a shared catalog (referred to by librarians as a union catalog) that itemizes the holdings of 72,000 libraries in 170 countries and territories. It is maintained and operated by the Online Computer Library Center (OCLC), of which participating libraries are members.

3. Incidentally, a book on bisexuality would be more properly placed in HQ74, but this book is classed in HQ71, which is designated for "Sexual practices outside of social norms." Although the discussion of shelf classification is reserved for the following chapter, it is worth noting that this Stekel text is not shelved with other books on bisexuality or homosexuality, but rather, it is among other books on sexual perversion and deviation. Surely, this is a case in which the book was cataloged eighty years ago and was never reshelved and the subject headings never manually revisited. Although this may be viewed as being more historically accurate because the author associated homosexuality with perversion, it is also troubling for a number of reasons and demonstrates the effects of time, power-knowledge structures, and the shifting, slippery nature of vocabularies for sexuality. It should also be noted that subsequent editions of Stekel's book are cataloged at UW–Madison with the heading "Homosexuality" instead of "Paraphilias."

4. I have verified that all of the texts currently assigned "Paraphilias" and published before 1942 did include the earlier heading "Sexual perversion" by comparing the titles to early catalog cards. Association of Research Libraries, *A Catalog of Books Represented by the Library of Congress Printed Cards*,

Issued to July 31, 1942, vols. 1–166 (Ann Arbor, Mich.: Edwards Brothers, 1942–1945). The global updating technology is conducted on a local level because libraries are responsible for maintaining the authority files for their systems. Assuming libraries keep up with the updates, their catalogs will include "Paraphilias." Some libraries, because of the time and labor required, irregularly update their authority databases, so those catalogs would contain "Sexual deviation."

5. Library of Congress, Linked Data Service, http://id.loc.gov/about/.

6. "Paraphilias," Library of Congress Authorities, http://lccn.loc.gov/ sh85120724.

7. "Sex crimes," Library of Congress Authorities, http://lccn.loc.gov/ sh85120572.

8. FAQ on SACO Subject Heading Proposals, http://www.loc.gov/aba/ pcc/saco/sacogenfaq.html.

9. *GLC Voice* 21 (March 1983): 4.

10. Eve Kosofsky Sedgwick, *Epistemology of the Closet* (Berkeley: University of California Press, 1990), 26.

11. It should be noted that a handful of these titles are assigned the Medical Subject Heading "Paraphilias" rather than the LC heading. I've decided to include these in the count for a number of reasons: The number of books with the *MeSH* heading is around twenty, and some records include both *MeSH* and LCSH headings. Additionally, they are included in the LC records in the LC catalog, and the records serve the public in the same way.

12. I've chosen only to use the texts written or translated into English because the inclusion of all languages would introduce a whole realm of issues surrounding translation that are beyond the scope of this book. Additionally, this study is limited to the United States, but note that LCSH is used in library catalogs worldwide, in translation in some parts of the world.

13. Charles Moser, "Paraphilia: A Critique of a Confused Concept" in *New Directions in Sex Therapy: Innovations and Alternatives*, ed. Peggy J. Kleinplatz (Philadelphia: Brunner-Routledge, 2001).

14. Charles Moser and Peggy J. Kleinplatz, "*DSM-IV-TR* and the Paraphilias: An Argument for Removal," *Journal of Psychology & Human Sexuality* 17, no. 3–4 (2006): 93.

15. D. Richard Laws and William T. Donahue, *Sexual Deviance: Theory, Assessment, and Treatment* (New York: Guilford, 2008), 1.

16. Élisabeth Roudinesco, *Our Dark Side: A History of Perversion*, trans. David Macey (Cambridge: Polity, 2009), 133.

17. "Paraphilias," Library of Congress Authorities, http://authorities.loc .gov/, emphasis added.

18. Harry Oosterhuis, *Stepchildren of Nature: Krafft-Ebing, Psychiatry, and the Making of Sexual Identity* (Chicago: University of Chicago Press, 2000), 47.

19. Richard von Krafft-Ebing, "Preface to the First Edition," in *Psychopathia Sexualis with Especial Reference to the Antipathic Sexual Instinct*, rev. trans. from the 12th German ed. (New York: Rebman, 1939), vii.

20. Deborah Britzman, *Lost Subjects, Contested Objects: Toward a Psychoanalytic Inquiry of Learning* (Albany: SUNY Press, 1998), 69.

21. Lisa Duggan, *Sapphic Slashers: Sex, Violence, and American Modernity* (Durham, N.C.: Duke University Press, 2000).

22. The discourse on congenital inversion, for instance, relied on masculine (active) and feminine (passive) attributes, and same-sex attraction was a symptom of the larger problem of males taking on female attributes and females embodying male characteristics. Near the end of his life Krafft-Ebing admitted his error in defining inversion as degenerate and immoral, and he corrected it by declaring that inversion should be explained in terms of genetics rather than disease. He also came to recognize that "all noble activities of the heart which can be associated with heterosexual love can be equally associated with homosexual love" and that, relatively speaking, heterosexuals tend to perform more depraved acts than homosexuals do. Krafft-Ebing, quoted by Victor Robinson, in "Introduction," *Psychopathia Sexualis*, 12th ed., viii.

23. Duggan, *Sapphic Slashers*, 160.

24. Michel Foucault, *Abnormal: Lectures at the Collège de France, 1974–1975*, trans. Graham Burchell (New York: Picador, 2003), 32–33.

25. Ibid., 34.

26. The German text and the 1949 English translation were placed in the Library of Congress's restricted Delta Collection—the subject of Chapter 2.

27. Sigmund Freud, *Three Essays on the Theory of Sexuality*, trans. James Strachey (New York: Basic Books, 1962), 37.

28. Juliet Mitchell, "Love and Hate, Girl and Boy," *London Review of Books* 36, no. 21 (2014): 12.

29. Others have cited the first volume of this series, *Nervöse Angstzustände und ihre Behandlung*, published in 1908, as featuring the first use of "paraphilias," but in combing through the text, I find only the use of "perversion" and "perversität." Later English translations of the text use "paraphilias." It seems that "paraphilie" is actually coined in 1917, in the second volume of the series, where it appears multiple times. This timeframe agrees with the notion that Stekel invented the term after his break from Freud around 1912. Wilhelm Stekel, *Storungen des Trieb- und Affektlebens*,

vol. 2: *Onanie und Homosexualität: Die Homosexuelle Parapathie* (Berlin: Urban & Schwarzenberg, 1917). The second edition (1921) was translated into English in 1922: William Stekel, *Bi-Sexual Love: The Homosexual Neurosis*, trans. James S. Van Teslaar (Boston: Richard G. Badger, The Gorham Press, 1922). It is available through the Internet Archive, at https://archive.org/details/bisexuallovehomooostekuoft. Although this book is not presently assigned "Paraphilias" in the Library of Congress catalog, local catalogs, including that of the University of Wisconsin–Madison, do include this heading in bibliographic records for this book.

30. Wilhelm Stekel, *Sexual Aberrations: The Phenomena of Fetishism in Relation to Sex* (New York: Liveright, 1930), v.

31. Ibid., 3.

32. Ibid., 4.

33. Ibid., 13, 18.

34. Ibid., 14.

35. Jacques André, "Immanent Masochism," trans. Claudia Vaughn, *European Journal of Psychoanalysis*, http://www.journal-psychoanalysis.eu/immanent-masochism/.

36. William Stekel, "Is Homosexuality Curable?" *Psychoanalytic Review* 17, no. 4 (1930). Jennifer Terry associates a shift in psychoanalysis and the more radical treatments like electric shock as aversion therapy in the 1930s with Stekel's more radical views. For an account of Stekel's falling out with Freud and his marginal position within the psychoanalytic community, see Jaap Bos and Leendert Groenendijk, *The Self-Marginalization of Wilhelm Stekel: Freudian Circles Inside and Out* (New York: Springer, 2007).

37. Jennifer Terry, *An American Obsession: Science, Medicine, and Homosexuality in Modern Society* (Chicago: University of Chicago Press, 1999), 323.

38. Paul Weiss, personal e-mail, June 26, 2009.

39. Library of Congress Catalog Division, *Library of Congress Subject Headings* (Washington, D.C.: LC, 1948).

40. Francis Miksa, *The Subject in the Dictionary Catalog from Cutter to the Present* (Chicago: American Library Association, 1983), 332.

41. Margot Canaday, *The Straight State: Sexuality and Citizenship in Twentieth-Century America* (Princeton, N.J.: Princeton University Press, 2009), 3.

42. American Psychiatric Association, Committee on Nomenclature and Statistics, *Mental Disorders: Diagnostic and Statistical Manual* (Washington, D.C.: American Psychiatric Association, 1952), 38.

43. Andreas De Block and Pieter R. Adriaens, "Pathologizing Sexual Deviance: A History," *Journal of Sex Research* 50, no. 3–4 (2013).

44. *DSM-III*, quoted in John K. Noyes, *The Mastery of Submission: Inventions of Masochism* (Ithaca, N.Y.: Cornell University Press), 20.

45. See Melissa Adler, "'Let's Not Homosexualize the Library Stacks': Liberating Gays in the Library Catalog, 1970–1988," *Journal of the History of Sexuality* 24, no. 3 (Fall 2015): 478–507.

46. I have argued elsewhere that this movement was influential in the emerging field of gay and lesbian studies. Ibid.

47. Robert L. Spitzer, "A Proposal About Homosexuality and the APA Nomenclature: Homosexuality as an Irregular Form of Sexual Behavior and Sexual Orientation Disturbance as a Psychiatric Disorder," *American Journal of Psychiatry* 130, no. 11 (1973): 1215.

48. De Block and Adriaens, "Pathologizing Sexual Deviance," 280.

49. Vern L. Bullough, *Sin, Sickness, and Sanity: A History of Sexual Attitudes* (New York: Garland, 1977), xi.

50. See LC Acquisitions and Bibliographic Access, *Program for Cooperative Cataloging, Statistics—NACO/BIBCO/CONSER/SACO Annual Compilation FY2015* (Washington, D.C., 2014), https://www.loc.gov/aba/pcc/stats/FY2015/SummaryStatisticsAnnual.pdf.

51. American Psychiatric Association, *Diagnostic and Statistical Manual of Mental Disorders* (Washington, D.C.: American Psychiatric Association, 1980), 261, 267.

52. Both *MeSH* and the *DSM* started using "Paraphilias" in place of "Sexual deviation" or "Sex deviations" in 1980.

53. John Money, *Lovemaps: Clinical Concepts of Sexual/Erotic Health and Pathology, Paraphilia, and Gender Transposition of Childhood, Adolescence, and Maturity* (New York: Irvington, 1986), 1.

54. Ibid., xvii. Money has been a highly controversial figure in the psychiatric profession, not least because he led a sex-reassignment surgery for a boy whose penis was seriously damaged during a surgical operation as a baby. Recall that Stekel's attitude toward homosexuals was one of contempt, and he believed that homosexuality was a diseased condition. Even for his day, Stekel's views were radically pathologizing, extending beyond prevailing beliefs about sexual variance. Whereas most psychiatrists held the view that homosexuals should be treated with a certain degree of sympathy, Stekel's view propelled the perception that homosexuals were dangerous. The controversies surrounding both Money and Stekel raise questions about the motivations and implications of using the term that they both promoted, "paraphilias."

55. De Block and Adriaens, "Pathologizing Sexual Deviance," 290.

56. John F. Noyes, *The Mastery of Submission*, 21.

57. Ibid.

58. American Psychiatric Association. *Diagnostic and Statistical Manual of Mental Disorders: DSM-IV-TR* (Washington, D.C.: American Psychiatric Association, 2004), STAT!Ref, http://online.statref.com.

59. Paul Weiss, personal e-mail, June 29, 2009.

60. Thirty books were cataloged by LC between 2007 and 2014 with the subject heading "paraphilias," but only nine of them contain "paraphilias" in the back of the book index, and among these are also uses of "deviation" and "perversion." Two of these use "paraphilias" in a cultural or historical context to explain to readers what the term means, and the other seven are quite clearly situated in psychiatry. In contrast, fifteen of the books use "perversion" as an index term, and those also primarily use this word in the title and the table of contents. Nine of the thirty books include "perversion" or "perverse" in the title, four use "deviation" or "deviance," and none use "paraphilias." The remainder simply don't use a version of this word, and their titles begin to reveal its inadequacy in capturing what the texts are about: *Sade: Queer Theorist*; *Kink: A Straight Girl's Investigation*; *Kiss My Relics: Hermaphroditic Fictions of the Middle Ages.*

61. Dean Spade, *Normal Life: Administrative Violence, Critical Trans Politics, and the Limits of Law* (Cambridge, Mass.: South End, 2011), 30.

62. Sanford Berman, "Inside Censorship," *Progressive Librarian* 18 (2001): 50.

63. Ibid., 49.

64. National Coalition for Sexual Freedom, "DSM Revision White Paper," https://ncsfreedom.org/key-programs/dsm-v-revision-project/dsm-revision-white-paper.html.

65. Berman, "Inside Censorship," 50.

66. Ibid.

67. American Psychiatric Association, "Timeline," http://www.dsm5.org/about/Pages/Timeline.aspx. The APA has gone back and forth on the significance of harm or distress to self or others as well as the difference between acting and not acting (which seems recall Krafft-Ebing's distinction between perversion and perversity).

68. The section that further elaborates a method of diagnosis seems to make this fuzzier, indicating that "if admitting individuals declare no distress, exemplified by anxiety, obsessions, guilt, or shame, about these paraphilic impulses, and are not hampered by them in pursuing other goals, and their self-reported, psychiatric, or legal histories do not act on them, then they could be ascertained as having sadistic sexual interest but they would not meet criteria for sexual sadism disorder." This seems to suggest that acting on sadistic impulses would be disordered, complicating and almost nullifying the significance of the distinction of acting with nonconsenting persons in Criterion B.

69. Lisa Downing, "Heteronormativity and Repronormativity in Sexological 'Perversion Theory' and the *DSM-5*'s 'Paraphilic Disorder,'" *Archives of Sexual Behavior* 44 (2015): 1139–1145.

70. Judith Halberstam, *Female Masculinity* (Durham, N.C.: Duke University Press, 1998), 53.

71. It should be noted that there seems to have been general agreement that fetishism, sadism, masochism, and other interests were unquestionably perverse. Even Magnus Hirschfeld, a sexologist and an invert who advocated fair treatment for homosexuals, wrote an extensive volume on pathological aberrations of the sexual instinct.

72. Anomaly, *The Invert, and His Social Adjustment* (Baltimore, Md.: The Williams & Wilkin Company, 1929), 19–20.

73. I counted the library holdings of all books with the heading "Paraphilias" in the LC catalog by searching WorldCat. For the books acquired between 1892 and 1945, Anomaly's ranks third among American libraries.

74. Terry, *An American Obsession*, 122.

75. Davis's study population was composed entirely of white, middle-class women.

76. Katharine Bement Davis, *Factors in the Sex Life of Twenty-Two Hundred Women* (New York: Harper and Bros., 1929), 248.

77. Library of Congress, *Library of Congress Classification: H, Social Sciences*, 2nd ed. (Washington, D.C.: Library of Congress, 1920). The 1972 reprint is assigned "Women—Sexual behavior" and "Lesbianism" and is classed as HQ29, which is the LC classification for the sexual behaviors and attitudes of women.

78. Marion Zimmer Bradley, *Checklist: A Complete, Cumulative Checklist of Lesbian, Variant, and Homosexual Fiction . . . for the Use of Collectors, Students, and Librarians* (Rochester, Texas, 1960); Jeanette Howard Foster, *Sex Variant Women in Literature: A Historical and Quantitative Survey* (New York, Vantage, 1956). Foster received the 1974 Gay Book Award from the ALA Gay Liberation Task Force for the reissue of this book. See Foster's biography: Joanne E. Passet, *Sex Variant Woman: The Life of Jeannette Howard Foster* (New York: Da Capo, 2008).

79. Barbara Gittings, "Gays in Library Land: The Gay and Lesbian Task Force of the American Library Association: The First Sixteen Years," in *Daring to Find Our Names: The Search for Lesbigay Library History*, ed., James V. Carmichael Jr. (Westport, Conn.: Greenwood, 1998), 86.

80. The memoir was authored pseudonymously by Diana Frederics, who has recently been determined to be the late Frances Remmel. Interestingly, the identity of the author was discovered by the *History Detectives*, by looking at the original copyright records at the Library of Congress. http://www.pbs.org/opb/historydetectives/investigation/diana/.

81. Gayle Rubin, "Thinking Sex: Notes for a Radical Theory of the Politics of Sexuality," in *Pleasure and Danger*, ed. Carole S. Vance (Boston: Routledge and Kegan Paul, 1984), 267–319. Also see Heather Love, "Doing Being Deviant: Deviance Studies, Descriptions, and the Queer Ordinary," *differences: A Journal of Feminist Cultural Studies* 26, no. 1 (2015), 74–95.

82. For an excellent review of scholarship during this time see Gayle Rubin, "Studying Sexual Subcultures: Excavating the Ethnography of Gay Communities in Urban North America," in *Out in Theory: The Emergence of Lesbian and Gay Anthropology*, ed. Ellen Lewin and William Leap (Urbana: University of Illinois Press, 2002), 17–68.

83. John H. Gagnon, William Simon, and Donald E. Carns, eds., *Sexual Deviance* (New York: Harper & Row, 1967), 2, 12.

84. Lars Ullerstam, *The Erotic Minorities* (New York: Grove, 1966), 123.

85. James M. Henslin, *Deviant Life-styles* (New Brunswick, N.J.: Transaction, 1977), 13.

86. Library of Congress, *Library of Congress Subject Headings*, 6th ed. (Washington, D.C.: Library of Congress, 1966).

87. Library of Congress. *Library of Congress Subject Headings*, 11th ed. (Washington, DC: Library of Congress, 1988).

88. Ellen Greenblatt, "Homosexuality: The Evolution of a Concept in the Library of Congress Subject Headings," in *Gay and Lesbian Library Service*, ed. Cal Gough and Ellen Greenblatt (Jefferson, N.C.: McFarland, 1990), 216.

89. Tillett to Berman, January 27, 2006, Sanford Berman papers, University of Illinois, Urbana/Champaign.

90. Ibid.

91. Berman to Tillett, February 6, 2006, Sanford Berman papers, University of Illinois, Urbana/Champaign.

92. Sanford Berman, "Personal LCSH Scorecard"; "Tretter Board Urges Library of Congress to Adopt New Cataloguing," Tretter Letter 2 no.1 (January 2007), Sanford Berman papers, University of Illinois, Urbana/Champaign.

93. Lauren Rosewarne, *Part-Time Perverts: Sex, Pop Culture, and Kink Management* (Santa Barbara, Calif.: Praeger, 2011).

94. Book description from the author's website: http://www.laurenrosewarne.com/main/page_books_part_time_perverts.html.

95. Lori Gottlieb, "A Love Life Less Ordinary," *New York Times Sunday Book Review* (February 2, 2009), http://www.nytimes.com/2009/02/08/books/review/Gottlieb-t.html.

2. LABELING OBSCENITY: THE DELTA COLLECTION

1. Eve Kosofsky Sedgwick, *Epistemology of the Closet* (Berkeley: University of California Press, 1990), 70.

2. Thanks to Polly Thistlethwaite for pointing out the likeness.

3. It was not until 1973 that the "Miller Test" defined obscenity as material that appeals to prurient interests, offends, and lacks artistic and literary merit.

4. Paul S. Boyer, *Purity in Print: Book Censorship in America from the Gilded Age to the Computer Age* (Madison: University of Wisconsin Press, 2002); James C. N. Paul and Murray L. Schwartz, *Federal Censorship: Obscenity in the Mail* (New York: Free Press of Glencoe, 1961); Douglas M. Charles, *The FBI's Obscene File: J. Edgar Hoover and the Bureau's Crusade Against Smut* (Lawrence: University Press of Kansas, 2012).

5. Paul and Schwartz, *Federal Censorship*, 273.

6. Alison Moore, "Arcane Erotica and National 'Patrimony': Britain's Private Case and the Collection de l'Enfer of the Bibliothéque Nationale de France," *Cultural Studies Review* 18 (2012): 199.

7. Works consulted include Jane Aikin and John Y. Cole, eds., *Encyclopedia of the LC: For Congress, the Nation & the World* (Washington, D.C.: LC, 2004); *Subject Collections: A Guide to Special Book Collections and Subject Emphases as Reported by University, College, Public, and Special Libraries and Museums in the United States and Canada* (New York: Bowker, 1958).

8. Ralph L. Henderson, [Memorandum], August 8, 1963, Keeper of the Collections Papers, Library of Congress Manuscript Division, Washington, D.C.

9. Congressional Record Appendix A4211, "The Mattachine Society of Washington: Extension of Remarks of Hon. John Dowdy of Texas in the House of Representatives, July 5, 1963," Kameny Papers, http://kameny papers.org/correspondence/congressionalrecord-1963.jpg.

10. Roy P. Basler to Judge Moore, June 10, 1960, Keeper of the Collections Papers, Library of Congress Manuscript Division, Washington, D.C.

11. Jennifer Terry, *An American Obsession: Science, Medicine, and Homosexuality in Modern Society* (Chicago: University of Chicago Press, 1999), 337–338.

12. "Congress Library to Get Big Haul of Obscene Items," *Evening Star* (January 29, 1958). Keeper of the Collections Papers. Library of Congress Manuscript Division, Washington, D.C.

13. Jerry Landauer, "Erotic Materials Seized at Businessman's Home," *Washington Post* (September 4, 1958). Keeper of the Collections Papers. Gichner's titles include *Erotic Aspects of Hindu Sculpture* (1949), *Erotic Aspects of Chinese Culture* (1957), and *Erotic Aspects of Japanese Culture* (1953).

14. Dwight D. Eisenhower, "Remarks at the Dartmouth College Commencement Exercises," Hanover, N.H., June 14, 1953. http://www .presidency.ucsb.edu/ws/?pid=9606.

15. Whitney Strub, *Perversion for Profit: The Politics of Pornography and the Rise of the New Right* (New York: Columbia University Press, 2013), 13.

16. Ibid., 14. See also George Chauncey, *Why Marriage? The History Shaping Today's Debate Over Gay Equality* (Cambridge, Mass.: Basic Books, 2004); Margot Canaday, *The Straight State: Sexuality and Citizenship in Twentieth-Century America* (Princeton, N.J.: Princeton University Press, 2009); Terry, *An American Obsession.*

17. Louise Robbins, *Censorship and the American Library: The American Library Association's Response to Threats to Intellectual Freedom, 1939–1969* (Westport, Conn.: Greenwood, 1996).

18. Ibid., 42.

19. American Library Association, *Intellectual Freedom Manual*, 10th ed. (Chicago: American Library Association, 2010). Rogers would become chief assistant librarian at the Library of Congress in 1957 after having worked at the New York Public Library.

20. Ibid., 158.

21. Eli M. Oboler, "Congress as Censor," *Library Trends* (July 1970): 69.

22. Ibid., 70.

23. Robbins, *Censorship and the American Library*, 90.

24. Terry, *An American Obsession.*

25. *Roth v. United States*, 354 U.S. 476 (1957). This is a necessarily selective summary of censorship. For an account of the FBI's treatment of obscenity, see Douglas M. Charles, *The FBI's Obscene File: J. Edgar Hoover and the Bureau's Crusade Against Smut* (Lawrence: University Press of Kansas, 2012).

26. Senate Document 241, quoted in Louise S. Robbins, "The Library of Congress and Federal Loyalty Programs, 1947–1956: No 'Communists or Cocksuckers,'" *Library Quarterly* 64, no. 4 (1994): 377.

27. John Gardener Race, "The World's Lewdest Library," n.d., 54, Keeper of the Collections Papers, Library of Congress Manuscript Division, Washington, D.C.

28. John Cole, LoC historian and director of the Center for the Book, confirmed that this was a plausible theory and noted that the archival records from this time are unfortunately sparse.

29. Carl Ostrowski, "'The Choice of Books': Ainsworth Rand Spofford, the Ideology of Reading, and Literary Collections at the Library of Congress in the 1870s," *Libraries and the Cultural Record* 45 (2010): 74.

30. Ainsworth Spofford, *A Book for All Readers: Designed as an Aid to the Collection, Use, and Preservation of Books and the Formation of Public and Private Libraries* (New York: G. P. Putnam's Sons, 1900), 20.

31. Spofford, quoted in Ostrowski, "'The Choice of Books,'" 74.

32. Moore, "Arcane Erotica and National 'Patrimony.'"

33. "Library of Congress Acquisitions," 1954, Keeper of the Collections Papers, Library of Congress Manuscript Division, Washington, D.C.

34. Librarian to Charles Booher, February 3, 1920, Library of Congress Central File. Library of Congress Manuscript Division, Washington, DC.

35. Herbert Putnam to Millard Caldwell, March 27, 1936, Library of Congress Central File, Library of Congress Manuscript Division, Washington, D.C.

36. The Keeper was also in charge of Defense planning for the protection of the collections, determining the effects of nuclear war on library materials, fire prevention, water-damage prevention, binding, preservation, organization and maintenance of the collection, thefts and mutilations, security of rare materials, door passes, security of exhibits, access controls, and allocating book stack space for protected collections.

37. Luther Evans, "The Library of Congress and the War," *Freedom's Fortress* (May 30, 1942), http://www.loc.gov/resource/mff.001022/#seq-1.

38. United States Bureau of Customs, *Customs Manual of 1943*, Amendment no. 288.12.40.e., 1952. Keeper of Collections Papers, Library of Congress Manuscript Division, Washington, D.C.

39. John W. Cronin to Alton Keller, 1953, Keeper of the Collections Papers, Library of Congress Manuscript Division, Washington, D.C.

40. Luther Evans to Frank Dow, January 17, 1952, Keeper of the Collections Papers, Library of Congress Manuscript Division, Washington, D.C.

41. *Annual Report of the Exchange and Gift Division, Processing Department, for the Year Ending June 30, 1956*, Library of Congress Manuscript Division, Washington, D.C.

42. Ibid.

43. Alvin W. Kremer, Diary, July 17, 30, 1956, Keeper of the Collections Papers, Library of Congress Manuscript Division, Washington, D.C.

44. Alvin W. Kremer, Diary, March 8, 1957, Keeper of the Collections Papers, Library of Congress Manuscript Division, Washington, D.C.

45. Alvin W. Kremer to Robert C. Gooch, February 19, 1957, Keeper of the Collections Papers, Library of Congress Manuscript Division, Washington, D.C.

46. Keeper of the Collections, *Annual Report for the Fiscal Year Ended June 30, 1957*, 2. Library of Congress Manuscript Division, Washington, DC.

47. Ralph Kelly, *Customs Manual* Amendment no. X-532, Keeper of the Collections Papers; Robert D. Stevens to Rutherford D. Rogers, August 27, 1958, Keeper of the Collections Papers, Library of Congress Manuscript Division, Washington, D.C.

48. Letter to Rutherford D. Rogers, Chief Assistant Librarian, and Lewis C. Coffin, Assistant Director Processing Dept., October 21, 1958, Keeper of the Collections Papers, Library of Congress Manuscript Division, Washington, D.C.

49. "Lot inventory of materials in Delta Collection selected from Customs and Post Office intercepts," December 19, 1960, Keeper of the Collections Papers, Library of Congress Manuscript Division, Washington, D.C.

50. Keeper of the Collections, *Annual Report for the Fiscal Year Ended June 30, 1961*, 72. Library of Congress Manuscript Division, Washington, D.C.

51. Ibid., 14.

52. George M. Hall to Robert C. Gooch, May 27, 1963, Keeper of the Collections Papers, Library of Congress Manuscript Division, Washington, D.C.

53. Nathan R. Einhorn to Paul E. Edlund, November 5, 1963, Keeper of the Collections Papers, Library of Congress Manuscript Division, Washington, D.C.

54. Alvin W. Kremer, Diary, February 25, 1960, Keeper of the Collections Papers, Library of Congress Manuscript Division, Washington, D.C.

55. Robert D. Stevens to Rutherford D. Rogers, March 14, 1960, Keeper of Collections Papers, Library of Congress Manuscript Division, Washington, D.C.

56. Office of Collections Maintenance and Preservation, *Annual Report for the Fiscal Year Ended June 30, 1963*. Library of Congress Manuscript Division, Washington, D.C.

57. Mr. Ladd to Mr. Rosen, Memorandum: "Unsub; Mutilation of Books, Library of Congress, August 6, 1953, Destruction of Government Property," 52–61613-3, August 12, 1953, Federal Bureau of Investigation, documents obtained through FOIA request.

58. Carl S. Voelker, Federal Bureau of Investigation, "Unknown Subject, Mutilation of Books, Library of Congress," 52–61613-6, October 16, 1953. Documents obtained through FOIA request.

59. Ibid.

60. Mr. Ladd to Mr. Rosen, Memorandum.

61. Carl S. Voelker, Federal Bureau of Investigation, "Unknown Subject, Mutilation of Books, Library of Congress," 52–61613-6, October 16, 1953.

62. Carl S. Voelker, Federal Bureau of Investigation, "Unknown Subject, Mutilation of Books, Library of Congress," 52–61613-9x, February 17, 1954.

63. Ibid.

64. Unknown author to Director, FBI Washington Field Office, 52–61613-2, August 11, 1953, Federal Bureau of Investigation. Documents obtained through FOIA request.

65. Carl S. Voelker, Federal Bureau of Investigation, "Unknown Subject, Mutilation of Books, Library of Congress," 52–61613-5, October 15, 1953.

66. Unknown author to Director, FBI Washington Field Office, 52–61613-5, October 12, 1953, Federal Bureau of Investigation. Documents obtained through FOIA request.

67. Carl S. Voelker, Federal Bureau of Investigation, "Unknown Subject, Mutilation of Books, Library of Congress," 52–61613-12, April 22, 1954.

68. Louis Loebl, "Report. Unknown subjects; Mary Frances Anderson," File no. 52–1479, March 22, 1939, Federal Bureau of Investigation. Documents obtained through FOIA request.

69. "FBI Hunts Ring in Library of Congress Thefts," unknown publication, n.d. Federal Bureau of Investigation. Documents obtained through FOIA request.

70. Carl S. Voelker, Federal Bureau of Investigation, "Unknown Subject, Mutilation of Books, Library of Congress," 52–61613-6, October 16, 1953.

71. A 1962 letter to an LoC employee is available at the Kameny Papers website, Holmes to Nevin Feather, June 28, 1962: http://www.kamenypapers .org/correspondence/NevinFeather-LOC%20Letter-062862.jpg.

72. I am borrowing this section heading from Sedgwick, *Epistemology of the Closet.*

73. Eleni Kefala, *Peripheral (post) Modernity: The Syncretist Aesthetics of Borges, Piglia, Kalokyris, and Kyriakidis* (New York: Peter Lang, 2007). Kefala draws a fascinating connection between Borges's stories of labyrinths and the Delta symbol: "On the one hand, Delta stands for Daedalus, the famous craftsman (maker) and inventor of carpentry who built the labyrinth for Minos—the king of Crete. The Minoan labyrinth is the one that Borges reinvented in order to house Asterión, his version of the Minotaur as the eternal inmate of the labyrinth . . . ; besides, the labyrinth of Daedalus naturally evokes Borges' famous labyrinthine structures of fiction" (81).

74. Jorge Luis Borges, "The Library of Babel," in *Collected Fictions*, trans. Andrew Hurley (New York: Penguin, 1998), 112.

75. Herbert Small, *Handbook of the New Library of Congress* (Boston: Curtis and Cameron, 1897), 80.

76. Ibid., 82.

77. Ibid., 19.

78. Vladimir Nabokov, *Lolita* (New York: Vintage, 1997), 119.

79. Frederick Whiting, "'The Strange Particularity of the Lover's Preference': Pedophilia, Pornography, and the Anatomy of Monstrosity in *Lolita*," *American Literature* 70, no. 4 (1998): 834.

80. Richard von Krafft-Ebing, *Psychopathia Sexualis with Especial Reference to the Antipathic Sexual Instinct: A Medico-Forensic Study*, 12th ed., trans. F. J. Rebman (New York: Rebman, 1939), 1.

81. Patricia MacCormack, "Perversion: Transgressive Sexuality and Becoming Monstrous," *thirdspace: a journal of feminist theory & culture* 3, no. 4 (2004).

82. Michel Foucault, *Death and the Labyrinth*, trans. Charles Ruas (London: Continuum, 2006), 89.

83. Canaday, *The Straight State*.

84. The account of the monstrous is provided in Foucault's *Abnormal*, and he famously made this claim about identifying homosexuals as a species in *History of Sexuality*.

85. Michel Foucault, *Abnormal: Lectures at the Collège de France, 1974–1975*, trans. Graham Burchell (New York: Picador, 2003).

86. Sedgwick, *Epistemology of the Closet*, 3.

87. Michel Foucault, "So Cruel a Knowledge," in *Essential Works*, vol. 2: *Aesthetics, Method, and Epistemology*, ed. James D. Faubion and Robert Hurley (New York: Norton, 1998), 66.

88. Ibid., 67.

89. "Procedures for Handling Customs Intercepts now on Deck 39," March 26, 1956, Keeper of Collections Papers, Library of Congress Manuscript Division, Washington, D.C.

90. This "delta collection" as keyword anywhere turns up records that have this phrase in the local 852 field of the MARC record. I would not have known to search for this if my copy editor hadn't asked me whether a specific title was included in the collection. Looking at the record for that specific title revealed this information. It is possible that there are other hidden records that I've not yet discovered.

91. Michael B. Goodman, "The Customs' Censorship of William Burroughs' *Naked Lunch*," *Critique: Studies in Contemporary Fiction* 22, no. 1 (1980): 92–104.

92. Nicholson Baker wrote in 1994 of his concerns about the loss of the historical record with the shift to computerized catalogs, and debates about the value of catalog cards continue today. Nicholson Baker, "Discards," *New Yorker* (April 4, 1994): 64–86.

3. MAPPING PERVERSION: HQ71, ETC.

1. There is not a specific class or subdivision for queer theory in the literature sections. Rather, works on or using queer theory are generally shelved in the range HQ75 through HQ76.8 in the social sciences.

2. Michel Foucault, "First Preface to *Histoire de la folie à l'âge classique* (1961)," *Pli* 13 (2002): 1–10.

3. Stuart Elden, *Mapping the Present: Heidegger, Foucault, and the Project of a Spatial History* (London: Continuum, 2001), 142.

4. For an analysis of the critique of Foucault's diminished account of the state, see Thomas Lemke, "An Indigestible Meal? Foucault, Governmentality, and State Theory," *Distinktion: Scandinavian Journal of Social Theory* 8, no. 2 (2007): 43–64.

5. Michel Foucault, "Questions on Geography," in *Power/Knowledge: Selected Interviews and Other Writings, 1972–1977,* ed. Colin Gordon (New York: Pantheon, 1980), 72.

6. I borrow this phrasing from Wendy Brown's analysis of tolerance discourses in *Regulating Aversion: Tolerance in the Age of Identity and Empire* (Princeton, N.J.: Princeton University Press, 2008), 84.

7. Michel Foucault, *Discipline and Punish*, trans. Alan Sheridan (New York: Vintage, 1995), 206; Alistair Black, "The Victorian Information Society: Surveillance, Bureaucracy, and Public Librarianship in Nineteenth-Century Britain," *Information Society* 17, no. 1 (2001): 63–80; Nan Dahlkild, "The Emergence and Challenge of the Modern Library Building: Ideal Types, Model Libraries, and Guidelines, from the Enlightenment to the Experience Economy," *Library Trends* 60, no.1 (2011): 11–42; Matthew R. Griffis, "Bricks, Mortar, and Control: A Multicase Examination of the Public Library as Organization Space," *Advances in Library Administration and Organization* 32 (2014): 1–106.

8. Foucault, *Discipline and Punish*, 205.

9. Ibid., 209.

10. I have described some of the various projects and set a research agenda to study the reach and influence of the LoC in "Broker of Information, the 'Nation's Most Important Commodity': The Library of Congress in the Neoliberal Era," *Information & Culture* 50, no. 1 (2015): 24–50.

11. U.S. House of Representatives, http://www.house.gov/content/learn/partners/library_of_congress.php.

12. Brown, *Regulating Aversion*, 81–82.

13. Scott does not speak in terms of governmentality, and he puts more responsibility on the state than Foucault would. James C. Scott, *Seeing Like a State: How Certain Schemes to Improve the Human Condition Have Failed* (New Haven, Conn.: Yale University Press, 1999), 83.

14. Brown, *Regulating Aversion*, 82–83.

15. Michel Foucault, *Society Must Be Defended: Lectures at the Collège de France, 1975–76*, ed. Mauro Bertani and Alessandro Fontana, trans. David Macey (New York: Picador, 2003), 224.

16. Ibid., 225.

17. Ibid., 226.

18. Theodore Roosevelt, "True Americanism," in *The Works of Theodore Roosevelt: American Ideals* (New York: P. F. Collier & Son, 1897), 34.

19. Foucault, *Society Must Be Defended*, 227.

20. Scott, *Seeing Like a State*, 2.

21. Jean-Luc Nancy, *Corpus*, trans. Richard Rand (New York: Fordham University Press, 2008), 115.

22. Foucault, *Discipline and Punish*, 148.

23. Ibid., 141.

24. Some people will take issue with this assessment, particularly now that electronic books and digital libraries are widely available. There is much talk about "libraries without walls." Nevertheless, it seems to me that this frame of restriction still applies. There are rules for use and access. Certainly, if we think only of printed books, the walled library fits, both historically and in the present.

25. Ibid., 143. Scholars in the information sciences will undoubtedly recognize a resonance with S. R. Ranganathan's laws for library science: Books are for use; *Every reader his book, every book its reader*; Save the time of the reader; The library is a growing organism.

26. Ibid.

27. Ibid., 146–147.

28. Foucault, "Questions on Geography," 77.

29. Gilles Deleuze, *Foucault*, trans. Seán Hand (Minneapolis: University of Minnesota Press, 1986), 36.

30. Foucault, *Discipline and Punish*, 23.

31. Michel de Certeau, *The Practice of Everyday Life*, trans. Steven Rendall (Berkeley: University of California Press, 1988), 147.

32. Jakub Zdebik, *Deleuze and the Diagram: Aesthetic Threads in Visual Organization* (New York: Continuum, 2012), 10.

33. Ibid., 10–11.

34. Michel Foucault, "Governmentality," in *The Foucault Effect: Studies in Governmentality*, ed. Graham Burchell, Colin Gordon, and Peter Miller (Chicago: University of Chicago Press, 1991), 102.

35. http://www.loc.gov/about/fascinating-facts.

36. Deleuze, *Foucault*, 19.

37. Online Computer Library Center (OCLC), "A Global Library Resource," https://www.oclc.org/en-CA/worldcat/catalog.html.

38. Personal e-mail. OCLC Customer support, January 13, 2012.

39. Gayle Rubin, "Thinking Sex: Notes for a Radical Theory of the Politics of Sexuality," in *Pleasure and Danger*, ed. Carole S. Vance (Boston: Routledge and Kegan Paul, 1984), 267–319.

40. This must be a mistake in cataloging or shelving, as editions or copies of the same title should be adjacent to one another.

41. Hope Olson's "The Power to Name" includes an analysis of the historical roots of universal library classifications and vocabularies, focusing on Cutter's *Rules for a Dictionary Catalog*, the Dewey Decimal System, and LCSH. Hope Olson, "The Power to Name: Representation in Library Catalogs," *Signs* 26, no. 3 (2001): 660.

42. Francis Miksa, *The Development of Classification at the Library of Congress*, Occasional Papers 164 (Champaign: University of Illinois, 1984), 22.

43. Francis Miksa, *The Subject in the Dictionary Catalog from Cutter to the Present* (Chicago: American Library Association, 1983), 206.

44. Ibid., 207.

45. Falkner was a professor of statistics who studied economics, crime, and prisons. His studies appear in government reports. See *Statistics of Prisoners, 1890* (Chicago: Wardens Association of the United States and Canada, 1892).

46. F. Leslie Hayford, "Roland Post Falkner, 1866–1940," *Journal of the American Statistical Association* 36, no. 216 (1941): 543–545.

47. Falkner drew from the Dewey Decimal Classification, the Cutter Classification for the social sciences, and the Classification of the Harvard University Library for Economics and Sociology. Of these systems, he found Cutter to be the most satisfactory, but with some problems regarding specifics of the Library of Congress's collection. Dewey was too general and better suited for organizing public libraries; the Library of Congress Classification was designed to be much more granular, allowing for deeper refinement of subjects. Roland Falkner to the Librarian of Congress, "Memorandum, Referring to Classification, Economics, etc.," July 17, 1901, Subject Cataloging Division Papers, Library of Congress Manuscript Division, Washington, D.C.

48. Ian Hacking, "How Should We Do the History of Statistics?" in *The Foucault Effect: Studies in Governmentality*, ed. Graham Burchell, Colin Gordon, and Peter Miller (Chicago: University of Chicago Press, 1991), 181.

49. Benedict Anderson, *Imagined Communities: Reflections on the Origin and Spread of Nationalism* (London: Verso, 2006), 168.

50. Ibid., 164.

51. Ibid., 166.

52. Although the HQ section did provide a "See also" reference to the general HV class, "Social pathology. Philanthropy, etc." The back-of-the-book index to the 1910 classification indicates that "sex and crime" is accounted for by HV6158, but upon turning to the classification itself we see that this is actually a class under causes of crimes, with related classes being "family," "age," "sex," and "education." "Sex" here refers to what we would be more likely to call gender today, and books assigned to this class tend to be more about crime and masculinity or gender in general. None of the works currently in the class are about sex crimes. The same back-of-the-book index indicates that "crimes," a category within "sex relations," are to be found with HQ71–HQ463, producing an association between criminality and abnormal sex relations that does not actually exist in the classification itself.

53. Estelle B. Freedman, "'Uncontrolled Desires': The Response to the Sexual Psychopath, 1920–1960," *Journal of American History* (1987): 83.

54. Jennifer Terry, *An American Obsession: Science, Medicine, and Homosexuality in Modern Society* (Chicago: University of Chicago Press, 1999), 323.

55. Freedman, "Uncontrolled Desires," 92.

56. Ibid., 103.

57. Ibid., 98.

58. I determined the coverage of homosexuality in the sample books by looking at the number of pages and chapters devoted to the subject in each book, and I found that nine of the fifteen do address homosexuality quite extensively. In each of these nine books, at least 20 percent of the content deals directly with homosexuality. As common practice among catalogers is to include headings for subjects that comprise at least 20 percent of a work's contents, it would be appropriate to include *Homosexuality* in these records.

59. Joseph Paul De River, *The Sexual Criminal, a Psychoanalytical Study* (Springfield, Ill.: Charles C. Thomas, 1956), xi.

60. Robin Thicke (feat. T.I. & Pharrell), "Blurred Lines" (Interscope Records, 2013); E. L. James, *Fifty Shades of Grey* (New York: Vintage, 2012).

61. Hortense Smith, "Why is Amazon Removing the Sales Rankings from Gay, Lesbian Books?" *Jezebel* (April 12, 2009), http://jezebel.com/5209088/why-is-amazon-removing-the-sales-rankings-from-gay-lesbian-books.

62. Mike Annany, "The Curious Connection Between Apps for Gay Men and Sex Offenders," *The Atlantic* (April 14, 2011), http://www.theatlantic.com/technology/archive/2011/04/the-curious-connection-between-apps-for-gay-men-and-sexoffenders/237340/.

63. Ann Laura Stoler, *Race and the Education of Desire: Foucault's History of Sexuality and the Colonial Order of Things* (Durham, N.C.: Duke University Press, 1995), 62.

4. ABERRATIONS IN THE CATALOG

1. Affonso Romano de Sant'Anna, "Libraries, Social Inequality, and the Challenge of the Twenty-First Century," *Daedalus* 125, no. 4 (1996): 267.

2. Roderick Ferguson, *Aberrations in Black* (Minneapolis: University of Minnesota Press, 2003), viii.

3. Ibid., viii.

4. "Railroad station, Manchester, Georgia," Prints & Photographs Online Collection, Library of Congress, http://www.loc.gov/pictures/item/fsa1997003449/PP/.

5. Library of Congress, *Thesaurus for Graphic Materials I: Subject Terms* (TGM I), last revised 1995, http://www.loc.gov/rr/print/tgm1/.

6. Wendy Brown, "Suffering Rights as Paradoxes," *Constellations* 7, no. 2 (2000): 235–236.

7. Roderick A. Ferguson, *The Reorder of Things: The University and Its Pedagogies of Minority Difference* (Minneapolis: University of Minnesota Press, 2012), 19, 27.

8. Nicholson Baker , *Double Fold: Libraries and the Assault on Paper* (New York: Vintage, 2001), 104.

9. Susan Leigh Star and Geoffrey Bowker, *Sorting Things Out: Classification and Its Consequences* (Cambridge, Mass.: MIT Press, 2000).

10. Ferguson, *Aberrations in Black*, 4.

11. Ibid., 20.

12. Theodor W. Adorno and Max Horkheimer, *Dialectic of Enlightenment* (London: Verso, 1997).

13. Theodor W. Adorno, *Problems of Moral Philosophy*, ed., Thomas. Schröder, trans., Rodney Livingstone (Stanford, Calif.: Stanford University Press), 19.

14. Judith Butler, *Giving an Account of Oneself* (New York: Fordham University Press, 2005), 4.

15. I also conducted a search with the specific subject heading "African American gay men" and retrieved 121 records. Some of these overlap with the search for "African," "American," and "gays," and the pattern is very similar to the one I describe in this section. I have chosen to focus on the terminology applied to the Ferguson text for this analysis. "African American gays" was authorized as a heading in 1986, and "African American gay men" was authorized in 2003. Library of Congress, Authorities, http://lccn.loc .gov/sh2003003398; http://lccn.loc.gov/sh86004765.

16. See Melissa Adler, Jeffrey T. Huber, and A. Tyler Nix, "Stigmatizing Disability: Libraries and the Marking and Marginalization of Books about People with Disabilities," *Library Quarterly*, in press.

17. Jasbir Puar, *Terrorist Assemblages: Homonationalism in Queer Times* (Durham, N.C.: Duke University Press, 2007).

18. Wendy Brown, *Regulating Aversion: Tolerance in the Age of Identity and Empire* (Princeton, N.J.: Princeton University Press), 61.

19. Women in politics first appeared in the J division, in a class for suffrage within constitutional law in the discipline of political science.

20. Intner and Futas offer a related explanation: "The answer that might be given is the Family is largely a woman's issue, or that the rest of the classification is gender neutral, except for HQ and the scattering of subclasses and sub-sub-subclasses devoted specifically to women. But it is these authors' opinion that the rest of the classification presumes any gender issues to be addressed relate solely to women because men are considered the norm." Sheila S. Intner and Elizabeth Futas, "The Role and Impact of Library of Congress Classification on the Assessment of Women's Studies Collections," *Library Acquisitions: Practice & Theory* 20, no. 3 (1996).

21. Colin Higgins, "Library of Congress Classification: Teddy Roosevelt's World in Numbers?" *Cataloging & Classification Quarterly* 50, no. 4 (2012): 249–262.

22. Michel Foucault, *Discipline and Punish: The Birth of the Prison*, trans. Alan Sheridan (New York: Vintage, 1995), 182–183.

23. Judith Butler, *Bodies That Matter: On the Discursive Limits of "Sex"* (New York: Routledge, 1993), 16.

24. See my website "Cruising the Library" for this list of classes.

25. Michael Omi and Howard Winant, *Racial Formation in the United States* (New York: Routledge, 2014).

26. Ann Laura Stoler, *Race and the Education of Desire: Foucault's History of Sexuality and the Colonial Order of Things* (Durham, N.C.: Duke University Press, 1995).

27. John Russell Young, *Report of the Librarian of Congress for the Fiscal Year Ended June 30, 1898* (Washington, D.C.: Government Printing Office, 1898), 4.

28. Ibid., 5–6.

29. Ibid.

30. John Russell Young, *Report of the Librarian of Congress* (Washington, D.C.: Government Printing Office, 1897), 20.

31. Library of Congress, *America: History and Geography, Preliminary and Provisional Scheme of Classification* (Washington, D.C.: Government Printing Office, 1901), http://babel.hathitrust.org/cgi/pt?id=njp.32101074713999;view=1up;seq=5.

32. The first edition of the H section, printed in 1910, included two classes related to African Americans: Negro charities in the Social Pathology

section at HV3181 (near a section on charities for "defectives") and Negro secret societies in a range between HS2251 and HS2265. The index to the classification at the end of the book indicates that works on Negro labor are found in "Other classes of labor, A–Z" in HD6305.

33. Robert H. Wiebe, *The Search for Order, 1877–1920* (New York: Hill and Wang, 1967), 156.

34. Jackson Lears, *Rebirth of a Nation: The Making of Modern America, 1877–1920* (New York: Harper Perennial, 2009), 2.

35. Hannah Arendt, *The Origins of Totalitarianism* (New York: Harcourt, 1968), 185.

36. Alfred McCoy, *Policing America's Empire: The United States, the Philippines, and the Rise of the Surveillance State* (Madison: University of Wisconsin Press, 2009), 22–23.

37. See Melissa Adler, "Classification Along the Color Line: Excavating Racism in the Stacks," *Journal of Critical Library and Information Studies*, in press.

38. Luther Evans, quoted in John Y. Cole, "The Library of Congress Becomes a World Library, 1815–2005," *Libraries & Culture* 40, no. 3 (2005): 391.

39. Much research has been conducted on library and book programs after World War II. See Greg Barnhisel, *Cold War Modernists: Art, Literature, and American Cultural Diplomacy* (New York: Columbia University Press, 2015); Pamela Spence Richards, Wayne A. Wiegand, and Marija Dalbello, eds., *A History of Modern Librarianship: Constructing the Heritage of Western Cultures* (Santa Barbara, Calif.: Libraries Unlimited, 2015); Pamela Spence Richards, "Cold War Librarianship: Soviet and American Library Activities in Support of National Foreign Policy, 1946–1991," *Libraries and Culture* 36 (Winter 2001): 193–203; Louise S. Robbins, "Publishing American Values: The Franklin Book Programs as Cold War Cultural Diplomacy," *Library Trends* 55, no. 3 (2007): 638–650.

40. The Library of Congress is currently working in partnership with a private company to develop a new encoding scheme eventually to replace MARC. The new system is called BibFrame.

41. The Library of Congress maintains Dewey's editorial office through a cooperative arrangement with the Online Computer Library Center (OCLC), which owns the copyright to the Dewey Decimal Classification. Dewey is the most widely used classification in the world, is used in 135 countries, and has been translated into more than thirty languages. Dewey is beyond the scope of this research, but a similar approach could certainly be taken to analyze the classification. OCLC, "Dewey Decimal Classification Summaries," https://www.oclc.org/dewey/features/summaries.en.html.

Some European, Asian, and African libraries often use the Universal
Decimal System, which was based on the Dewey Decimal System. For a
list of the countries that use that system, see UDC Consortium, "UDC
Users Worldwide," http://www.udcc.org/index.php/site/page?view=users
_worldwide.

42. Library of Congress, Cataloging Distribution Service, "Library of
Congress Subject Headings," http://www.loc.gov/cds/products/product
.php?productID=214.

43. Edward Said, *Culture and Imperialism* (New York: Vintage, 1993), 290.

44. Adorno and Horkheimer, *Dialectic of Enlightenment*, 84.

45. Toni Morrison, *Playing in the Dark: Whiteness and the Literary Imagination* (Cambridge, Mass.: Harvard University Press, 1992), 8.

46. Ibid., 49.

5. THE TROUBLE WITH ACCESS / TOWARD REPARATIVE TAXONOMIES

1. Sergey Brin and Lawrence Page, "The Anatomy of a Large-Scale
Hypertextual Web Search Engine," Seventh International World-Wide Web
Conference (WWW 1998), April 14–18, 1998, Brisbane, Australia, http://
ilpubs.stanford.edu:8090/361/1/1998-8.pdf.

2. Anna Lauren Hoffmann, "Google Books, Libraries, and Self-
Respect," *Library Quarterly: Information, Community, Policy* 86, no. 1
(2016): 87.

3. Nanna Bonde Thylstrup, "Archival Shadows in the Digital Age,"
Nordisk Tidsskrift for Informationvidenskab og Kulturformidling 3, no. 2/3 (214):
29–39.

4. For example, Geoffrey Bowker and Susan Leigh Star conducted similar studies in their book *Sorting Things Out: Classification and Its Consequences*
(Cambridge, Mass.: MIT Press, 1999), in which they analyzed such systems
as the International Classification of Diseases and racial classifications in
Apartheid-era South Africa.

5. These searches were conducted on July 19, 2015, in Toronto, Canada,
from my laptop. I searched again on September 26, 2016, from my work
computer in Lexington, Ky., and got almost identical results. I should note
that I did similar searches with other search engines.

6. Safiya U. Noble, "Google Search: Hyper-visibility as a Means of Rendering Black Women and Girls Invisible," *InVisible Culture* 19 (2013).

7. Robert Darnton, *The Case for Books: Past, Present, and Future* (New
York: Public Affairs, 2009). For example, librarians have teamed up to assemble vast digital libraries like HathiTrust, which houses digitized materials
from over one hundred partner research libraries; the Internet Archive, a
nonprofit organization which preserves digital texts and artifacts, including

video and software, and provides access to researchers, historians, scholars, and the public; and the Digital Public Library of America, which aggregates metadata from participating libraries, including HathiTrust and the Internet Archive. Libraries of all types and sizes offer digital libraries that feature images, videos, and audio of local or topical interest.

8. Thomas Mann, "The Changing Nature of the Catalog and Its Integration with Other Discovery Tools. Final Report. March 17, 2006. Prepared for the Library of Congress by Karen Calhoun: A Critical Review," prepared for AFSCME 2910, Library of Congress Professional Guild (Washington, D.C., 2006), 4.

9. Ibid., 8.

10. To be sure, the findability of library materials by their subjects, even if conducted by keyword searches, is only as good as the metadata contained within the records. Keyword searches of catalogs will only retrieve records that contain the words searched. A library catalog record that includes the LC subject heading "Paraphilias" won't be found with a keyword search using the terms "perversion" or "deviance" unless those words are in the title, note, or other descriptive field. There are techniques that can improve retrieval power, like adding keywords, providing table of contents in the records, and offering library users the option to add tags directly to catalog records. All of these things increase the likelihood that seekers of knowledge and information will find books that are relevant to their desires.

11. John M. Budd, "The Library, Praxis, and Symbolic Power," *Library Quarterly* 73, no. 1 (2003): 19–32; Christine Pawley, "Beyond Market Models and Resistance: Organizations as a Middle Layer in the History of Reading," *Library Quarterly* 79, no. 1 (2009): 73–93; Douglas Raber, "Librarians as Organic Intellectuals: A Gramscian Approach to Blind Spots and Tunnel Vision," *Library Quarterly* 73, no. 1 (2003): 33–53; John Buschman, *Dismantling the Public Sphere: Situating and Sustaining Librarianship in the Age of the New Public Philosophy* (Westport, Conn.: Libraries Unlimited, 2003); Michael H. Harris, "State, Class, and Cultural Reproduction: Toward a Theory of Library Service in the United States," *Advances in Librarianship* 14 (1986): 211–252.

12. Christine Pawley, "Hegemony's Handmaid? The Library and Information Studies Curriculum from a Class Perspective," *Library Quarterly* 68, no. 2 (1998): 123–144.

13. James C. Scott, *Seeing Like a State: How Certain Schemes to Improve the Human Condition Have Failed* (New Haven, Conn.: Yale University Press), 183.

14. Dean Spade, *Normal Life: Administrative Violence, Critical Trans Politics, and the Limits of Law* (Cambridge, Mass.: South End, 2011), 68.

15. Ibid., 28.

16. Emily Drabinski, "Queering the Catalog: Queer Theory and the Politics of Correction," *Library Quarterly* 83, no. 2 (2013): 109; Hope Olson, revered among library scholars for her pioneering critical feminist theory within library and information science, suggested in 2001 that it is not necessary to dismantle the existing systems, but rather we need "to renovate the master's house to make space for the voices of excluded others." Olson has advocated the reappropriation of the master's technological tools to create redemptive technologies. She has suggested a number of ways we might apply a redemptive technology to LCSH, including developing systems designed for multilingual catalogs to allow more than one authoritative heading for a topic, using transaction logs to determine the kind of language users actually use when searching a catalog, and encouraging users to create links for future users.

17. Roderick A. Ferguson, *The Reorder of Things: The University and Its Pedagogies of Minority Difference* (Minneapolis: University of Minnesota Press, 2012), 127.

18. Ibid., 221. Also see Lisa Duggan, *The Twilight of Equality? Neoliberalism, Cultural Politics, and the Attack on Democracy* (Boston: Beacon, 2003). Similarly, Alison Hearn suggests that interdisciplinarity has been taken up as an instrument of the corporate university: "Interdisciplinarity/Extradisciplinarity: On the University and the Active Pursuit of Community," *History of Intellectual Culture* 3, no. 1 (2003): 1–15.

19. Michel Foucault, *The Order of Things* (London: Routledge, 1989), xv.

20. Ibid., xvi.

21. Jean-Luc Nancy, "On the Soul," in *Corpus*, trans. Richard Rand (New York: Fordham University Press, 2008), 128.

22. Michel Foucault, *Discipline and Punish: The Birth of the Prison*, trans. Alan Sheridan (New York: Vintage, 1995).

23. Ibid., 29.

24. Jean-Luc Nancy, *The Birth to Presence*, trans. Brian Holmes, et al. (Redwood City, Calif.: Stanford University Press, 1993).

25. Judith Butler, *Bodies That Matter: On the Discursive Limits of "Sex"* (New York: Routledge, 1993), 33.

26. Ibid., 34.

27. Ibid., 16.

28. Ibid., 190.

29. Foucault, *Discipline and Punish*, 305.

30. Nancy Fraser, "Rethinking Recognition," *New Left Review* 3 (May/June 2000): 119.

31. Ibid., 119.

32. This is inspired by Wendy Brown's discussion of rights discourses. Wendy Brown, "Suffering Rights as Paradoxes," *Constellations* 7, no. 2 (2000): 239–240.

33. Judith Halberstam, *The Queer Art of Failure* (Durham, N.C.: Duke University Press, 2011), 10.

34. Ferguson, *The Reorder of Things*, 230.

35. Michael Ryan, "Deconstruction and Radical Teaching," *Yale French Studies* 63 (1982): 45–58.

36. Ibid., 7.

37. Rosi Braidotti, *Nomadic Subjects: Embodiment and Sexual Difference in Contemporary Feminist Theory* (New York: Columbia University Press, 2013), 13, 90.

38. Ibid., 137.

39. Michel Foucault, "Sade: Sergeant of Sex," in *Essential Works*, vol. 2: *Aesthetics, Method, and Epistemology*, ed. James D. Faubion and Robert Hurley (New York: Norton, 1998), 227.

40. Ferguson, *The Reorder of Things*, 223.

41. Judith Butler, "Against Proper Objects," *differences: A Journal of Feminist Cultural Studies* 6, no. 2/3 (1994): 21.

42. Lesbian Herstory Archives, "Virtual Tour: Subject Files," http://www.lesbianherstoryarchives.org/tourcoll2.html.

43. Lesbian Herstory Archives, "Special Collections," https://herstory specialcollections.wordpress.com/1979–1983/.

44. One needs only look at the lineup for the 2016 LGBTQ* Libraries, Archives, Museums, and Special Collections conference in London to see the huge range of local and transnational projects, many of which are centered around taxonomic practice. http://lgbtqalms.co.uk/conference-programme/.

45. Eve Kosofsky Sedgwick, "Paranoid Reading and Reparative Reading, or, You're So Paranoid, You Probably Think This Essay Is About You," in *Touching Feeling: Affect, Pedagogy, Performativity* (Durham, N.C.: Duke University Press, 2003), 128.

46. Ellis Hanson, "The Future's Eve: Reparative Reading After Sedgwick," *South Atlantic Quarterly* 110, no. 1 (Winter 2011): 105.

47. Eve Kosofsky Sedgwick, "Shame in the Cybernetic Fold," in *Touching Feeling: Affect, Pedagogy, Performativity* (Durham, N.C.: Duke University Press, 2003), 106.

48. Eve Kosofsky Sedgwick, *Epistemology of the Closet* (Berkeley: University of California Press, 1990), 23.

49. Donna J. Haraway, "A Game of Cat's Cradle: Science Studies, Feminist Theory, Cultural Studies," *Configurations* 2, no. 1 (1994): 69–70.

50. Ibid., 69–70.

51. Gilles Deleuze and Félix Guattari, *A Thousand Plateaus: Capitalism and Schizophrenia* (Minneapolis: University of Minnesota Press, 1987), 3.

52. Ibid., 21.

53. Elizabeth Grosz, *Becoming Undone: Darwinian Reflections on Life, Politics, and Art* (Durham, N.C.: Duke University Press, 2011), 41.

EPILOGUE. SADOMASOCHISM IN THE LIBRARY

1. Franz Kafka, "In the Penal Colony," trans. Ian Johnston. I've chosen this translation for the use of the term "Inscriber." Other translations use the term "designer" for the German *der Zeichner*. All quotes from the piece can be found at https://records.viu.ca/~Johnstoi/kafka/inthepenalcolony.htm.

2. Jane Bennett, "Kafka, Genealogy, and the Spiritualization of Politics," *Journal of Politics* 56, no. 3 (1994): 650–670.

3. Hanna Arendt, "Franz Kafka, Appreciated Anew," in *Reflections on Literature and Culture*, ed. Susannah Young-ah Gottlieb (Stanford, Calif.: Stanford University Press, 2007), 109.

4. Ibid., 108.

5. Judith Butler, "How to Read Kafka" (2011), https://www.youtube.com/watch?v=OSIA6qXoIio.

6. Julia Kristeva, *Powers of Horror: An Essay on Abjection*, trans. Leon S. Roudiez (New York: Columbia University Press, 1982).

7. Réda Bensmaïa, "Foreword: The Kafka Effect," trans. Terry Cochran, in Gilles Deleuze and Félix Guattari, *Kafka: Toward a Minor Literature*, trans. Dana Polan (Minneapolis: University of Minnesota Press, 1986), xiv.

8. Bennett, "Kafka, Genealogy, and the Spiritualization of Politics."

9. The debacle surrounding the ownership of Kafka's papers cannot go unmentioned. See Judith Butler, "Who Owns Kafka?" *London Review of Books* 33, no. 5 (2011).

10. Deleuze and Guattari, *Kafka: Toward a Minor Literature*, 17.

11. Anna Katharina Schaffner, "'Seasick in the Land of Sexuality': Kafka's Eroticisms," in *Modernist Eroticisms: European Literature After Sexology* (Basingstoke: Palgrave Macmillan, 2012), 80.

12. Clayton Koelb, "'In der Strafkolonie': Kafka and the Scene of Reading," *German Quarterly* 55, no. 4 (1982): 512.

13. Margot Norris, "Sadism and Masochism in Two Kafka Stories: 'In der Strafkolonie' and 'Ein Hungerkünstler,'" *MLN* 93, no. 3 (1978): 437.

14. Gilles Deleuze and Félix Guattari, *A Thousand Plateaus: Capitalism and Schizophrenia* (Minneapolis: University of Minnesota Press, 1987), 76.

15. Andreas Gailus, "Lessons of the Cryptograph: Revelation and the Mechanical in Kafka's 'In the Penal Colony,'" *Modernism/modernity* 8, no. 2 (2001): 299.

16. Bennett, "Kafka, Genealogy, and the Spiritualization of Politics," 650.

17. Ronald E. Day, "Death of the User: Reconceptualizing Subjects, Objects, and Their Relations," *Journal of the American Society for Information Science and Technology* 62, no. 1 (2011): 78–88.

18. John K. Noyes, *The Mastery of Submission: Inventions of Masochism* (Ithaca, N.Y.: Cornell University Press, 1997), 5.

19. Jean Paulhan, "The Marquis de Sade and His Accomplice," in Marquis de Sade, *Justine, Philosophy in the Bedroom, and Other Writings*, ed. and trans. Richard Seaver and Austryn Wainhouse (New York: Grove, 1965).

20. Élisabeth Roudinesco, *Our Dark Side: A History of Perversion*, trans. David Macey (Cambridge: Polity, 2009).

21. Both Paulhan and Roudinesco refer to *120 Days of Sodom* as a catalog of perversions.

22. Slavoj Žižek, "The Ambiguity of the Masochist Social Link," in *Perversion and the Social Relation*, ed. Molly Anne Rothenberg, Dennis A. Foster, and Slavoj Žižek (Durham, N.C.: Duke University Press, 2003), 112–125.

23. Michael Uebel, "Psychoanalysis and the Question of Violence: From Masochism to Shame," *American Imago* 69, no. 4 (2012): 473–505.

24. Amber Musser, "Masochism: A Queer Subjectivity?" *Rhizomes* 11/12 (Fall 2005/Spring 2006), http://www.rhizomes.net/issue11/musser.html.

25. Roudinesco, *Our Dark Side*, 52.

26. Gilles Deleuze, "From Sacher-Masoch to Masochism," trans. Christian Kerslake, *Angelaki* 9, no. 1 (2004): 129.

27. Michel Foucault, "Sex, Power, and the Politics of Identity," in *Ethics: Subjectivity and Truth*, ed. Paul Rabinow, trans. Robert Hurley et al. (New York: The New Press, 1997), 169.

28. Eve Kosofsky Sedgwick, "A Poem Is Being Written," *Representations* 17 (1987): 132.

29. Lillian Faderman, in the foreword to Joanne Passett, *Sex Variant Woman: The Life of Jeannette Howard Foster* (Philadelphia: Da Capo, 2008), xii. The book to which Faderman refers is the first book-length bibliography on lesbians in literature, first published in 1956. Foster was a librarian at the Kinsey Institute for Sex Research when she wrote the book.

30. Žižek, "The Ambiguity of the Masochist Social Link," 119.

31. Giorgio Agamben, *Homo Sacer: Sovereign Power and Bare Life* (Stanford, Calif.: Stanford University Press, 1998).

Adorno, Theodor, 126–127; and Max
    Horkheimer, 126, 140, 141
Agamben, Giorgio, 13
American Library Association: and
    cataloging, 19, 34, 46, 145, 187–188n;
    on intellectual freedom, 69–70,
    145; Statement on Labeling, 69–70;
    Library Bill of Rights, 69; Task Force
    on Gay Liberation, 43–44
Anderson, Benedict, 112
anomaly, 53–54, 195n
Arendt, Hannah, 138, 167–168

Baker, Nicholson, 125, 202n
Barthes, Roland, 26, 171
Bennett, Jane, 166, 168, 172
Bensmaïa, Réda, 168
Bentham, Jeremy, 98–99, 100
Bergner, Daniel, 61–62
Berman, Sanford, 44, 46, 49, 59–60; on
    bibliocide, 49, 166
bibliographic classification: definition,
    xiii, 92
biopolitics, 135, 137
bisexuality, 28–29, 40, 115, 118, 189n
Bishop, William Warner, 16
Black, Diane, 11
bodies of literature, xi–xii, 6–7, 9, 12–13,
    104, 123, 140, 150, 152, 157, 166
Borges, Jorge Luis, 27, 82–84, 150–151,
    174, 201n
Britzman, Deborah, 5, 38, 144
Brown, Wendy, 101, 124, 131–132, 154
Buchanan, Ian, 6
Bullough, Vern, 46
Butler, Judith, 126–127, 134, 152–153,
    157, 168

Caldwell, Millard, 73
Canaday, Margot, 85–86

catalog cards, 19, 88–89, 189n, 202n
Certeau, Michel de, 104
Clapp, Verner, 69
closet (the), xv, 63, 82, 84, 85, 87
Cold War, 69–71, 86, 139
Collins, Samuel, 10
Comstock Act, 69
cruising, xii, xvi, 121, 127, 129, 178
Cruz, Ted, 11

Daedalus, xv, 82, 85, 201n
Darnton, Robert, 147
Davis, Katherine Bement, 54–55
Day, Ronald E., xii, 15, 173, 175
De Block, Andreas, and Pieter R.
    Adriaens, 43, 45
De River, Paul, 117
Deleuze, Gilles, xiv, 6, 7, 104, and
    Félix Guattari, 7, 162–163; and Félix
    Guattari on Kafka, 168–169, 171; on
    masochism, 175
Delta Collection, xiii–xiv, xv, 57; and la-
    beling, 70; and U.S. Postal Service and
    Customs Bureau, 68, 70–71, 74–75,
    76; archival records, 66; catalog rec-
    ords, 88–91, 202n; delta symbol, 82,
    201n; description, 63–65; early history
    (19th c.–1936), 71–73; management of,
    74–77; quantity of holdings, 76–77,
    88; theft from, 78–82; use of, 67, 73
Derrida, Jacques, 26
Dewey, Melvil, 17
Dewey Decimal Classification, 107, 139,
    209–210n
*Diagnostic and Statistical Manual of Mental
    Disorders*, 35, 37, 42–45, 47–50
diagram, xvi, 98, 103–106, 108, 168, 171
Dollimore, Jonathan, 59, 144
Dowdy, John, 67
Downing, Lisa, 50